THE FUTURE FOR OLDER WORKERS

New perspectives

Edited by Wendy Loretto, Sarah Vickerstaff and Phil White

First published in Great Britain in 2007 by

The Policy Press
University of Bristol
Fourth Floor
Beacon House
Queen's Road
Bristol BS8 1QU
UK

Tel +44 (0)117 331 4054
Fax +44 (0)117 331 4093
e-mail tpp-info@bristol.ac.uk
www.policypress.org.uk

British Library Cataloguing in Publication Data
A catalogue record for this book is available from the British Library.

Library of Congress Cataloging-in-Publication Data
A catalog record for this book has been requested.

ISBN 978 1 86134 896 8 hardcover

Cover design by Qube Design Associates, Bristol.
Printed and bound in Great Britain by MPG Books, Bodmin.

Contents

List of tables and figures

Tables

Figures

Foreword

The contributors to this publication represent a cross-section of the leading researchers, thinkers and writers about the implications of changing demographics on the world of work. Collectively they have had a substantial influence on public policy and on the actions of employers, employees and public agencies. It is welcome to see their expertise brought together in this book.

The subtitle of this book is 'New perspectives' on the future of older workers. This is appropriate because its appearance coincides with a turning point. Legislation against age-based employment and training practices came into force in 2006. For a decade it had been a topic of discussion. Now it is a reality.

Also, the improved employment rate of older workers is well established. After a 30-year decline in the employment of older people, notably men, up to the mid 1990s, the over-50s employment rate has grown strongly over the past decade. Now the growth is extended to those over state pension age.

It might be concluded that we have all woken up to the reality of longer lives, less good pensions and the need to extend working life in the face of a reduced flow of young people into the workforce. Nothing further need be done.

This is the new complacency which threatens us. It explains why new perspectives and new drivers of government, individual and employer action are needed. Three facts illustrate why we cannot sit back:

1. The duration of time spent on welfare benefits among the over-50s has got longer, reflecting the difficulty of getting back into work, while for the under-50s it has got shorter.
2. There are as many people aged between 50 and state pension age who are not active in the economy as there were in 1997, despite the improved employment rate.
3. The number of adults aged over 50 in government-funded learning activity has almost halved in the last two years in order to fund learning by young people, even though government says that adult learners have never been more important.

The authors rightly emphasise that there is no such thing as a standard older worker or older person. There is a world of difference between those with occupational pensions, qualifications and their own resources and those with none of those things. The ability to make choices about the future is much discussed; it is reality for some people, not for others.

New perspectives must include:

Quality of work as well as quantity of work. Most of the increased work for older people is low paid, low quality and without prospects to advance. Under-utilisation of the skills and experience of older workers is almost as bad as no utilisation of them. It is also bad for productivity and for their prospects of retention in the workforce. The next stage is to focus on quality of opportunity in work.

Career advice and training. Despite statements of intent and many major reports for government, the opportunities for workers over the age of about 30 to up-skill or retrain are currently (spring 2007) going backwards. Our educational policy establishment is in denial about demographic change because of the scale of under-performance of the 16-25 age group compared to our major international competitors.

Corporate culture. The phases and age-based stages of working life in hierarchical corporations and public services are still largely locked in place. The changing pattern of women's careers is doing most to break them down. The new perspective is to move towards a workplace in which there are flexible working patterns, moving up, down, or sideways at any stage. It is to be hoped that in the next few years this will include the ending of the concept of a fixed retirement age.

These themes and much more are elaborated throughout this book. I hope that it will make an important contribution to change.

Patrick Grattan
The Age and Employment Network (TAEN)

Acknowledgements

We would like to thank the Economic and Social Research Council (award number 451-26-0308) for funding the seminar series that gave rise to this text. Our thanks also to all who contributed, attended and helped organise the seminars. We are enormously grateful to the Equal Opportunities Commission for its financial support in producing the book, and in particular to Dr Dave Perfect for his personal support and enthusiasm. We are indebted to all the authors who agreed to contribute chapters. We also wish to note our appreciation for the administrative support provided by various individuals at the Universities of Kent and Edinburgh – many thanks to Paul Kydd, Judy Lee, Charis Stewart and Lynn Walford. A final note of thanks to Emily Watt and all staff at The Policy Press for their invaluable support and guidance, and to the reviewers for their advice and constructive comments.

List of abbreviations

ACAS	Advisory, Conciliation and Arbitration Service
ADEA	Age Discrimination in Employment Act (US)
APP	Appropriate personal pension
ASP	Alternatively secured pension
AVC	Additional voluntary contribution
BFOQ	Bona fide occupational qualification
CEC	Commission of the European Communities
CEHR	Commission on Equality and Human Rights
CIPD	Chartered Institute of Personnel and Development
CIS	Co-operative Insurance Society
CRE	Commission for Racial Equality
DDA	Disability Discrimination Act
DfES	Department for Education and Skills
DH	Department of Health
DSS	Department of Social Security
DWP	Department for Work and Pensions
EEOC	Equal Employment Opportunity Commission (US)
EFA	Employers' Forum on Ageing
ELSA	English Longitudinal Study of Ageing
EOC	Equal Opportunities Commission
EPFDP	Equal Programme Forward Development Partnership
ESF	European Social Fund
ESRC	Economic and Social Research Council
FRS	Family Resources Survey
FSA	Financial Services Agency
FSS	Futureskills Scotland
GCE	General Certificate of Education
GROS	General Register Office for Scotland
HBOS	Halifax Bank of Scotland
HEFCE	Higher Education Funding Council of England
HSBC	Hong Kong and Shanghai Banking Corporation Ltd
HSE	Health and Safety Executive
IB	Incapacity Benefit
ILO	International Labour Organization
IMF	International Monetary Fund
JIL	Japan Institute of Labour
JRF	Joseph Rowntree Foundation
JSA	Jobseeker's Allowance

LFS   Labour Force Survey
LGPC   Local Government Pensions Committee
LSC   Learning and Skills Council
MHLW Ministry of Health, Labour and Welfare (Japan)
NAO   National Audit Office
NI   National Insurance
OECD Organisation for Economic Co-operation and Development
ONS   Office for National Statistics
OPEC   Organization of the Petroleum Exporting Countries
PIU   Performance and Innovation Unit
RAKM Research Analysis and Knowledge Management
RFOA   Reasonable factors other than age
S2P   State second pension
SERPS State earnings related pension scheme
SPA   State pension age
TAEN   The Age and Employment Network (formerly Third Age Employment Network)
TDB   Teikoku Databank Bankruptcy
TSO   The Stationery Office
UKIP   UK Independence Party
UN   United Nations
WERS Workplace Employment Relations Survey
WTO   World Trade Organization

Glossary of UK-based institutions and programmes

Adult Learning

This is a government initiative that promotes and supports a wide range of adult and continuous learning, from enhancing basic literacy skills to training and workplace learning.

www.direct.gov.uk/en/EducationAndLearning/AdultLearning/index.htm

Age Concern

Age Concern is a large charity whose aim is to promote the well-being of older people. It provides a range of services and information across the UK for people over 50. The organisation also campaigns on issues such as pensions and age discrimination.

www.ageconcern.org.uk

Age Positive

This is a team working in the Department for Work and Pensions, 'responsible for strategy and policies to support people making decisions about working and retirement'. The Age Positive campaign promotes the benefits of employing a mixed-age workforce that includes older and younger people. It was set up to raise awareness, disseminate information and promote good practice in preparation for the 2006 Employment Equality (Age) Regulations.

www.agepositive.gov.uk

B&Q

This is a UK-wide chain of 'DIY' (hardware, gardening and home improvement) stores that has had widespread publicity over its positive approach to employing older workers.

www.kingfisher.co.uk/index.asp?pageid=221

Careers Scotland

Operating throughout Scotland, Careers Scotland aims to help people to make the most of their working lives by providing information on available jobs and careers, learning and skills. It works in partnership with schools, colleges and businesses, and with those who are out of work as well as those in employment.

www.careers-scotland.org.uk

City and Guilds

This is the UK's leading vocational awards body. It offers over 500 qualifications across a wide range of industry sectors.

www.city-and-guilds.co.uk

Commission for Equality and Human Rights

This was established by the 2006 Equality Act, and will come into being in October 2007. Its aim is to 'bring together the expertise and resources to promote equality and tackle discrimination in relation to gender, gender reassignment, disability, sexual orientation, religion or belief, age, race and promote human rights'.

www.cehr.org.uk

Equal Opportunities Commission

The Equal Opportunities Commission is an independent, non-departmental public body, funded primarily by the government. It provides information and advice, and commissions and publishes research in furtherance of its aim to 'eliminate sex discrimination in 21st century Britain'. From October 2007 it will be part of the Commission for Equality and Human Rights.

www.eoc.org.uk

Fresh Talent Initiative

This is a scheme of managed migration that seeks to attract people to live and work in Scotland.

www.scotland.gov.uk/Topics/Government/Promoting-Scotland/18738/14640

GCE 'O' levels

The General Certificate of Education at 'O' (Ordinary) level is an entry requirement to many diploma and polytechnic programmes, and to GCE 'A' (Advanced) level courses. The subject areas covered include Languages, Humanities, Social Sciences, and Maths and Science subjects. There are some vocational subjects, too. Students of 'O' level courses (who are usually of school age) attain a mix of practical skills and theoretical knowledge.

Health and Safety Executive (HSE)

Working in support of the Health and Safety Commission (HSC), and in cooperation with local government, the HSE is responsible for controlling and enforcing workplace health and safety. The HSE and HSC are sponsored by the government Department for Work and Pensions (DWP).

www.hse.gov.uk

Incapacity Benefit (IB)

This is a benefit for people who cannot work because of illness or disability and who are under state pension age. There are different rates, depending on the length of time out of work. A medical assessment is required.

http://direct.gov.uk

Inland Revenue

In 2005, Inland Revenue was merged with HM Customs and Excise Departments to form HM Revenue and Customs. The 'Revenue' part continues to collect and administer both direct (for example, income tax) and indirect (for example, VAT) taxes. It also pays benefits, such as child benefit.

http://hmrc.gov.uk

Jobcentre Plus (JCP)

Through its various offices throughout the country, Jobcentre Plus seeks to support people of working age, to shift from welfare either directly into work, or by way of preparatory training. It also assists employers in recruiting employees. A key goal of Jobcentre Plus is to regard employment 'as the best form of welfare'. Jobcentre Plus is part of the Department for Work and Pensions.

http://jobcentreplus.gov.uk

Jobseeker's Allowance (JSA)

This is a benefit for unemployed people. It can be claimed if people are able to work, available for work and actively looking for work. It is not available to those who are over state pension age (that is, men, 65; women, 60).

http://jobcentreplus.gov.uk

New Deal programmes

There are several programmes within the overall New Deal programme. They include New Deal 50+ (see below), New Deal for Disabled People, New Deal for Young People, New Deal for Lone Parents, New Deal for Musicians, New Deal 25+ and New Deal for Partners. Their collective aim is to provide certain groups of unemployed people with help and support to get work.

New Deal 50+

New Deal 50+ is a voluntary scheme, open to people aged 50 and over, who have been unemployed and in receipt of certain benefits (including JSA and IB) for at least six months. Jobcentre advisers make available such facilities as a tax-free employment credit for up to 52 weeks, clothing and other financial support for job interviews, and an in-work training grant after work has started. Since April 2003, the over-50s have been given some working tax credits that were not hitherto available to them.

www.jobcentreplus.gov.uk/JCP/Customers/New_Deal

Pathways to Work

This government programme has been developed, through various pilots, to provide greater support for those people claiming IB either to move into employment, or to move closer to the labour market. A key objective is for JCP advisers to play a supportive and informational role for claimants.

http://jobcentreplus.gov.uk

Pensions Commission

Chaired by Lord Turner, the Pensions Commission was established by the government in 2002 to consider long-term trends in saving for pensions and retirement. Its key remit was to deliberate on, and make recommendations for, the balance between state, occupational and private pension provision. The Commission produced two reports between 2002 and 2006.

http://pensionscommission.org.uk

Regional Development Agencies (RDAs)

These were established by statute in 1998. There are eight regional agencies in England; there is separate provision in Scotland, Northern Ireland and Wales. The aim of the RDAs is to regenerate and develop the socioeconomic situations of the regions. Partnerships between public bodies and private industry are encouraged, as are community action groups. There are separate websites for each agency, such as

www.seeda.co.uk (for the South East), or

http://nwda.co.uk (for the North West)

State pension age (SPA)

Age at which people are eligible to claim the state old age pension. In the UK, this is currently 60 for women and 65 for men. However, by 2020 women's state pension age will also be 65.

The Age and Employment Network (formerly Third Age Employment Network)

The Age and Employment Network is a not-for-profit network of public, private and voluntary organisations committed to 'open opportunities, free from artificial barriers, for everyone to choose whether and how they extend working life, retrain, change direction, stay fit, save for retirement and retire'. It provides information and advice on a broad spectrum of third-age employment issues to individuals and organisations.

www.taen.org.uk

Turner Report (see Pensions Commission)

Worker Registration Scheme (WRS)

Under the aegis of the Home Office, the WRS applies to most nationals of most EU member states that have acceded in recent years. Where those nationals wish to work in the UK for more than one month, they must register under the WRS. Once people have worked for more than 12 months without a break, they are no longer required to register. They can then get a residence permit for the UK.

www.workingintheuk.gov.uk

Notes on contributors

Christina Beatty is a Principal Research Fellow in the Centre for Regional Economic and Social Research at Sheffield Hallam University (www.shu.ac.uk/cresr/staff/c-beatty.html).

Bernard Casey is Visiting Fellow in Personal Finance, Cass Business School, London, and Principal Research Fellow at the Institute for Employment Research, University of Warwick.

Mike Danson is a Professor of Scottish and Regional Economics in the Centre for Contemporary European Studies at the University of Paisley (www.paisley.ac.uk/business/cces/researchers/mike-danson.asp).

Steve Fothergill is a Professor in the Centre for Regional Economic and Social Research at Sheffield Hallam University (www.shu.ac.uk/cresr/staff/s-fothergill.html).

Amanda Griffiths is a Professor of Occupational Health Psychology at the Institute of Work, Health & Organisations, University of Nottingham (www.nottingham.ac.uk/iwho/).

Donald Hirsch is an independent consultant and writer on social policy, currently Special Adviser to the Joseph Rowntree Foundation (www.hirsch.demon.co.uk/).

Wendy Loretto is a Senior Lecturer in Employment Relations/ Organisation Studies in the Management School and Economics, University of Edinburgh (http://webdb.ucs.ed.ac.uk/management/ school_new/people/WendyLoretto.html).

John Macnicol is Visiting Professor in Social Policy at the London School of Economics and Political Science (www.lse.ac.uk/ people/0000015630/publications.htm).

Tony Maltby is Research Fellow and Deputy Director at the Centre for Research into the Older Workforce (CROW), at the National Institute of Adult Continuing Education – England and Wales (www. niace.org.uk/crow).

Chris Phillipson is Professor of Applied Social Studies and Social Gerontology in the School of Criminology, Education, Sociology and Social Work at Keele University (www.keele.ac.uk/research/lcs/membership/philipson.htm).

Sarah Vickerstaff is Professor of Work and Employment at the School of Social Policy, Sociology and Social Research at the University of Kent (www.kent.ac.uk/sspssr/staff/vickerstaff.htm).

Sue Ward is a freelance journalist and researcher on pensions issues.

Phil White is an Honorary Fellow in the Management School and Economics, University of Edinburgh (http://webdb.ucs.ed.ac.uk/management/school_new/people/PhilWhite.html).

ONE

Introduction

Wendy Loretto, Sarah Vickerstaff and Phil White

The future for older workers has recently become an issue of major concern to individuals, employers and governments. For many people confronted with diminishing pension savings or entitlements and extensions to state pension ages, the prospects for an early and smooth transition to retirement appear to be diminishing. For employers facing a more regulated labour market with the advent of age discrimination legislation and in the context of changing demographics and potential skills shortages, there is an increasing need to rethink their management of the older workforce. For governments, concerns about the tendency for people to retire earlier and live longer and the concomitant strains on the public purse in terms of state pensions and health service costs have fuelled an increasingly urgent commitment to 'extending working life'. This volume brings together a range of up-to-date research findings by many of the leading writers and researchers on older workers. It examines, from various angles, the opportunities and constraints that face older workers in advanced post-industrial societies in the 21st century.

The book was inspired by a series of seminars, supported by a grant from the UK Economic and Social Research Council (ESRC),[a] on the subject of 'Employability of Older Workers'. The series identified a number of underdeveloped themes that are considered critical to extending working lives:

- the heterogeneity of work experiences among the older population;
- the impact of work culture and ageism on older workers' employment participation;
- the need to think about older workers before they become older;
- the significance of choice and flexibility for older workers' employment aspirations and well-being;
- the strategic importance of work organisation and design in creating an older worker-friendly environment;

- the crucial role that occupational health and welfare will have in sustaining decent working lives and providing opportunities for people to re-enter work;
- the importance of extending training and career development opportunities through the work lifecycle.

This book seeks to pursue these themes from an interdisciplinary perspective, drawing on academic and policy-related research from the UK, mainland Europe, the US and Japan.

This opening chapter provides an introduction to the national and international context for the current interest and concern about older workers, herein defined as those aged 50 years and older. Two recent reports (OECD, 2006; Zaidi and Fuchs, 2006) have confirmed the worldwide concern over population decline and ageing populations. In its review of the situation in 21 countries, the Organisation for Economic Cooperation and Development (OECD) noted that in 2004, the average employment rate for those aged 50-64 was under 60%, and that there was 'substantial scope' (OECD, 2006, p 9) for increasing the employment of older workers. In particular, the report highlighted the importance of keeping people in employment, as early exit (leaving employment before official retirement or state pension age) is a 'one-way street' (OECD, 2006, p 10).

Zaidi and Fuchs (2006, p 13) argue that paying attention to the employment of older workers will tackle both parts of the dependency ratio – by engendering more 'taxable capacity' within economies, as well as reducing dependency of future older people on the state. Drawing on analysis of the European Union (EU) Labour Force Survey, they note that, across the EU25, early retirement seems to have slowed down and may even be reversing, in that participation rates of older workers are rising, as are average retirement ages. However, a closer examination of the figures reveals that, within the overall trends, there are significant differences between countries (for example, according to 2005 figures, Sweden leads the EU10 with employment rates of 73% for workers aged between 50 and 64, with Italy reporting only 41% participation), as well as between men and women (men generally higher than women, but women's participation rates increasing faster because of the greater propensity of the current generation to work). Based on OECD statistics, Table 1.1 illustrates the employment rates of men and women aged 55-64 across 30 countries in 2005.

In all countries, those older workers with the highest levels of educational qualification are those most likely to work, and the majority of the over-50s who are in employment work on a full-time

Table 1.1: Employment rates, 2005

Country	Working-age population (15–64 years) Men	Women	Population aged 55–64 years Men	Women
Australia	80.5	65.6	63.9	43.4
Austria	76.3	62.4	41.3	22.9
Belgium	68.2	54.4	41.3	23.0
Canada	78.5	69.3	63.1	46.8
Czech Republic	74.2	56.8	59.4	31.0
Denmark	82.0	71.5	66.8	52.9
Finland	70.2	67.0	52.5	52.7
France	68.1	57.2	43.8	37.6
Germany	72.5	60.2	53.6	37.6
Greece	76.2	46.8	58.8	25.8
Hungary	63.6	51.2	40.6	26.8
Iceland	91.6	83.5	89.3	80.2
Ireland	78.3	58.6	65.7	37.4
Italy	71.2	45.6	42.7	20.8
Japan	87.7	62.5	78.9	49.4
Korea	79.4	56.1	72.2	45.7
Luxembourg	73.5	53.8	38.3	24.8
Mexico	84.7	43.0	77.4	30.3
Netherlands	78.6	65.2	55.1	34.5
New Zealand	84.1	69.4	78.3	61.3
Norway	80.1	73.3	73.1	62.1
Poland	60.4	74.9	37.9	21.4
Portugal	78.7	65.5	58.1	43.7
Slovak Republic	64.9	51.1	47.9	15.7
Spain	77.0	52.2	59.7	27.4
Sweden	77.7	72.6	72.2	66.9
Switzerland	86.1	71.7	74.8	55.4
Turkey	70.1	24.4	45.3	16.9
UK	80.5	67.9	65.7	48.2
US	80.6	67.9	67.0	55.1

Source: Compiled from OECD statistics (http://stats.oecd.org/wbos/default.aspx? DatasetCode=LFS_SEXAGE_I_R).

basis (OECD, 2006; Zaidi and Fuchs, 2006). Moreover, analysis by age group shows a sharp drop-off in employment rates at age 60 onwards. For example, in the UK in 2005, 79% of those aged 50-54 were in employment, compared with 69% of 55- to 59-year-olds, and only 42% of those aged 60-64 (Zaidi and Fuchs, 2006, p 14).

Taking stock of these facts and figures, we find a situation in which, despite general trends towards increased working among older workers, employment rates still fall short of EU targets[b] in many countries, retirement still occurs at a fairly fixed time, and opportunities for (extending) work are not uniformly available. Opportunities are affected by a range of institutional and individual circumstances. The chapters that follow aim to explore the significance and impact of the various stakeholders – governments, employers and the (older) individuals themselves – in shaping the future prospects for older workers.

Chapter Two, written by Mike Danson, provides more contextual detail for the debates surrounding the employment implications of an ageing population. Focusing initially on Scotland, it explores the significance of examining demographic trends over time, before widening the focus to consider the demography of Europe and beyond.

Chapters Three (John Macnicol) and Four (Bernard Casey) expand on the international comparisons by reviewing experiences and trends in two very different world economies. Macnicol's focus is on the United States, where legislation outlawing discrimination against older workers has been in place since the late 1960s. This chapter considers the effectiveness of the legislation and assesses the possible implications for the recent implementation of the 2006 Employment Equality (Age) Regulations in Great Britain. In Chapter Four, Casey considers the example of Japan, where employment rates among older people are high, and draws attention to the importance of national traditions and work cultures for debates on the employability of older workers. Japan has often been seen as a special case, but Casey argues that harsher economic conditions may mean that Japan increasingly experiences the pressures and problems facing other industrialised countries.

In Chapter Five, Christina Beatty and Steve Fothergill address a neglected aspect of the debate about extending working lives, namely the demand-side question of whether there is work in the labour market for older workers. Looking at the particular case of workers who have left the labour market and are in receipt of incapacity benefit, they present a detailed analysis of regional variations in the availability of job opportunities across Great Britain. In a critical assessment of New Labour's welfare-to-work policy reforms, they argue that job-creation policies are needed to address the job shortfall.

In Chapter Six, Sue Ward picks up on a key aspect of the different situations of older men and women. It is well documented that more women than men are likely to live in poverty in retirement (Ginn, 2003). By exploring the extent to which women's and men's attitudes towards pensions and financial planning for retirement differ, Ward assesses the ways in which these differences may affect their attitudes towards remaining in work.

The remaining contributions (Chapters Seven to Eleven) consider ways in which older workers can be retained and sustained in employment. In Chapter Seven, Donald Hirsch draws together some of the key findings from the Joseph Rowntree Foundation's Transitions after 50 programme to highlight the importance of thinking about the employment of older workers in new ways, and especially in adopting a life-course perspective. Chapters Eight and Nine present a more detailed treatment of some of the routes to extending working lives raised by Hirsch. Amanda Griffiths (Chapter Eight) examines the role and importance of occupational health in ensuring a healthy and active workforce across the life course. She argues for a shift in focus away from work modifications for particular individuals towards designing and managing healthy work for all workers and hence for older workers too. Using data from the Great Britain Labour Force Survey, Wendy Loretto, Sarah Vickerstaff and Phil White (Chapter Nine) profile the current patterns of flexible working among the over-50s, finding that opportunities for working flexibly are currently limited. They then consider future prospects and possibilities. The focus in Chapter Ten (Tony Maltby) turns to those older workers who are outside the labour market. Reporting on EU-funded action research, Maltby considers the fundamental practical issues of getting older people (back) into work. Chapter Eleven by Chris Phillipson presents a critical review of the options for extending working lives, paying particular attention to the heterogeneity of circumstances, attitudes and desires of older workers, and posing the question of whether we should simply accept the extending working life agenda.

The editors of the volume conclude, in Chapter Twelve, with a detailed consideration of the future prospects for older workers. Drawing out the main themes across the contributions, the discussion critically evaluates the opportunities and constraints for extending and sustaining working lives.

Notes

[a] Award number 451-26-0308.

[b] In March 2001, the Stockholm Council set a target, to be attained by 2010, to raise the average employment rate of men and women aged 55-64 to 50%.

References

Ginn, J. (2003) *Gender, Pensions and the Lifecourse: How Pensions Need to Adapt to Changing Family Forms*, Bristol: The Policy Press.

OECD (Organisation for Economic Co-operation and Development) (2006), *Live Longer, Work Longer*, Paris: OECD Publishing.

Zaidi, A. and Fuchs, M. (2006) *Transition from Work to Retirement in EU25*, Policy Brief December 2006, Vienna: European Centre for Social Welfare Policy and Research.

TWO

Older workers in the labour market: the demographic context

Mike Danson

Introduction

Critical to the determination of the supply of labour to an economy is the number of people who are fit and able to work. In determining this 'working population', there is a host of factors to be considered, including most fundamentally the age structure and health of people in the economy. With the rise in joblessness of those of 'working age', and especially among those over 50, has come an interest in matters of 'employability' and the perceived reasons for higher rates of economic inactivity among older workers. This chapter addresses the demographic aspects behind these employability debates, focusing initially on Scotland and then demonstrating that many of its specific problems are replicated elsewhere. It is argued that lessons learnt in Scotland should be of wider application and concern, as similar challenges are being faced in most economies across the world.

Background

Generally, three key and related phenomena are leading to extensive and divergent population changes across economies and societies: extended longevity for both men and women; declining fertility and birth rates; and nationally and regionally specific issues, such as differential trends among minority ethnic communities and migration between and within areas.

Yet, while these demographic trends are increasingly being recognised – for instance, demographic ageing has been debated in Canada since 1980 – it is only recently that their impact has begun to be addressed significantly. A key area of increasing interest in most member countries of the Organisation for Economic Cooperation and Development (OECD) has been the growing number of older men and women of working age outside the labour force (Hollywood et al, 2003). For example, in England, the Performance and Innovation Unit (2000) estimated that there were 2.8 million workless people in the 50- to 65-year age group alone in 2000, a figure projected to increase by a further million by 2010. Indeed, many are leaving the labour force at progressively younger ages, even though the population is ageing and living longer (Anyadike-Danes, 2002). Progress on addressing such ageing issues in Europe was recently criticised by the International Monetary Fund (IMF), which argued: 'As long as Europe fails to adequately reinvigorate its inflexible labor markets and better prepare to deal with the consequences of its rapidly aging population, its growth rate will likely continue to lag' (Rogoff, 2002). The IMF also highlighted the taxation effects of this phenomenon: 'The problem of the aging population with its concomitant higher tax burdens will raise the burden of taxes, thereby also potentially lowering growth' (Rogoff, 2002). Rather than uncritically accept such broad analyses and neoliberal policy prescriptions, it is necessary to explore the experiences with the ageing agenda across Europe as a range of strategies are adopted for diverse environments.

Beneath general trends, demographic ageing effects are differentiated between nations and regions. For example, birth rates are falling in certain regions and countries, including Scotland, the north east of England and Germany, so that fewer people are joining the labour force and the population is actually declining. For other regions, such as parts of Portugal, Spain and France and the south west and the east of England, in-migration of older retirees is a specific challenge. By contrast, key regions in North America and Australasia continue to attract young adults. These trends are causing concern about the future supply of labour and economic competitiveness, and there is particular concern that changes in the 'dependency ratio' will have significant implications for the financing, provision and staffing of health, social care and pension systems.

Yet, although the language in which much of this debate takes place is unnecessarily pejorative, ageing should not be seen simply as a 'problem' or a 'challenge'. While these supply-side changes are occurring, the distribution of wealth in many developed countries is adjusting so that more economic resources are in the control of some sections of the older community, providing new economic development opportunities (Metz and Underwood, 2005). This pattern is made more complex by the differential geographical distribution of older and younger populations, with the population distribution in some rural sub-regions in the UK being skewed to older age groups. This trend was graphically illustrated in the Haskins review of the impact of foot and mouth disease in Cumbria, which highlighted the importance of non-wage income such as pensions in the survival of Cumbria's economy during the crisis (Haskins, 2003). In other countries, patterns of ageing are very different, with Finland offering a model of proactive retirement (Kahila and Rinne-Koski, 2006) where part-time work is an important component of 'flexible lifestyles' for older people. In New Zealand, latest figures confirm that older workers are a large and growing section of the labour force, with their numbers increasing more quickly than any other group. From surveys across six countries in Europe, this diversity of activity has been recorded and examined to show that even within these variations many remain workers and volunteers, socially aware long after the labour market may have consigned them to joblessness elsewhere (Droogleever Fortuijn and van der Meer, 2003).

Demographic ageing is the focus of substantial international and national policy initiatives. The UN Conference on Ageing in Madrid in October 2002 updated the international action plan on ageing to prioritise the following areas: societal participation by older persons; political representation and social inclusion; solidarity between generations; migration of members of the younger generation and its impact on older people; protection of older persons from abuse and violence; greater sensitivity to older persons in rural areas or those belonging to minority ethnic groups; and, promotion of life-course planning for better health and well-being in older years (UNRISD, 2002). Within Europe, the policy implications of demographic ageing at the regional level have been highlighted in the *Third Cohesion Report* published by the European Commission (CEC, 2004). In particular, this recent publication identifies the ageing of the population as one of the four key drivers to cohesion policy and proposes performance indicators for the 2007-13 European Social Fund linked to the promotion of active ageing and of lifelong learning.

In the UK, as an example of moves to recognise the need for coherence between EU and national strategies, the government has established a cabinet subcommittee on ageing, which has focused on a number of programmes linked to this agenda. These have included the code of practice on age diversity in employment and the Age Positive website; the promotion of involvement of older people in local planning through the Better Government for Older People programme; and the NHS National Service Framework for Older People, which intends to improve the quality and focus of health and social care services. Within the academic community, there has been a long tradition of research on demographic ageing and, again using the UK as an example, some of this research has been supported by a number of research programmes on demographic ageing sponsored by the Joseph Rowntree Foundation (Transitions after 50), the Economic and Social Research Council (Growing Older Programme and the Cross-Council Programme on Ageing), the Nuffield Foundation and the Lifespan Trust. However, perhaps most notable has been the work of the Old People's Unit at the Scottish Executive, which has been a leader within the UK in addressing the implications of a demographic change (Scottish Executive, 2006). This has been driving forward the publication of a strategy for an ageing society in late 2006, following extensive academic research and other evidence gathering, commentary from a high-powered and inclusive advisory group, and a wide-ranging consultation.

Scotland, therefore, is an especially appropriate focus for this introduction to the issues raised by demographic ageing. This specific strategy highlights a realisation across government and civic society of the dimensions, importance and implications of changes in population structure. Scotland has been concerned with aspects of demographic change for many decades, with depopulation, emigration and – more recently – ageing all having social, economic and political significance (Ascherson, 2002; Watson, 2003; Paterson et al, 2004). Furthermore, an enhanced appreciation of the benefits generated by in-migration (Ascherson, 2002; Watson, 2003) and cosmopolitanism (CRE, 2005; Florida, 2002a,b,c), arising from centuries of emigration (Hunter, 1994; Whyte, 2000) and greater willingness to accept incomers, suggests a readiness to address demographic issues positively and proactively. This can obviously be contrasted with a position of reluctance underpinned with racism, xenophobia and ageism, as demonstrated by such actors as the UK Independence Party (UKIP, 2005), Migrationwatch (2006) and the Home Office Secretary (Reid, 2006). This openness to solutions (Scottish Executive, 2004; Independence Convention, 2005; Joshi and Wright, 2005) is consistent with a strategic approach to engaging with the needs of an ageing society (Scottish Executive, 2006). The UK, along with Ireland and Sweden, from the start of the most recent enlargement of the European Union, has not used the possibility of invoking a seven-year moratorium on opening its borders to mobile labour from the accession countries. As a result, there were 427,000 successful applications under the UK's Worker Registration Scheme in the two years from May 2004 to June 2006 by migrant workers from the new members states, with 32,000 coming to Scotland, mostly from Poland. An important reason for the welcome offered to these migrants has been their role in tackling the implications of an ageing workforce and associated labour and skill shortages (Boyle and Watt, 2006).

In coming to the conclusion that addressing the implications of an ageing population can be inextricably linked with a positive and open approach to immigration, Scotland potentially has lessons for the rest of the EU, and especially for those who do not recognise or yet do not accept the link (CEC, 2005).

There are signs, then, of the 'mainstreaming' of ageing issues within the academy of the social sciences, with new emphasis on cross-cutting themes, as seen with the Cross-Council Programme on Ageing and policy arenas. Beyond the UK, there has been a growth in research and active policy formation and analyses in a number of countries, offering the opportunity to compare experiences and strategies across different environments. Where transnational studies (see, for instance, Droogleever Fortuijn and van der Meer, 2003) have been undertaken, these confirm both similarities and variations of experience and approach to ageing and its impacts according to cultural, economic, historical and other dimensions of society.

Neither demography nor any individual discipline can address all the issues raised by these population developments, so that an eclectic response is required. So here the foundations are laid to give an evidence base to the arguments and policy debates in this volume. This chapter provides an exploration of the demographic changes and variations underpinning the research developments below, hopefully offering a cross-cutting examination of the population changes that should inform any analysis of ageing and employability. It goes on to present data and discussion on demographic change for Scotland – a nation that has long been confronted by population stagnation and has recently been at the forefront of policy interventions to address decline and ageing. It then contrasts these specific Scottish developments with UK, European and global structural changes and trends. A consideration of the range of national and regional responses to these developments, in particular the ageing dimension, precedes the concluding remarks.

Demographic change: tales from an old and declining population

Until relatively recently, for many countries and societies facing the threat of an ageing population there has been an emphasis on the uniqueness of their particular situation, with a failure to appreciate the universality of the main trends. Scotland is fairly typical in that respect, with both government and opposition becoming increasingly concerned at the demographic prospects of a population both in decline and getting older. So, according to the Scottish First Minister,

Jack McConnell, the nation's declining population is 'the single biggest challenge facing Scotland as we move further into the 21st century' (Scottish Executive, 2004, p 1). The Scottish Executive (2004, p 3) policy document that spotlights this continues:

> If this decline is not stemmed then our economy will suffer, there will be a severe strain on our public services as an ever ageing population struggles to cope with the challenges of the global economy, and our cultural life will be diminished ... If Scotland is to achieve a balanced economy, with a stable tax base to support strong public services, then we must boost the working population, particularly the 25–45 age group.

This brings home how 'ageing' has had a critical impact on the mainstream Scottish establishment policy agenda. Much of the recent interest in Scottish population change has been driven by this concern, with a predicted decline in numbers below the totemistic five million, albeit with a recognition of concomitant ageing. This contrasts with earlier periods when emigration was seen as the dominant concern and actual depopulation was experienced in many localities, especially in remote rural areas and former mining and textile communities. Rural regions have been similarly affected in many other parts of Europe (CEC, 2004); nevertheless, the issue dominating the public debate has been concern over immigration. This divergence of priorities will be returned to later.

The threat of population decline in Scotland, forecast by the General Register Office for Scotland since the late 1990s (GROS, 2005), contrasts with the other countries of the UK, where unremitting growth is expected to continue well into the future (GROS, 2005). However, in a climate of almost unprecedented interest and scrutiny in demographic change, the Scottish population has been avoiding a fall and is now expected to increase marginally to 5.1 million by 2019 before a slow and steady decline. Significantly for the topic of this volume, commentary has been growing on the associated structural changes in the population – reporting that there have been progressively fewer young people and more older citizens and forecasting that these trends are set to continue. It is now predicted that, between 2004 and 2031, the numbers of children under 16 will have fallen by a further 15% and those of working age by 7% while those of pensionable age will have increased by 35% (all forecasts incorporating the raising of women's pensionable age to 65 by 2020). The numbers of young people entering the labour market have begun to decline as the declining birth rate has worked its way through successive age cohorts. Considering the components of these gross changes, in every year from 1997 to 2004 there was a natural decrease of about four thousand as deaths outnumbered births; but in 2004 migrants boosted the population by a net 26,000 – 15,500 from the rest of the UK, 11,700 from the rest of the world. Migration has thus again become a key element to overall changes against a background of overall anticipated population decline, but now compensating for losses rather than balancing for gains as in the past.

To explore and so understand these demographic developments and forecasts, it is helpful to look at historical changes. Over the past 140 years, Scotland's share of the population of the UK (as currently constituted) fell from 12.5% in 1861 to 8.6% in 2001, confirming that significant population shifts are nothing new and that they reflect long-term differentials in economic growth rates. Migration has been an important part of these changes, with both in- and out-migration capturing attention, and with the host and origin countries for these movements varying over time. However, what is most remarkable in the case of Scotland is the stability in the aggregate population; it has hardly changed in a century (from 1921 to 2021 it will have varied within a narrow band between 4.9 and 5.2 million) and in reality relatively little change is expected for the next few decades.

Figure 2.1: Scotland's population, 1901–2004

Source: Clark (2005)

© Crown copyright. Data supplied by General Register Office for Scotland

As the graph shows, apart from the apparently minor effects of the First World War on the total numbers and the more important long-term impacts of the Second World War, there has been stability over a century. This hides massive emigration throughout the 20th century, especially in the 1920s and 1960s, and as migration is dominated by pull factors, with people leaving to take advantage of better opportunities rather than being pushed out by problems, there are certain lessons for today (an argument that will be returned to later). That level of emigration from Scotland has inevitably left a legacy of non-growth, as these migrants and their children were not there to contribute to the renewal of the population naturally; the counter-argument obviously applied to their new homelands.

So projections in the early part of the new millennium suggested that as Scotland was facing decline it was in a unique position in the UK, where further significant strong growth was expected, and it was also practically unique in the EU. The main reasons for its decline were attributed to the falling and low birth rate, which was less than necessary to grow or keep the population stable. This represented a change from the previous history when high natural growth just about balanced high net emigration.

Figure 2.2: Net migration and natural change in Scotland, estimated and projected, 1951–2031

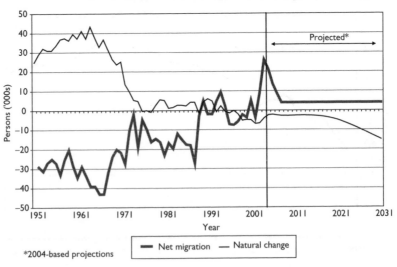

*2004-based projections

Source: Clark (2005)

© Crown copyright. Data supplied by General Register Office for Scotland

Natural change was now no longer contributing to net growth, as the number of births had dropped by half since the early 1960s. By the early part of the new century, although reduced from previously, Scotland still had a net outward migration of 41,000 over that decade (1992-2001) compared with the UK net inward migration of 875,000. Projections suggested that these trends would continue into the future as past changes inevitably work their way forward, becoming endemic to each cohort in the absence of large-scale movements of people into Scotland or a raising of the birth rate. Within this context of a stable population with fewer births, inevitably the idea of an ageing population and fewer school leavers came to be considered as creating dependency problems for the working population and increasing labour shortages for the employment market. Table 2.1 illustrates why the government and others became increasingly concerned as the scale of the challenge became apparent. The net changes were to be driven by fewer children, more older people, and fewer of working age.

This would lead to dependency rates worsening: slowly at first, arrested after 2010 to an extent by the rising pension age for women (increasing from 60 to 65 between 2010 and 2020), but eventually there would be high proportions of the very old and fewer young people dependent on the reducing 'working age' population.

This is illustrated graphically – in more ways than one – in Figure 2.3, with the structure evolving away from the classical pyramid through

Table 2.1: Scotland's changing age structure

2004–based age group*	Projected age structure of Scotland's population	
	2004	2031
Children	18.4%	15.7%
Working age	62.5%	58.5%
Pension age	19.1%	25.8%
	Projected number of dependants per 100 population of working age, Scotland	
	2004	2031
Children	29.5	26.8
Pensioners	30.5	44.2
All dependants	60.0	70.9

* Children defined as under 16. Working age and pensionable age populations based on state pension age for given year. Between 2010 and 2020, state pension age will change from 65 years for men and 60 years for women, to 65 years for both sexes.

Source: GROS (2004)

© Crown copyright. Data supplied by General Register Office for Scotland

Figure 2.3: Estimated and projected age structure in Scotland, 1911–2031

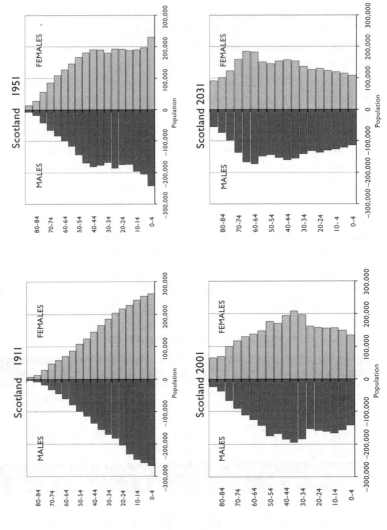

the effects of world wars and selective out-migration to a shape that resembles a supertanker or coffin in the middle of the current century. The traditional model of the actuaries and manpower planners has broken down, and this has been exacerbated as many postpone full entry into the labour market by continuing into higher education. Within Scotland, these aggregate national changes are not uniform, with core cities, old industrial areas and the rural periphery in decline, and the commuting suburbs and communities around Edinburgh growing. There are also more local divergences; within the Highlands, for example, most landward areas and islands continue their century-long decline, while the service and administrative capital of Inverness maintains a rapid growth. These past trends are expected to proceed into the future with continuing net population movements from the west to the east of the country, and a decline of the periphery and old industrial areas. Although the Registrar General for Scotland regularly modifies the demographic predictions as new data become available, with migration an especially erratic factor, the basic messages of the past decade have remained clear and firm: over the coming decades, Scotland will experience slow, very gradual population decline due to low and decreasing levels of fertility (births are at their lowest levels since records began in 1855) and assumed reduced levels of net migration (although, as discussed later, there appears to have been substantial immigration recently). This will be associated with spatial population change within the country based on differing economic performances, and, crucially, the population will be ageing and ageing fastest where economic problems present the greatest difficulties in sustaining jobs and populations. The conclusion in the late 1990s was that these trends marked Scotland out as unique and as such it could and should address this peculiar demographic challenge through a tailored Fresh Talent Initiative, which would seek to attract new Scots to be employed and to settle there. Why this tale of the unique Scottish circumstances is worthy of wider attention is explored later.

Demographic change: comparisons with UK, European and global trends

Over the Census period 1991-2001, the UK population grew by 3.4%, and, significantly, London's population grew by 400,000.

Regionally, the south of the country was growing fast, driven by the booming economy of the capital, which itself marked a turnaround from the position prior to 1980 (Gordon, 2004). By contrast, with the decline of manufacturing and the reorientation of the UK economy

Table 2.2: UK regions: percentage population change, 1997–2002

London	6.2
South West	2.9
Eastern	2.9
East Midlands	2.4
South East	2.3
United Kingdom	1.8
Northern Ireland	1.5
Wales	1.0
West Midlands	0.8
Yorkshire and the Humber	0.6
North West	0.0
Scotland	–0.6
North East	–1.6

Source: GAD

away from the Commonwealth and the North Atlantic and towards Europe, the old northern industrial regions and the rest of the periphery, away from the core South East, have been and remain in decline. External migration flows into the UK reinforced the internal moves to the South East so that a clear North–South divide was established. This attention to the changing fortunes of London is deliberate: although losing about a fifth of a million people through mobility out of the city, a very high proportion (over 90%) of international in-migration to the UK (almost 900,000 over the decade) was to the Greater London conurbation, more than compensating for suburbanisation tendencies. Concerns over the scale of these immigration flows has set the UK agenda on population policies, with a consequent lack of awareness or subordination of some of the ageing and structural developments that are most apparent in the North. As the latter, and Scotland in particular, has been facing these challenges since the millennium, innovation notably has been generated away from the capital.

In a European context, although the decline in fertility has been stronger than average in Scotland and is now low, it is not very different from much of the rest of the continent.

Patterns of change vary substantially across Europe but undoubtedly there are indications that population stability is an issue across the continent. Whereas the initial concerns in Scotland were raised on the basis of Figure 2.4, crucially only the pre-2004 member states of the EU15 were included.

Table 2.3: European total fertility rates, 2004

EU25	1.50[(e)]
EU15	1.52[(e)]
Euro-zone	1.48[(e)]
Scotland	1.60
Belgium	1.64[(e)]
Czech Republic	1.23
Denmark	1.78
Germany	1.37[(e)]
Estonia	1.40[(e)]
Greece	1.29[(e)]
Spain	1.32[(e)]
France	1.90[(p)]
Ireland	1.99[(e)]
Italy	1.33
Cyprus	1.49[(p)]
Latvia	1.24
Lithuania	1.26
Luxembourg	1.70
Hungary	1.28
Malta	1.37
Netherlands	1.73
Austria	1.42
Poland	1.23
Portugal	1.42[(e)]
Slovenia	1.22[(e)]
Slovakia	1.25
Finland	1.80
Sweden	1.75
United Kingdom	1.74[(e)]
Bulgaria	1.29
Croatia	1.35
Romania	1.29
Turkey	2.20[(e)]
Iceland	2.03
Liechtenstein	1.45[(p)]
Norway	1.81
Switzerland	1.42[(p)]
European Free Trade Association (Iceland, Liechtenstein, Norway, Switzerland)	1.55[(p)]

(e) = Estimated value.

(p) = Provisional value.

Source: GROS (2005) and Eurostat (2005)

When all 27 existing and accession countries are compared, Scotland appears to be typical of the picture in the poorer parts of the European Union; that is, declining. Indeed, UN and EU statistics (UN, 2002; CEC, 2005) predict that the European population is entering a period of decline, and by 2050 is expected to have fallen by 100 million (or by over 12%) from 730 million. Pre-accession, the EU15 were generally suffering decline, with the four large countries only stable through large-scale in-migration. Of the 2004 new member states, six out of the 10 were already in decline on entry to the EU and this is forecast to continue. Importantly for ageing issues and employability, those over the age of 65 were expected to increase both absolutely and proportionately to reach 27.6% of the total in 2050.

If this analysis is extended to the global scale, some of the fastest-ageing societies are also the largest, with both China and India expected to suffer particularly rapid structural changes (UN, 2002). As will be discussed later, national solutions to future changes in dependency ratios and reductions in the numbers of young people entering semi- and unskilled labour markets cannot rely on sustained flows of talented, graduate migrant workers from apparently people-rich countries. In the global marketplace, such competitors are raising their stock of human capital resources on the one hand, and having to face the evolution of their own labour shortages caused by this upgrading and ageing on the other. There is but limited evidence, however, on how these international and transnational trends will develop, although Casey and Macnicol in this volume provide some insights from their comparative studies.

Figure 2.4: Population projections across the EU27

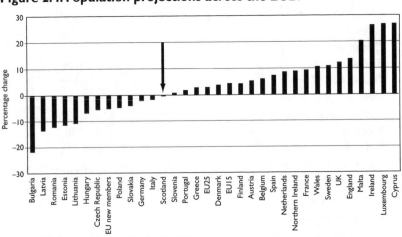

Source: GAD (UK and constituent countries) and Eurostat.
Note: Eurostat also produces an alternative UK projection not shown here.

Ageing and declining populations are therefore global phenomena. Scotland is not unique, although it perhaps has recognised, and so has started to appreciate, many of the consequences of these developments before the rest of the UK, where the other nations can expect continuing population growth for some decades. The rest of the UK is therefore the anomaly in the wider European environment and Scotland has much in common with its other continental neighbours from which it can learn. Indeed, while the Fresh Talent Initiative has been welcomed as a progressive and strategic approach to certain aspects of these changes, it is not acting in vacuum. The strategy has been broadly welcomed within Scotland (see CRE, 2005, for example), although there have been difficulties reconciling the details with UK-wide legislation and interpretations of central government's intentions. However, other countries, and especially those in central and eastern Europe, can be expected to react to their own problems and perhaps specifically to any Scottish initiative. So far, there is evidence that immigration from the new EU member states has been significant, with estimates that the decline in Scottish population had been reversed by 2005 (Ernst & Young, 2006). Migrant workers coming from Poland especially, making up 60% of newcomers from the accession states, are filling the sorts of low-paid, low-skilled jobs traditionally taken by incomers initially. However, overall there is little room for manoeuvre within the EU framework, and this degree of flow is not believed sustainable beyond 2007, when net migration is again predicted to approach a balance. Furthermore, opportunities to address ageing and dependency challenges through the attraction of migrants are limited further by the restrictions imposed by the UK central state. Under the 1998 Scotland Act (TSO, 1998), Westminster has ensured that it has retained control over migration by reserving these powers. In a unitary state, although there is some advantage in 'the importance of being unimportant', the Fresh Talent Initiative offers limited choice and constrained options to the devolved government[a].

Given that a primary rationale for attracting migrant workers has been to address the falls in the working population and labour and skill shortages, this reaffirms the need to consider the role of, and policies for, those who currently suffer low rates of economic activity (DWP, 2002; Blyth, 2006). In particular, the socially excluded, those with low qualifications, the long-term sick and disabled, and, in the context of this volume, older workers have all been targeted for special attention as alternative recruits from the reserve army of labour. Accepted wisdom (DWP, 2002; Blyth, 2006; McQuaid and Lindsay, 2006) considers that 'employability' is a useful concept to analyse why members of some of these groups are inactive and it is to a brief exploration of the dimensions of this that we now turn.

Older people, older workers: social and policy responses

Consistent with the description above, Jess Barrow (Age Concern Scotland, seconded to the Older People's Unit) (Scottish Executive, 2006) has argued that net out-migration and a declining birth rate, combined with increased longevity, means that Scotland faces significant demographic challenges. As here, she contrasts how the political response has been focused on encouraging younger people to stay in Scotland and encouraging greater immigration (including the Fresh Talent Initiative), while little has been said about the positive contribution of older people. In Chapter Five of this volume, Beatty and Fothergill extensively discuss wider UK attempts to move more of the over-50s back into employment. Their research has been conducted against a continuing lack of effective demand in those regions that traditionally have suffered from industrial restructuring, unemployment and low growth. Critically, and consistent with market-induced responses to disequilibria in regional labour markets, the regions facing these job shortfalls are also the regions with the lowest population growth, or actual decline, over the past two decades, with associated significant net out-migration. They also tend to have older and more rapidly ageing populations and lower participation rates of older workers, as demonstrated earlier.

However, and in contradistinction to Beatty and Fothergill's (2002 and in Chapter Five of this volume) prognosis, labour markets have been tightening across the UK, with significant job growth. For example, estimates in Scotland have consistently shown that labour shortages are important in many secondary labour market sectors (FSS, 2004). As Beatty and Fothergill demonstrate, more attention is being paid, therefore, to the potential offered by attracting many of the inactive to the low-paid, low-skilled jobs unfilled in the service sectors, a root cause of the approach favoured by the DWP (2005) and Treasury. Complementing this approach to identifying new reserves of labour, inward migration has risen sharply with the entry of central and east European countries into the EU (Home Office, 2006), so that competition for many of the secondary labour market jobs is coming from this new source of young, fit, skilled workers (Boyle and Watt, 2006).

As 'soft' skills such as customer handling, oral communication, team working and problem-solving skills are proving the most difficult for employers to source in the Scottish context (FSS, 2004), and probably elsewhere, there is evidence (Danson et al, 2006) that companies are recruiting from the migrant communities in preference to older workers. This will probably only be of short-term gain as the flow of young immigrants reduces naturally or is controlled by government (Ernst & Young, 2006). This contradiction between short- and long-term imperatives confirms the need to address the challenges of an ageing workforce through improving the capacities of older workers to stay in the labour market. That suggests better routes back to work for the inactive (DWP, 2002, 2005; Blyth, 2006; and see Beatty and Fothergill in Chapter Five of this volume) and better and more careers advice and support. Interestingly, Scotland has an all-age service, Careers Scotland, which has been favourably reviewed by the OECD as having adopted practices that 'are comparable to leading good practice across the world' (Watts, 2005, p 37) to complement these other actions.

Conclusion

In a significant, though often ignored publication, the European Commission forecast that:

> Europe is facing … unprecedented demographic change. In 2003, … the new Member States, with the exception of Cyprus and Malta, all saw falling populations. In many countries, immigration has become vital to ensure population growth. The fertility rate everywhere is below the threshold needed to renew the population (around 2.1 children per woman), and has even fallen below 1.5 children per woman in many Member States. (CEC, 2005, p 2)

With an ageing and declining population, Scotland is fairly typical and so its experiments in both trying to attract migrant workers and improve the activity rates of those over 50 offer the opportunity to gauge such initiatives more broadly. Similarly, the experiences of Finland in promoting more inclusion for older workers also hold lessons for elsewhere. Indeed, as countries across the globe come to recognise the challenge of an ageing and healthier society and the potential for introducing more progressive strategies to address this development, there is advantage in transnational research. Neither policy changes nor markets alone can remove barriers to raising their employability, as changes in attitudes and behaviour are also necessary (Worsley, 1996). As recently noted:

> Reflecting on the differing needs identified and legislation in place, the efforts of government bodies are currently focused primarily on race and disability; however, age, where legislation is forthcoming, features less prominently in government bodies' main priorities. (NAO, 2004, p 6)

Note

[a] Interestingly, both Quebec and Catalonia have secured the capacity to regulate immigration to their respective territories, raising the possibilities for divergence within the UK to reflect specific area needs.

References

Anyadike-Danes, M. (2002) 'Why is our employment rate the lowest in the UK?', *Labour Market Bulletin*, no 16, pp 48-53.

Ascherson, N. (2002) *Stone Voices: The Search for Scotland*, London: Granta Books.

Beatty, C. and Fothergill, S. (2002) 'Hidden unemployment among men: a case study', *Regional Studies*, vol 36, no 8, pp 811-23.

Blyth, B. (2006) 'Incapacity Benefit reforms – Pathways to Work pilots performance and analysis', Working Paper No 26, Sheffield: Department for Work and Pensions (www.dwp.gov.uk/asd/asd5/wp26.pdf).

Boyle, S. and Watt, P. (2006) 'Scottish economic review' (13th edn), Edinburgh: Scottish Executive, pp 92-9 (www.scottishexecutive.gov.uk/Publications/2006/06/27171110/13).

CEC (Commission of the European Communities) (2004) *Third Cohesion Report*, Brussels: CEC.

CEC (2005) *Green Paper 'Confronting Demographic Change: A New Solidarity Between the Generations'*, 94 final, Brussels: CEC.

Clark, E. (2005) *Setting the Demographic Scene*, Edinburgh: General Register Office for Scotland.

CRE (Commission for Racial Equality) (2005) 'Broadening our horizons' (www.cre.gov.uk/downloads/broadening_our_horizons_summary_report.pdf).

Danson, M., Gilmore, K., Helinska-Hughes, E. and Wyper, J. (2006) *Employability and Employer Attitudes to the Unemployed and Inactive in Scotland*, Report to EQUAL – Access, Paisley: University of Paisley.

Droogleever Fortuijn, J. and van der Meer, M. (2003) 'Daily activities of older adults in urban and rural areas in six European countries', Paper presented at the Regional Studies Association Seminar Series on Demography and Ageing 'Demographic Ageing and the Built Environment', Nottingham Trent University, 7 November.

DWP (Department of Work and Pensions) (2002) *Pathways to Work*, London: DWP.

DWP (2005) *Department for Work and Pensions Five Year Strategy: Opportunity and Security throughout Life*, London: DWP.

Ernst & Young (2006) 'Scottish Item Club – Economic prospects 2006' (www.ey.com/global/download.nsf/UK/ITEM_Club_Scotland_23-11-05/$file/051121_ITEM_club_scotland_2006.pdf).

Florida, R. (2002a) *The Rise of the Creative Class: And How It's Transforming Work, Leisure, Community and Everyday Life*, New York, NY: Basic Books.

Florida, R. (2002b) 'The economic geography of talent', *Annals of the Association of American Geographers*, vol 92, no 4, pp 743-55.

Florida, R. (2002c) 'Bohemia and economic geography', *Journal of Economic Geography*, vol 2, no 1, pp 55-71.

FSS (Futureskills Scotland) (2004) *Skills in Scotland 2004*, Glasgow: Scottish Enterprise.

Gordon, J. (2004) 'A disjointed dynamo: the South East and inter-regional relationships', *New Economy*, vol 11, no 3, pp 40-4.

GROS (General Register Office for Scotland) (2005) *Projected Population of Scotland (2004-Based)*, Edinburgh: GROS.

Haskins, C. (2003) *Rural Delivery Review: A Report on the Delivery of Government Policies in Rural England*, London: Department for Environment, Food and Rural Affairs.

Hollywood, E., Brown, R., Danson, M. and McQuaid, R. (2003) *Older Workers in the Scottish Labour Market: A New Agenda*, Universities of Stirling and Strathclyde: Scotecon (www.scotecon.net/publications/McQuaid%20older%20workers%20Full%20Report.pdf).

Home Office (2006) *Accession Monitoring Report*, May 2004 – December 2005 (www.ind.homeoffice.gov.uk/6353/aboutus/accessionmonitoringreport1.pdf).

Hunter, J. (1994) *A Dance Called America*, Edinburgh: Mainstream.

Independence Convention (2005) Commemorative DVD of the official launch of the Independence Convention (www.independenceconvention.org/).

Joshi, H.E. and Wright, R.E. (2005) 'Starting life in Scotland', in D. Coyle, W. Alexander and B. Ashcroft (eds) *New Wealth for Old Nations: Scotland's Economic Prospects*, Princeton, NJ: Princeton University Press, pp 166-85.

Kahila, P. and Rinne-Koski, K. (2006) 'New mode of ageing? Flexible lifestyle as an alternative', *Regions*, vol 2, no 1, pp 14-15.

McQuaid, R. and Lindsay, C. (2006) 'The concept of employability: transcending the orthodoxies of supply and demand?', *Urban Studies*, vol 42, no 2, pp 197-219.

Metz, D. and Underwood, M. (2005) *Older, Richer, Fitter*, Powys: Age Concern Books.

Migrationwatch (2006) www.migrationwatchuk.org/outline_of_the_problem.asp

NAO (National Audit Office) (2004) *Delivering Public Services to a Diverse Society*, London: NAO.

Paterson, L., Bechhofer, F. and McCrone, D. (2004) *Living in Scotland: Social and Economic Change since 1980*, Edinburgh: Edinburgh University Press.

Performance and Innovation Unit (2000) *Winning the Generation Game*, London: Stationery Office.

Reid, J. (2006) Speech to Demos, 9 August.

Rogoff, K. (2002) Transcript of a Press Briefing on the World Economic Outlook, International Monetary Fund, 25 September, Washington, DC.

Scottish Executive (2004) *New Scots: Attracting Fresh Talent to Meet the Challenge of Growth*, Edinburgh: Scottish Executive.

Scottish Executive (2006) 'Older people' (www.scotland.gov.uk/Topics/People/older-people).

TSO (The Stationery Office) (1998) 'The Scotland Act' (www.opsi.gov.uk/ACTS/acts1998/19980046.htm).

UKIP (2005) 'UK Independence Party 2005 General Election manifesto' (www.ukip.org/index.php?menu=manifesto2005&page=manifesto2005homeaffairs).

UN (2002) *World Population Prospects*, New York, NY: UN.

UNRISD (2002) Conference on Global Ageing, UN 2nd World Assembly on Ageing, Madrid, 6-9 April.

Watson, M. (2003) *Being English in Scotland*, Edinburgh: Edinburgh University Press.

Watts, A.G. (2005) *Careers Scotland: Progress and Potential: A Review Benchmarked against the OECD Career Guidance Policy Review*, Glasgow: Careers Scotland.

Whyte, I. (2000) *Migration and Society in Britain 1550–1830*, London: Palgrave MacMillan.

Worsley, R. (1996) *Age and Employment: Why Employers Should Think Again About Older Workers*, London: Age Concern England.

THREE

The American experience of age discrimination legislation

John Macnicol

Introduction

In 2006, the United Kingdom finally passed legislation against age discrimination in employment. The essentials can be summarised quickly: both direct and indirect discrimination are outlawed; improved employment protection has been granted to older workers; and the opportunity to work past the age of 65 is now negotiable with employers. Over the coming years, numerous legal decisions will test the legislation's defences, and other political pressures will be brought to bear which may abolish mandatory retirement for all but a few occupations.

Ostensibly, the new Age Regulations are a direct response to the European Union Employment Directive on Equal Treatment of November 2000 (2000/78/ET), which obliges member states to redesign their existing legislation on race, sex and disability discrimination, while universalising legislative action against age discrimination. However, in the medium term, the British legislation represents the culmination of a revival of interest in the problems of older workers that has intensified since the early 1990s, in response to concerns over the fall in older men's economic activity rates since the 1970s (although these have risen since 1994), a future ageing population, skills shortages and human capital wastage, and those overall labour-supply considerations that are central to the New Deal. Action against age discrimination is part of the government strategy of attaining an 80% overall employment rate and getting one million people aged between 50 and state pension age back into work. The largely voluntarist approach of John Major's Conservative government (1990-97) was followed by New Labour's post-1997 initiatives – notionally more proactive, but still very cautious. From 2000, however, legislation became inevitable and the example of other countries has been arousing growing interest.

In designing legislation against age discrimination in employment, the obvious country to examine is the United States, which has had, at federal level, an Age Discrimination in Employment Act (ADEA) since 1967 (with subsequent amendments). The ADEA provides protection against age-based discrimination in hiring, firing, promotion, demotion, retraining, working hours, compensation, workplace harassment and other aspects of employment. Since 1986, mandatory retirement has been abolished for all but a few key occupations where public safety is an issue (notably, firefighters, bus drivers, civilian airline pilots, prison guards and uniformed police officers). Interestingly, the ADEA does not protect elected officials, their personal staff and other high-level policy makers. Nor has it affected minimum ages for certain public offices and age-based legal protections for young people (as in the minimum age for alcohol consumption). Age-targeted social security benefits are, of course, exempt. Unless covered by certain defences, age stipulations in job advertisements are illegal. Evidence of discrimination need not only be overt; it can be adduced from statistical discrimination tests and other measures of outcome (following the civil rights doctrine of 'adverse impact') – though in the case of age this kind of evidence can be elusive: demonstrating indirect age discrimination is always problematic.

This chapter will examine the origins and subsequent development of the ADEA, and draw some parallels with Britain. In doing so, it will not accept tacitly the policy maker's assumption that the benefits of such legislation are unproblematic, and that the issues are mere technocratic ones relating to minor adjustments. Instead, it will analyse the ADEA's origins, aims and achievements from a more critical perspective.

The growth of interest in age discrimination

In the US, as in most other industrialised economies, the late 19th century saw the beginnings of a debate over the 'worn-out' older worker who was being increasingly displaced by new technology and a 'speeding up' of industrial production methods. The labour force participation rates of American men aged 65+ fell from 68.3% in 1890 to 55.6% in 1920 and 41.8% in 1940. Undoubtedly, the recession of the interwar years exacerbated this technology-driven displacement: urban industries had to innovate in order to survive, and this involved workforce downsizings and the shedding of older employees. At the same time, American agriculture (which employed high proportions of older men) was in severe recession in the 1930s.

In the absence of any federal old age pension scheme, most retirees had to rely on the support of relatives, neighbours, charities and almshouses. Such state old age pension schemes as existed were few in number and paid meagre benefits. However, there was some local-level legislation against age discrimination in employment, via state laws: Colorado passed one as early as 1903, and other states gradually followed suit – though these laws were of limited effectiveness.

In interwar America, the very evident plight of the older worker engendered an interesting discussion, which is still highly relevant. Some commentators speculated that there seemed to be, as the statistician Louis I. Dublin put it:

> ... a very widespread and intense prejudice against the employment of older workers.... There are many instances on record of middle-aged men and women who find it extremely difficult to get a new job because of their age, even though it is obvious that they have many years of useful work ahead of them. Probably there is no greater tragedy in modern life than this forced retirement of workers still in the prime of life. (Dublin, 1928, p 161)

To some observers, age discrimination appeared to be growing (Barkin, 1933). However, others argued that the worsening job prospects of older workers were not caused by 'discrimination' per se but by economic restructuring, the 1930s recession and related factors (notably older workers' concentration in long-established industrial sectors experiencing greatest labour force shake-up, their displacement by new technology, or their lack of skills relevant to the new expanding industries) (Macnicol, 2006, p 37).

Those who argued that economic restructuring was more important had their case immensely strengthened by the events of the Second World War. Military call-up and the stimulation to heavy manufacturing opened up job opportunities for older workers (and others who had previously had weak labour force attachment, such as unskilled ethnic minorities, women, juveniles and disabled people). By 1944, about two million more men and women aged 55+ were in the labour force compared with 1940 (Bancroft, 1952, p 56). Older workers were successfully trained for demanding and skilled positions in industry, indicating how much latent working capacity there existed in the older population (Sheppard, 1976, p 296). Interestingly, the postwar economic boom (armaments manufacturing continuing at a high level, owing to the Korean War) stimulated labour market demand in those sectors that employed older workers: as a result, the labour force participation rate of men aged 65+ was virtually the same in 1950 (41.4%) as it was in 1940 (41.8%). The introduction of social security was seen by contemporaries as having little incentive effect on retirement: federal old age and survivors' social security benefits were simply too low. Older people tried to work as long as possible past the age of 65, largely for economic reasons (Stecker, 1951, pp 15, 17). As in Britain in the 1950s, there was a considerable 'spread' of retirement ages in the US at this time. Male labour force participation rates peaked between the ages of 35 and 44, and then declined with advancing age: at ages 65 to 69, about half of all men were in the labour force, that proportion dropping to one quarter above age 70 (Gordon, 1960, p 300).

In the US in the 1950s, there was much discussion – at both expert and populist level – of age discrimination, mandatory retirement, working capacity at later ages, the ageist 'prejudices' held by employers, the shortening of working lives yet the lengthening of chronological lives, the possibility of 'flexible' or 'phased' retirement, and so on (Drake, 1958). To take but one example, in 1953 *Time* magazine expressed concern over long-run retirement trends and a future ageing population, in the light of existing labour shortages, and praised those companies that had dropped their mandatory retirement policies; it urged corporations to review their 'prejudices' against hiring workers aged 40+ and to abandon compulsory retirement at age 65 (*Time*, 1953). The majority of informed contemporaries realised that retirement had continued to spread despite overall economic growth and an expansion of employment, because of declining labour market demand in those sectors that employed older people (Clague, 1949). Nevertheless, it was felt that certain policies at the margins might offer some help to older workers – notably the abolition of mandatory retirement (and its replacement by individualised testing), more retraining programmes, and persuading employers to abandon their 'prejudices' (Tibbitts, 1954, p 303). However, no great claims were ever made that legislation could reverse the trend to male early retirement.

The origins of the 1967 ADEA

Why did the US – a 'welfare laggard' in so many other areas of social policy, with a far less developed welfare state than most European societies, and with relatively little employment protection – pass into law a measure in 1967 which Britain has only now introduced? While there had been a build-up of interest in the labour market problems of older workers, age was not a central political issue in the way that race was; it might well have been largely ignored, as it was in Britain. The origins of the ADEA are complex, being rooted in the wider social, economic and political changes occurring in American society; in this chapter, only a brief summary can be provided.

An obvious key factor was the civil rights movement, which – because of America's unique racial history – was much more highly developed in the US than in Britain. Most contemporaries realised that there was not the same 'animus' or 'bigotry' towards older people as there was towards ethnic minorities, and that ageism was somewhat different from racism or sexism (age being a 'relative characteristic', whereas race and sex are 'immutable characteristics'). Nevertheless, age became part of the package of civil rights measures so much discussed in the 1960s. Age discrimination was originally included in the 1964 Civil Rights Bill, but was postponed pending an official enquiry into the problems of older workers (US Department of Labor, 1965), and then made the subject of separate legislation three years later.

Another factor was the growth of grey power pressure groups (such as the American Association of Retired Persons, founded in 1958), which have always argued the 'social justice' case against ageism in social attitudes and age discrimination in employment. There was also increasing concern over the economic status of the retired, as part of the 'rediscovery of poverty' of the early 1960s: official statistics showed that, in 1958, 60% of Americans aged 65+ had incomes of less than $1,000 per annum, where the federal standard of adequacy for a retired couple in an urban area in 1959 ranged from $2,681 to $3,304 per annum (Harrington, 1962, p 104 and ch 6). A final, very important, factor was that the slow transition from a manufacturing economy to a service-based one was both eroding the job prospects of those disadvantaged by factors such as ethnicity, age, lack of education or skills and leading to demands that labour power potential in the US be maximised in order to meet the new challenges of automation and modernisation in the economy. In the case of older workers, it appeared that valuable human capital was being lost by the use of crude 'age proxies' – seemingly based on irrational, 'false stereotypes' of their industrial obsolescence – and the imposition of mandatory retirement at age 65. Labour supply considerations were therefore important.

However, the origins of the ADEA are especially puzzling when one considers that middle-aged American men had not experienced falling labour force participation rates since the Second World War, and their unemployment rates were actually lower than those of young men: in 1964, on average only 3% of males aged 45-54 were unemployed, whereas for males aged 14-19 the rate was 15% (though, of course, the average older worker, once unemployed, experienced a longer and arguably more corrosive period of joblessness) (US Department of

Labor, 1965, p 99). Indeed, in its original form, the ADEA was not even about old age: it was, instead, a job-protection measure for middle-aged workers. The upper age limit was set at 65 (the lower eventually being set at 40), and was raised to 70 in 1978. Only in 1986 was the limit uncapped (with some key exceptions), and this was bound to have little effect, since by 1990 only 16.3% of men and 8.6% of women aged 65+ were still in the labour force. The final point of interest concerns the apparent insignificance of mandatory retirement: surveys at the time appeared to demonstrate that, on the face of it, the proportion of retirees who were still work-fit but unwilling to leave work was a mere 5-7% (Levine, 1988, pp 27-8). Of course, the 'true' extent of compulsory retirement is always difficult to measure: categories like 'voluntary retirement', 'involuntary retirement', 'mandatory retirement' or 'ill health', are porous and overlapping. It has also long been known that interview-based surveys can yield unreliable results, for many reasons (for example, retirees may not know the real reason for their retirement, or the disappearance of a job may be masked by self-defined ill health). The length of time spent in retirement can also affect responses (Bone et al, 1992, p 55). Finally, within a firm or sector there may develop a strong tradition, or what Michael Fogarty called 'a pattern of custom and practice', which may cause workers to leave at a certain age without explicit compulsion being needed (Fogarty, 1980, p 11).

The justifications for the ADEA were therefore uncannily similar to the mixture of 'social justice' and 'labour supply' ones that figure prominently in today's British debate. Ageism in social relations was little discussed (and certainly never seen as amenable to legislation). There was provision in the ADEA for the Secretary of Labor to introduce policies to re-educate employers and make them less ageist; however, this was never properly implemented. The emphasis was on tackling 'irrational' or 'arbitrary' age discrimination in employment. The overarching principle was that discrimination that was clearly job-related was permissible: individualised testing for job competence would be more effective than crude age proxies in weeding out unproductive workers. Legal rulings have thus tended to reinforce the principle that, if a test of employment is job-related, it can be a rational basis for compulsory retirement.

The working of the ADEA

The ADEA has engendered an enormous legal controversy, only a very small part of which can be mentioned here. Its legal procedures for bringing an age discrimination charge against an employer are quite complex: several 'procedural wrinkles' have to be negotiated, reflecting its intention to resolve disputes by conciliation if at all possible. Only at a relatively late stage does the supervisory body, the Equal Employment Opportunity Commission (EEOC), become involved. If all else fails, cases go to court. The history of the ADEA since 1967 has involved a series of fascinating courtroom disputes and 'landmark' cases where legal interpretation has collided head-on with the latest medical evidence on health status, working capacity and the biology of ageing. The legal decisions have reflected the difficulties inherent in demonstrating age discrimination.

Some of these difficulties can be summarised briefly. Proof of intent and motive is problematic, given that evidence tends to be circumstantial. (If a defendant articulates a reasonable explanation for their alleged discriminatory actions, the burden of proof falls on the plaintiff.) Ageist remarks uttered by managers in the workplace can, of course, be cited in court as strong evidence. But employers have become more adept at avoiding charges of age discrimination, and are now much more careful of what they say; workplace ageism may therefore have been driven deeper into whispered, off-the-record conversations behind boardroom walls. Most age discrimination probably occurs in hiring – and this is the most difficult for job applicants to detect. At a later stage, statistical discrimination tests can operate – for example, where the average age of those dismissed by a firm is clearly higher than those retained. But these can be more difficult to operate on an individual level: if an older employee is unfairly replaced by a younger one, and both are within the 'protected group', there must be sufficient 'daylight' between the individual ages. One problem is, of course, that there is a natural tendency for senior employees to be replaced by more junior ones. Differentials in earnings or status may be the result of discrimination; but they are more likely to derive from differentials in skill, education, productivity and so on. Again, the average age of a firm will tend to reflect the type of business it conducts rather than discrimination: for example, newly established enterprises, such as those in computing, will tend to have youthful workforces. (This alone can make the ideal of an 'age-balanced' workforce impossible to attain.) Adverse impact is also more problematic in the case of age compared with race or sex. Following the landmark civil rights case of *Griggs v. Duke Power Company* (1971), it was established that a facially neutral policy (with no overt intent to discriminate) could be held to be discriminatory if it had an adverse impact on the protected group, and there was no justification of 'business necessity'. In the case of race or sex, there may be no correlation between an individual characteristic and productivity; but this is more difficult to apply in the case of age, given that productivity *does* tend, on average, to decline with age (though, arguably, modern technology has mitigated this). As with everything else, much depends on the reasonableness of the age proxy.

Since 1967, much legal wrangling has taken place over the three principal ADEA defences:

1. Where age is a bona fide occupational qualification (BFOQ) reasonably necessary to the normal operation of the particular business, or where the differentiation is based on reasonable factors other than age (RFOA);
2. To observe the terms of a bona fide seniority system or any bona fide employee benefit plan such as a retirement, pension, or insurance plan, which is not a subterfuge to evade the purpose of the Act, except that no such employee benefit plan shall excuse the failure to hire any individual;
3. To discharge or otherwise discipline an individual for good cause.

Of these, BFOQ and RFOA have occasioned most controversy. In BFOQ, the employer admits age discrimination, but offers an explanation that the courts will find acceptable (an 'affirmative defence'). The employer must demonstrate that the job requirements allegedly being fulfilled less and less effectively because of advancing age are necessary to the essential operation of the business. In RFOA, the employer denies that age played a part: declining job performance (or some factor other than age) need only be demonstrated by a properly administered performance evaluation. In other words, the ADEA only outlaws 'irrational', 'arbitrary' or 'unjustified' discrimination. 'Justified' or 'rational' discrimination (that is, job-related discrimination) is permissible, and, arguably, even encouraged by the ADEA.

BFOQ cases are probably more interesting. They have covered instances where public safety is an issue, or where age is necessary for authenticity (as in the case of actresses). For example, in the 1960s there was much discussion of whether age was an occupational requirement for airline stewardesses: the airlines argued that youth and beauty (enhanced by workplace codes relating to lipstick, hairstyles and general grooming) were what their business-class customers wanted. The unions representing the stewardesses successfully countered with the argument that these personal characteristics were irrelevant in emergency situations or in everyday passenger care. Another perennial example is the question of whether civilian airline pilots should be required to retire at age 60. The controversies revolve round the ability of modern medical science to predict heart attacks but are complicated by the elaborate structures of seniority whereby pilots, as they age, expect to move up to better positions or more prestigious routes. It is the classic argument for mandatory retirement – that it keeps open the channels to promotion, and facilitates employee rotation. Other fascinating courtroom battles have occurred over questions such as the employment-based tests of physical fitness that might decide the right of firefighters to work later in life: what simulation could ever replicate the 'real world' experience of climbing many flights of stairs in searing heat and extreme danger, carrying a heavy hose? Many other legal cases have clarified the ADEA since 1967.

Evaluating the ADEA

Pronouncing a verdict on the ADEA is very difficult, for several reasons. Social policies can only be evaluated in relation to their notional aims, and therefore a verdict would depend on which of its aims one considered most important. Again, we cannot construct a counterfactual regarding what the US would have been like without the ADEA. For example, improving the quality of labour supply was undoubtedly one aim; but did the ADEA lead to 'better' older workers being retained? We simply cannot know.

Another major problem is that the ADEA was shortly followed (in 1973) by the OPEC-led oil price shock, triggering a virtual 'second industrial revolution': manufacturing (which employed many older men) went into decline; the new service-based jobs (often part-time) tended to be filled by women and younger workers; and those firms that survived sought productivity improvements by downsizing their workforces via early retirement inducements. Any rigorous evaluation of the ADEA's effect would need to take these multidimensional changes into account, and somehow control for them: methodologically, this would be well-nigh impossible. There are many other structural or policy-based differences between the US and Britain which make comparison problematic: for example, the US health insurance system probably makes employers reluctant to hire or retain older workers because of their higher costs, and, paradoxically, encourages employees to work later in life so that they can retain health benefits for as long as possible.

A final difficulty is that policy evaluation is always affected by the 'background noise' of prevailing political ideology. Thus in the 1990s, when legislative action was ruled out, most British commentators argued that the ADEA had had little discernible effect on the employment prospects of older Americans. This was the line taken by the Blair government until forced into accepting legislation by the EU. For example, *Action on Age* (1998), having examined the experience of other countries, was unenthusiastic, arguing that a US Congressional review of the ADEA in 1992 had concluded that 'its effectiveness was open to question' (DfEE, 1998, p 10). However, since 2000 (and especially in the aftermath of the EU Directive) there has been an increasing tendency to search for empirical justification for legislation. Hence *Winning the Generation Game* (2000) acknowledged that the international evidence of the effectiveness of age discrimination legislation was 'by no means decisive', but claimed that there was 'some positive evidence' from the US in the form of the recent rise in employment rates (Cabinet Office. Performance and Innovation Unit, 2000, pp 57-8). Likewise, Sarah Spencer and Sandra Fredman, in *Age Equality Comes of Age* (2003), stated that:

> The most promising evidence is from the United States where age legislation has been associated with (but not the sole cause of) significant increases in post retirement age employment rates. Thirty per cent of men aged 60-5 (and 19% of women) are still working, as are 18% of men aged 70-4. (Spencer and Fredman, 2003, p 17)

Such comparisons are, however, too simplistic. Granted, the fall in the labour force participation rates of American men aged 65+ has been slower since 1970 than that of their British counterparts, but several cautionary points need to be considered.

First, since 1930 the labour force participation rates of older American men have *always* been higher than those in Britain (see Table 3.1). Second, in the decade 1970-80, immediately after the ADEA, the rate of decline was slower in the US than in Britain, but this must have been for reasons other than legislation, since the ADEA's upper age limit was only raised to 70 in 1978. For most of that decade, therefore, men aged 65+ were not covered by the ADEA. Third, a valid comparison would have to answer several intriguing questions, such as why Britain, with no protective legislation, experienced a much slower fall in older men's economic activity rates in the 1960s. Fourth, there has certainly been a rise in the employment rates of older American men and women since the early 1990s, and this is projected to continue (see Table 3.2).

However, a similar rise has also taken place in Britain. The employment rates of British people aged between 50 and state pension age have risen

Table 3.1: Labour force participation rates/economic activity rates of men aged 65+ in the US and UK

US	UK
1930: 54.0%	1931: 47.9%
1940: 41.8%	1941: no census
1950: 41.4%	1951: 31.1%
1960: 30.5%	1961: 24.4%
1970: 24.8%	1971: 23.5%
1980: 19.0%	1981: 10.3%
1990: 16.3%	1991: 8.7%
2000: 17.7%	2001: 7.5%

Table 3.2: US labour civilian force participation rates by age: percentages and numbers (millions)

	1980	1990	2000	2010*
Men:				
Aged 65+	19.0%	16.3%	17.7%	19.5%
	1.9m	2.0m	2.5m	3.1m
Aged 55-64	72.1%	67.8%	67.3%	67.0%
	7.2m	6.6m	7.8m	11.1m
Aged 45-54	91.2%	90.7%	88.6%	87.8%
	9.9m	11.1m	16.3m	18.9m
Women:				
Aged 65+	8.1%	8.6%	9.4%	11.1%
	1.2m	1.5m	1.8m	2.3m
Aged 55-64	41.3%	45.2%	51.9%	55.2%
	4.7m	4.9m	6.6m	10.1m
Aged 45-54	59.9%	71.2%	76.8%	80.0%
	7.0m	9.1m	14.8m	17.9m

* = Projections.

Source: US Census Bureau (2003, p 385)

from 62.5% in 1994 to 69.9% in 2004, and those above state pension age from 4.9% to 5.9%. This is probably because of improved economic conditions, a tighter labour market and concerns over the erosion of private pensions (Whiting, 2005, p 287; Phillipson, 2006, pp 225-6). In any case, it would be distinctly odd to postulate that ADEA suddenly started working in the US from the mid-1990s.

The average age of permanent labour force exit in the two countries between 1960 and 1995 does not show a great difference. On this evidence, if the ADEA has had an effect, it is of the order of only 0.6 years:

Table 3.3: Average age of transition into inactivity among older male workers

	1960	1995	Decrease 1960–95
United Kingdom	66.2	62.7	–3.5
United States	66.5	63.6	–2.9

Source: Auer and Fortuny (2000, p 13)

Finally, both Britain and the US have witnessed a rise in the economic activity or labour force participation rates of middle-aged women since the 1970s, owing to the expansion of feminised jobs: for example, the rate for American women aged 45-54 rose from 54.4% in 1970 to 76.8% in 2000. This would seem to confirm that age discrimination in employment plays a relatively small part in determining employment opportunities compared with demand-side factors.

There have been some more fine-grained attempts to measure the effect of the ADEA. For example, David Neumark has recently argued, on the basis of state-by-state comparison, that age discrimination legislation has improved the employment prospects of protected workers under age 60 by less than one percentage point, and those over age 60 by six percentage points. But Neumark is rightly cautious of any such evaluation, emphasising the limits to our knowledge of the precise effects (Neumark, 2001, pp 56-9). Another example is Scott Adams's recent comparison between those US states with and without their own age discrimination laws in the period 1964-67, before the ADEA came into force: his conclusion is that workers covered by such laws were less likely to retire, though the effect on hiring was not great. Legislation thus had a mildly beneficial effect. If this finding is valid, and operated nationally after 1967, the ADEA has indeed kept the labour force participation rates of older American men more buoyant than they would otherwise have been. However, once again many awkward methodological questions arise, such as how one should control for each state's local economic conditions. Adams's conclusions are, in fact, hedged in with reservations – and rightly so (Adams, 2004). Such an analysis focuses too much on 'incentive effects' at the micro-level of the individual firm and ignores the macroeconomic background (including the crucial changes in sectoral labour market demand).

Much critical comment has been made that the ADEA has been a 'litigation bonanza' for middle-aged, middle-class, white males, who form a majority of plaintiffs (Friedman, 1984, pp 45-7). However, the explanation for this is quite simple: women and ethnic minorities are much more likely to bring a charge (even if age is a contributory factor in such 'compounded discrimination' cases) under Title VII of the 1964 Civil Rights Act (Shaw, 1988). Between the fiscal years 1992 and 2001, 320,485 charges of race discrimination and 274,474 charges of sex discrimination were resolved, compared with only 167,959 relating to age. Prior to 1967, the most egregious instances of age discrimination in employment seemed to be at the hiring stage, via age stipulations in 'help wanted' job advertisements. But this is where the ADEA has been least effective: hence Daniel O'Meara's analysis found that 75.9% of cases related to termination of employment, with only 9.4% over refusal to hire (O'Meara, 1989, pp 25-7). As noted earlier, age discrimination at the hiring stage is the most difficult for an injured party to detect.

Organisations and individuals who work daily with the victims of age discrimination in employment are convinced that the ADEA has had a beneficial effect – and that more legislation is needed (Gregory, 2001). EEOC statistics undoubtedly represent only a tiny proportion of actual age discriminatory incidents. Again, the everyday job protection offered by the ADEA is not amenable to measurement: evidence is only forthcoming when a dispute occurs. In other words, good news is no news. It is also worth remembering, when considering the accusation that the ADEA has been used somewhat frivolously, that plaintiffs face many obstacles in bringing a charge (emotional stress, adverse publicity, potential findings of liability, an out-of-court settlement). In the fiscal year 1999, a mere 5.3% of charges were settled in favour of the plaintiff; in 59.4%, 'no reasonable cause' was found; and a further 23.3% were closed administratively (Neumark, 2001, p 48). Employers will only allow those cases to come to court that they think they can win.

If an unequivocal verdict on the ADEA is difficult to pronounce, therefore, this may be simply because an unequivocal verdict is impossible. What is clear is that the US attempted – for reasons that combined 'social justice' with 'labour supply' motivation – to eliminate 'arbitrary' and 'irrational' age discrimination in employment as far as possible, while also improving its social security pension. Unlike in Britain today, working later in life was not seen as a necessary consequence of a failure to improve state pensions.

Note

This chapter is based on the author's book, *Age Discrimination: An Historical and Contemporary Analysis* (Macnicol, 2006), chs 8 and 9. Readers wishing more elaboration should consult therein.

References

Adams, S. (2004) 'Age discrimination legislation and the employment of older workers', *Labor Economics*, vol 11, no 2, pp 219-41.

Auer, P. and Fortuny, M. (2000) *Ageing of the Labour Force in OECD Countries: Economic and Social Consequences*, Geneva: International Labour Organisation.

Bancroft, G. (1952) 'Older persons in the labour force', *Annals of the American Academy of Politics and Social Science*, vol 279, January, pp 52-61.

Barkin, S. (1933) *The Older Worker in Industry: A Study of New York State Manufacturing Industries*, Albany, NY: J.B. Lyon and Company.

Bone, M., Gregory, J., Gill, B. and Lader, D. (1992) *Retirement and Retirement Plans. A Survey Carried Out by the Social Survey Division of OPCS on Behalf of the Department of Social Security*, London: HMSO.

Cabinet Office. Performance and Innovation Unit (2000) *Winning the Generation Game. Improving Opportunities for People Aged 50-65 in Work and Community Activity*, London: The Stationery Office.

Clague, E. (1949) 'The working life span of American workers', *Journal of Gerontology*, vol 4, no 4, pp 285-9.

DfEE (Department for Education and Employment) (1998) *Action on Age: Report of the Consultation on Age Discrimination in Employment*, London: DfEE.

Drake, J.T. (1958) *The Aged in American Society*, New York, NY: Ronald Press.

Dublin, L.I. (1928) *Health and Wealth. A Survey of the Economics of World Health*, New York, NY: Harper.

Fogarty, M.P. (1980) *Retirement Age and Retirement Costs*, London: Policy Studies Institute.

Friedman, L.M. (1984) *Your Time Will Come. The Law of Age Discrimination and Mandatory Retirement*, New York, NY: Russell Sage Foundation.

Gordon, M.S. (1960) 'Changing patterns of retirement', *Journal of Gerontology*, vol 15, no 3, pp 300-4.

Gregory, R. (2001) *Age Discrimination in the American Workplace. Old at a Young Age*, New Brunswick, NJ: Rutgers University Press.

Harrington, M. (1962) *The Other America*, New York, NY: Macmillan.

Levine, M.L. (1988) *Age Discrimination and the Mandatory Retirement Controversy*, Baltimore, MD: The Johns Hopkins University Press.

Macnicol, J. (2006) *Age Discrimination. An Historical and Contemporary Analysis*, Cambridge: Cambridge University Press.

Neumark, D. (2001) 'Age discrimination legislation in the US: assessment of the evidence', in Z. Hornstein (ed) *Outlawing Age Discrimination. Foreign Lessons, UK Choices*, Bristol: The Policy Press.

O'Meara, D.P. (1989) *Protecting the Growing Number of Older Workers. The Age Discrimination in Employment Act*, Philadelphia, PA: University of Pennsylvania Wharton School of Industrial Relations Unit.

Phillipson, C. (2006) 'Extending working life: problems and prospects for social and public policy', in L. Bauld, K. Clarke and T. Maltby (eds) *Social Policy Review 18: Analysis and Debate in Social Policy, 2006*, Bristol: The Policy Press.

Shaw, L.B. (1988) 'Special problems of older women workers', in M.E. Borus, H.S. Parnes, S.H. Sandell and B. Seidman (eds) *The Older Worker*, Madison, WI: Industrial Relations Research Association.

Sheppard, H. (1976) 'Work and retirement', in R.H. Binstock and E. Shanas (eds) *Handbook of Aging and the Social Sciences*, New York, NY: Van Nostrand Reinhold.

Spencer, S. and Fredman, S. (2003) *Age Equality Comes of Age: Delivering Change for Older People*, London: Institute for Public Policy Research.

Stecker, M.L. (1951) 'Beneficiaries prefer to work', *Social Security Bulletin*, vol 14, no 1, pp 15-17.

Tibbitts, C. (1954) 'Retirement problems in American society', *American Journal of Sociology*, vol LIX, no 4, pp 301-8.

Time (1953) 'The older worker: the US must make better use of him', 19 October, p 100.

US Census Bureau (2003) *Statistical Abstract of the United States: 2003*, Washington, DC: US Government Printing Office.

US Department of Labor (1965) *The Older American Worker. Age Discrimination in Employment. Report of the Secretary of Labor to the Congress under Section 715 of the Civil Rights Act of 1964*, Washington, DC: US Department of Labor.

Whiting, E. (2005) 'The labour market participation of older people', *Labour Market Trends*, vol 113, no 7, pp 285-95.

FOUR

The employment of older people: can we learn from Japan?

Bernard Casey

Japan is frequently remarked upon for its very high level of labour force participation among older workers and particularly older men. In the year 2000, nearly 95% of men aged 55-59, nearly three quarters of those aged 60-64 and a third of those aged over 65 were still economically active. Almost all of the economically active were working rather than being unemployed: the relevant employment rates were 90%, 63% and 33%, respectively.[1] A brief comparison with other countries is given in Figure 4.1.

The high employment rates exist alongside a relatively low mandatory retirement age operated in many sectors of the economy – 60, having risen from 55 over the past 30 years. They also exist alongside a payment system that makes older workers relatively more expensive. The 'lifetime employment' system sets pay according to seniority and thus, effectively, in accordance with age. This chapter asks why, under these circumstances, and given the relatively poor performance of the Japanese economy over the past decade, such high rates of employment

Figure 4.1: Employment rates for older men, 2000

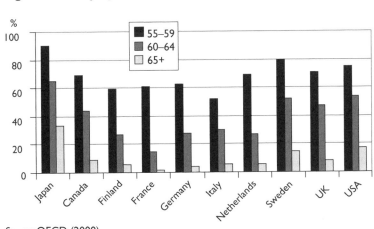

Source: OECD (2000)

have been maintained. It then goes on to ask whether they are likely to be maintained in the future.

Some conventional, and some less conventional, explanations

The lifetime employment system has its roots in a mixture of culture and late industrialisation. According to some commentators, it resulted from industrial workers being recruited from rural communities and moved from being the dependent members of one closed community to the dependent members of another. The firm replicated many of the practices of the village, particularly in having no concept of an individual job – and so of individual pay – but rather a concept of cooperative work – and so of pay, according to the type of worker. The concept is associated with a high degree of job flexibility, which, in turn, has been used to explain high levels of productivity (Koike, 1997). Within the firm, wage differentials between men and women were perpetuated, but pay also reflected assumed responsibilities, and these were recognised as rising with age (Sano, 1997). According to other commentators, the lifetime employment system was a rational response to labour shortages in periods of rapid growth, and it was a way by which firms sought to reduce turnover among skilled workers. It first manifested itself in the 1920s but did not gain importance until the 1950s (Matsuzuka, 2002). Whatever the origins of the system, many observers have pointed out how 'compared to [countries for which equivalent data is available], the age-earnings profile of Japanese workers remains steeper over a longer time period (OECD, 1996, p 105).

Precisely because of this pronounced age–earnings profile, firms impose mandatory retirement. Indeed, this is a classic case of 'why there is mandatory retirement' (Lazear, 1979). Such retirement is presumed to occur a few years after domestic responsibilities have peaked. A mandatory retirement age is operated by almost all large firms and by most but the very smallest ones. Its level has been set by employers, or by collective agreements, but increases have been encouraged by the government, which has sought to keep it aligned with the age of eligibility of a public pension. The latter has, effectively, been 60, but since the mid-1990s various steps have been taken to raise it to 65. Under current legislation, however, this will not be achieved until 2013 for men and 2018 for women.[2] The earlier, upward movement of the mandatory retirement age that occurred in the 1980s and 1990s was matched by an upward movement of the age at which earnings peaked. In 1980, this stood at around 52, in 1999 at around 57 (JIL, 2000).

The practices of employers that allow some of the consequences of an age-related payment system and the associated mandatory retirement age to be circumvented are suggested to be an important reason as to why the rate of employment among older people is high. Many employers offer forms of re-employment to those reaching mandatory retirement age. Such re-employment is often on a temporary basis, and it might involve a change in terms and conditions. Drawing on data from private sector enterprises, with at least 30 employees, the Organisation for Economic Cooperation and Development (OECD) concluded that, among firms with a retirement age under 65, the proportion offering continued employment until that age has now reached 55%, although only a quarter of these firms give a job to all those who apply for one (OECD, 2004).

Frequently referred to is the practice by which employees who are in their mid-50s are moved from their career jobs to jobs with subcontracting firms under arrangements such as *shukko* and *tenseki*. *Shukko* is a practice by which the transferred worker remains an employee of the sending firm; *tenseki* is a practice by which the transferred worker becomes an employee of the receiving firm. A period of transfer on *shukko* can be followed by a termination of the original contract and re-employment on *tenseki* (Sato, 1996).

Where there is no re-employment opportunity, and no opportunity for transfer, the employing firm might use its best efforts to assist in finding subsequent work or even help departing employees – who will receive a lump-sum retirement payment – to establish themselves in self-employment (Rebick, 1995).

The change in job, employment status and/or employer in later life is usually associated with some form of wage reduction. Thus, the age–wage curve shifts sharply downwards after having reached its peak, but more than in many other countries. It must be stressed, however, that most age–wage curves are cross-sectional, and do not show the development of cohorts, let alone individuals. Thus, they seldom show how individuals' wages progress with age, and they cannot capture any changes associated with changes in the nature of jobs that the individuals concerned might experience. That caveat aside, among those who stay with their old firm, the average wage reduction is estimated to be some 30%; among those who change employer, it is close to 50% (JIL, 2000).

Total income, however, falls by somewhat less. Under the rules of the public pension system, someone eligible for an earnings-related pension can draw this benefit but go back to work. Until the age of eligibility of the earnings-related pension was lifted to 65, this provision applied to people aged 60-64. An 'earnings test' reduced the pension by at least 20% and by a taper to 100% once earnings exceeded those of the average for an industrial worker. Under these provisions, someone taking a job paying about half the average industrial wage would be able to increase his gross income by about 50%. As Figure 4.2 shows, about 30% of men aged 60-64 who were drawing an earnings-related public pension were also working. Since 2002 a further, but somewhat less severe, 'earnings rule' with respect to the second-tier pension has been applied for people working between 65 and 69 (OECD, 2004).

Employment practices such as offers of re-employment or a transfer to a subsidiary, together with the ability to combine work with receipt of a pension, constitute only part of the explanation for why older people remain in work beyond the mandatory retirement age. The importance of the lifetime employment system has often been exaggerated. Those who have analysed it closely suggest that it applied to maybe some 20-30% of all employees – full-time, male workers in larger enterprises (Lincoln, 2001). Moreover, as Table 4.1 shows, in the year 2000, only about one in four men in their late 40s who worked in the private, non-agricultural sector was in an enterprise with 1,000 or more employees and less than one in three worked in one with 500 or more employees. As a proportion of all men of that age who were at work, these shares fall to a fifth and a quarter.

Figure 4.2: Employment and pension receipt among older men

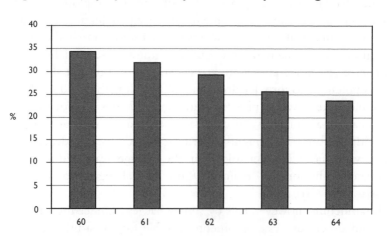

Note: Includes people whose pension is totally suspended – up to one quarter.

Source: Social Insurance Agency, Annual Operational Report FY 2000

Table 4.1: Employment of men aged 45–49 by firm size, 2000

	Men aged 45–49 (%)	
All	100	
Agricultural sector	3	
Non-agricultural self-employed	2	
Government sector	11	
Private sector employees	84	100
in a firm with <10 employees	13	15
in a firm with <30 employees	24	28
in a firm with >499 employees	24	29
in a firm with >1,000 employees	19	23

Source: Management and Co-ordination Agency, Statistics Bureau (2000a); author's calculations

Small enterprises are somewhat less likely to operate mandatory retirement ages than larger ones. In the mid-1990s, while almost all enterprises with 300 or more employees had a mandatory retirement age, only 72% of those with between 10 and 29 employees, and only 31% of those with under 10 employees, had one (Sato, 2000). In addition, small enterprises are more likely than larger enterprises to offer to continue the employment of people who reach mandatory retirement. Thus, some 55% of firms with 10-29 employees did so, compared with 35% of those with 5,000 or more employees. Small firms are not, however, any more likely to extend the offer to all who wish to work than are larger enterprises. This means that a substantial proportion of older people receive no structured assistance at all from their employer in finding post-retirement age work. Obtaining a picture of what happens to them is difficult because most surveys of employer practice do not sample firms with less than 30 employees, yet these firms employ about a quarter of all those working in the private sector. It might be expected that, in the small and micro-enterprise sector, personal relationships are such that many employees are retained into older age and few are involuntarily retired.

On the other hand, and as in most countries, conditions in the small firms sector are markedly inferior to those in the large firms sector. Pay is lower, coverage by supplementary pension plans is lower, and payment of a lump sum on retirement is less frequent. Those older employees who move into the small firms sector, and who do not continue an employment contract with their career employer, experience a substantial drop in their earnings. Some of this is compensated for by the partial pension they will be able to draw and the severance payments they have received from their former employer. Those older employees who move from one small firm to another, and move without assistance from the previous employer, usually do so without any severance payment and can suffer a significant fall in their income (Yamada, 2000).

An understanding of the role of job transfers and of shifts to new employers throws light on why such a high proportion of people in their late 50s and early 60s are still in work. It throws much less light on why such a high proportion of those aged 65 and over are still in work. To make sense of this, it is necessary to look more closely at what the very oldest workers in Japan actually do. This is done in Table 4.2.

Table 4.2: Characteristics of older male employment, 2000 (%)

	All ages (%)	Aged 55–64 (%)	Aged 65 and over (%)
Participation rate	76	84	33
Employment rate	72	78	26
of which, working in			
agriculture	5	6	31
construction	14	16	14
retailing	19	17	19
agriculture, construction or retailing	38	39	64
in agricultural sector			
self-employed	76	85	86
family worker	12	3	10
part-time	34	30	49
in retailing			
self-employed or family worker	3	6	10
in non-agricultural sector			
self-employed	11	18	44
family worker	1	*	4
part-time	6	5	15
dispatched worker	3	7	15
temporary or daily	6	7	24
Unemployment rate	5.2	7.1	3.7

* Less than 0.5.

Source: Management and Co-ordination Agency, Statistics Bureau (2000a, b); author's calculations

Self-employment is clearly important as a means of working beyond 65. The rate of self-employment increases steadily by age from 17% for those aged 55-59, to 30% for those aged 60-64, and to 48% for those aged 65 and older. Taken together with family working (paid or otherwise), in the year 2000, self-employment accounted for nearly two thirds (62%) of all those at work after 65. Also important is part-time working – one in four of those working beyond the age of 65 do so as part-timers. The agricultural sector accounts for nearly one third of those working beyond 65, and most of its older labour force is self-employed or working in the family. The wholesale and retail sectors account for one fifth, and construction for one seventh of those working beyond 64. Together, these three sectors account for two thirds of the oldest members of the male workforce, making their over-representation almost twofold.

Movement into self-employment at the end of a career job, often with the encouragement of the former employer, has already been mentioned. Movements into the wholesale and retail sectors are also common, in particular where there is a family connection. Most important are movements back to the agriculture sector. This reflects the fact that, outside the metropolitan areas, many middle-aged agricultural workers are *kengyo nouka*, or have part-time jobs alongside their industrial jobs. It also reflects the fact that others, on retiring from the industrial community, return to the rural community, perpetuating a family link with the land and the small plots that are maintained in the name of the family.

System strains

For over a decade, the Japanese economy has been suffering from slow growth and the prospect of an ageing labour force. Unemployment, while low by international standards, rose to levels that were high by Japanese standards. As continued poor performance became intolerable, enterprises were obliged to restructure and cut costs. The banking system, in part under government and external pressure, was obliged to be more strict about lending policy, to call in bad loans and to force non-performing firms to close. Finally, the government, again in part under external pressure, started to deregulate important sectors of the economy and thereby force enterprises to adopt more efficient practices.

The consequence was that those personnel practices and policies that served high growth and an expanding labour force ceased to be appropriate. The lifetime employment system that, together with *shukko* and *tenseki*, ensured continued employment opportunities for some older workers no longer functioned as effectively as it once did. Large firms, as well as merely reducing their hiring, started to declare redundancies. Early in 1993, there was already survey evidence that firms were feeling an excess of older (here, aged 45 and above) clerical and managerial workers and that, in the vast majority of cases, this surplus was structural rather than cyclical. Moreover, the larger the firm, the greater the problem (Sato, 1994). More extreme still, major companies started announcing large-scale redundancies as part of their plans to restructure (Osawa and Kingston, 1996). Some of these redundancies were even 'involuntary' (Araki, 1995). In other cases, early retirement opportunities were introduced, offering enhanced early pensions or lump-sum severance payments, sometimes to workers as young as 50 (Sato, 1994). Recently, the incidence of such 'un-Japanese' practices has appeared only to grow, as Table 4.3 illustrates.

What is of interest in Table 4.3 is the appearance of major motor manufacturing firms in the list. In the past few years, both Nissan and Mazda have been taken over by foreign companies. The new managements that were put in place there were not Japanese and were not beholden to Japanese practices. The first, and most well known, of the *gaijin* was Carlos Gohsan from Renault, who took charge of Nissan (Ibson, 2001). What these managements sought to do, when pushing through their restructuring plans, was very much what they were doing when they restructured at home (in France or America). They laid workers off and, in particular, offered early retirement programmes. And where they did, take-up has been high. Companies have reported over-subscription within days and even within hours, reflecting a fear among employees that job cuts were unavoidable and such terms would not be offered a second time (*Yomiuri Shimbun*, 2001). Also of relevance here is the oft-described case of Japan Tobacco – see Table 4.3. Japan Tobacco revealed that 5,800 rather than the expected 3,500 employees volunteered for early retirement under its cost-cutting programme (Associated Press, 5.1.05).

The problems experienced by large firms had repercussions for the operation of the *shukko* and *tenseki* systems. The sectors comprising the companies receiving transferred workers suffer the same slowdown in demand growth and face the same needs to restructure as the sector comprising the companies wishing to transfer. As a consequence, the transfer system has hit an impasse. The ability of firms to receive workers on transfer has been made worse by two further developments. First, the restructuring plans of many large firms involve them rationalising their supply systems – Nissan, under new foreign management, is often

Table 4.3: Major companies announcing/implementing early retirement plans: press announcements since 1999

Company	Sector	Date	Additional details
Arabian Oil	Oil refining	Announced Mar 2000	
Dainippon Ink	Chemicals	2000–01	
Fujisawa Pharmaceutical Co Ltd		End Nov 2004 to mid-Jan 2005	716 employees, of which 218 were from subsidiaries, applied; part of preparation of merger with Yamanouchi Pharmaceutical Co Ltd to form Astellas Pharma Inc.
Japan Energy Corp	Oil refining and manufacturing	2000–03	
Showa Shell	Oil refining	1999–2001	Also transfers to affiliates.
Isuzu	Motors	2000–01	
Mazda (of Ford)	Motors	Mar 2000	Plant closures and losses. 2,210 early retirements (8% of labour force); plan offered to all over 40 with at least 10 years' service.
Nissan (of Renault)	Motors		Plans to cut 3-5% of labour force each year. Renault has early retirement programme for all aged 57+ in France.
Anritsu	Electronics	May 2002	Offered to regular employees aged from 45 to 59, with at least 10 years of service; 312 leavers (including 57 employees dispatched to other companies).
Fujitsu	Electronics	Summer 2001	Voluntary early retirement offered to all aged 45 and over in Japan. Part of plan to cut global workforce by 21%.
Hitachi	Electronics	Spring 1999	Repeated programmes in subsequent years.

Table 4.3: Major companies announcing/implementing early retirement plans: press announcements since 1999

Company	Sector	Date	Additional details
Matsushita (Panasonic)	Electrical/ electronics	Mar 2000-01 and Jan 2005	Seeking 5,000 early retirements as part of plan to cut workforce by 13,000. Also making subcontractors more cost-efficient. Further 3,000 early retirements sought as of 2005.
Mitsubishi Electrical Co	Electronics	2000–01	Part of 10% cut in labour force.
Sega	Electronics	First half year 1999	
Toshiba	Electronics	August 2001	Voluntary early retirement for people over 40, with severance payment of 2½ years' pay. Expected cost of ¥60bn. Part of 10% cut in workforce.
Kawasaki	Heavy engineering/ steel	From mid-2000	In merger talks with NKK (see below).
Nippon Steel	Steel	1999–2000	
NKK	Steel		In merger talks with Kawasaki.
Japan Tobacco	Tobacco	1999 and 2003–04	Financial year 1999-00, cutting 10% of labour force at home and similar proportion abroad; 2003-04 workforce reduction of 25% including early retirement offered to employees aged 40-59 with minimum 15 years' service; take-up by 5,800 of eligible 12,000 (had expected only 3,500).
Kirin	Brewing	1999–2001	Also transfers to affiliates.

Table 4.3: Major companies announcing/implementing early retirement plans: press announcements since 1999

Company	Sector	Date	Additional details
Snow Brand Milk	Food processing	2000	Part of repercussions of food-poisoning case.
JAL	Air transport	Spring 2000	
NTT	Telecommunic-ations	Sept 2000 onwards	6,500 volunteers on top of 21,000 job cuts already planned (cutting 17% of workforce). Offering all employees aged 47-60 10 months' basic pay plus a retirement allowance.
Daiei	Retailing	1999-2000	Sold businesses to cover early retirement costs.
Kanematsu	General trading house	Announced mid-1999	Major restructuring forced by banks.
Mitsukoshi Ltd	Department store group	Reported Oct 2004	Seeking voluntary early retirement of 800 workers over 40 years old.
Mycal	Retailing	Jan 2001	Store closures. Requires bank loans to cover early retirement costs.
Seiyu (38% owned by Wal-Mart)	Supermarket chain	Reported Dec 2003	Voluntary early retirement programme as part of plan to reduce staff by 1,613 (or approx. one fifth).
Chiyoda and Dai-Tokyo	Insurance	Spring 2000	As part of merger.
Nikko Securities	Financial services	1998–2000	Open to employees aged 40+.
Sanawa	Banking	1999–2000	
Various private junior colleges	Education	Reported Mar 2001	Falling student numbers.

Source: Financial Times search 'Top World Sources' plus Google search Japan + 'early retirement'

cited as one of the leaders in this respect. Large firms have been seeking to reduce the number of subcontractors, to enforce greater efficiency and even to source from abroad. A study by the Mitsubishi Research Institute expected 143,000 job losses in the automobile industry, of which nearly 80% would be amongst suppliers, mainly small firms (*Financial Times*, 5.9.01).

The second development concerns small firms. These have been particularly threatened by attempts to force the banking sector to reduce bad loans – and their position is made yet weaker by the withdrawal of contracts to supply larger firms. Although such financial surgery has been performed only slowly, the number of bankruptcies has been rising. In 2000, there were 12% more than in the previous year, and bankruptcies reached their highest level since 1987. Small and medium-sized firms were hit twice over – both because the banks were putting their finances under greater scrutiny and because parent companies were seeking to extricate themselves from debt at the expense of sacrificing poorly performing subsidiaries (TDB, various issues).

Figure 4.3 illustrates the trends in the incidence of lay-offs, early retirements and external transfers since the mid-1990s. It reports the proportion of firms having adopted particular measures to help them adjust to downturns in demand. The overall rate of unemployment

Figure 4.3: Share of firms reporting lay-offs, transfers or early retirements

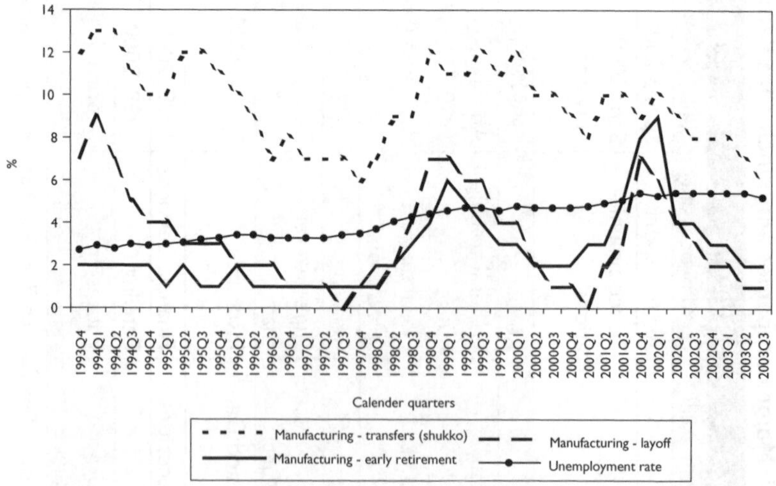

Source: Management and Co-ordination Agency, Statistics Bureau, Survey on Labour Economy Trends, quarterly (www.dbtk.mhlw.go.jp/toukei/kouhyo/data-rou15/jikei/jikeiretu-02.xls), OECD (standardised unemployment rates)

is also shown as a reference point. Although only a small minority of employers indicate they have had resort to it, the incidence of early retirement has risen substantially. At the same time, the incidence of external transfers has fallen.

It was primarily large firms that engaged in the practice of early retirement. Table 4.4 shows how nearly one in five of the largest offered early retirement in the year 2002. Manufacturing firms were heavy users of early retirement, but it was by firms in the financial services sector that its use was most intense.

The struggle on the part of the government to meet demands for greater financial rectitude is likely to have a further negative impact on the employment chances of older people. Table 4.2 showed the importance of the construction sector as an employer of older workers. This sector has been one of the principal beneficiaries of the many supplementary expenditure programmes by means of which the government has sought to sustain the 'post-bubble' economy. Many public works programmes have been criticised as inefficient uses of resources, at best no more than a form of disguised unemployment benefit, and at worst an instrument of political patronage (OECD, 2000). In August 2001, the government approved the 'largest ever' reduction of planned expenditure – of some 2% – whereby the brunt was to fall on infrastructure projects. Overall, public investment as a proportion of gross domestic product has fallen from a peak of some 8.5% in 1997 to some 4.5% in 2004 (OECD, 2005, p 86).

Last, the ability of those sectors that have in the past absorbed some of the older people not benefiting from transfers arranged by their career employers is increasingly in doubt. International and domestic pressures

Table 4.4: Share of firms reporting early retirements, by sector and size

	2000	2001	2002
All industries	2.1	3.7	4.8
Manufacturing	2.8	6.3	6.7
Financial services	6.3	10.6	10.8
5,000+ employees	13.9	17.6	19.5
1,000–4,999 employees	8.1	13.9	17.3
300–999 employees	5.1	6.0	9.7
100–299 employees	2.6	5.5	6.7
30–99 employees	1.5	2.6	3.3

Source: Management and Co-ordination Agency, Statistics Bureau, Survey on employment management

have required substantial deregulation of the two other sectors critical to older people's employment – retailing and agriculture. A succession of 'deregulation plans' have facilitated the opening of large supermarkets and department stores – the development of which had been impeded by local governments seeking to protect the livelihoods of small traders – and the breakdown of monopolies in the wholesale sector – over which domestic manufacturers had an effective stranglehold. If the relevant legislation is enforced, it will lead to the closure of many small shops and distribution companies currently employing older people, either on a self-employed basis or as family workers (Yahata, 1995).

Agriculture is being forced to accept World Trade Organisation rulings – particularly those following the 1994 'Uruguay Round' – to open up its markets to imported rice and beef. Although agricultural employment fell by a fifth during the 1990s, the number of people aged 65 and older at work in the sector remained almost constant, so that they made up over 40% of the workforce by 1996 compared with a quarter in 1989.[3] In 1995, the government committed itself to a six-year programme to promote agricultural adjustment, and, as the OECD observed, 'given the relatively old age of the farm labour force, most of the adjustment would be between generations' (OECD, 1996, p 81). If agricultural reform is carried to its logical conclusion, the scope for 'sheltered employment' provided by the highly regulated sector is bound to diminish rapidly.

Policy responses

Although they remain high by international standards, employment rates for older people in Japan have been falling since the late 1990s. Unemployment rates among older males were more than half as high again as the overall unemployment rates, while those for men in their early 60s exceeded 10% in 1998 and only fell back to a single-digit level in 2002.

Nevertheless, a 'work ethic', if this protestant concept can be applied to what is more a Confucian society, continues to be strong in Japan. Older people there appear to want to work more than do older people in most other countries. An exception is the 'protestant' Netherlands. According to a multi-country survey of people over 60, carried out in the late 1980s and early 1990s, just over 70% of respondents in the Netherlands said that they would like to work because, otherwise, life would be too boring, and only about 20% said that they would like to work because they needed the money. These are the same proportions as in Japan, where the gradual decline of the lifetime employment system

Figure 4.4: Trends in employment and unemployment rates

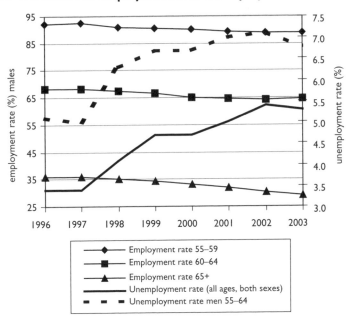

Source: Management and Co-ordination Agency, Statistics Bureau, Annual Report on the Labour Force Survey: 2003

and, in particular, the increased incidence of redundancy and early retirement seems to have had a profound effect on the psychological well-being of older men. The increase in suicides among men in their later middle age has been remarkable, as Figure 4.5 testifies.

Policy actors have sought to respond in a variety of ways. Although the government had been supportive of lifting the mandatory retirement age from 55 to 60, it was not until 1998 that legislation prohibiting employers to operate mandatory retirement at 60 became operative. The trade unions made the raising of the mandatory retirement age a critical element of their claims in the 2000 and 2001 wage rounds, but insofar as the government has backed them it has been through its traditional strategy of exhortation. The Law on the Stabilisation of Employment of Older Persons has been revised, but this law does little more than make recommendations. Employers *should make efforts* to secure employment opportunities for their older employees, by taking measures for the development and improvement of occupational ability working facilities and other conditions, and they *should make efforts* to provide necessary assistance to employees in designing an

Figure 4.5: Trends in suicide by older men

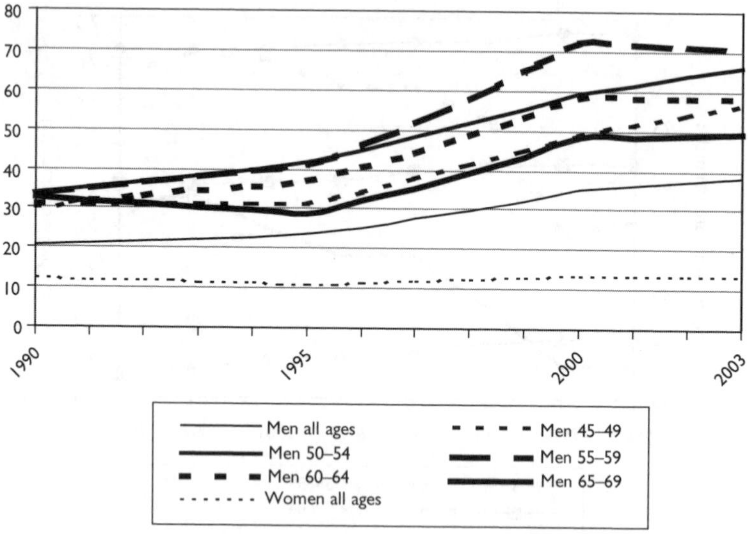

Source: Ministry of Health, Labour and Welfare, Suicide Statistics;
Management and Co-ordination Agency, Statistics Bureau, Annual Report on the
Labour Force Survey: 2003

'occupational life plan' as they become older. Where they operate a mandatory retirement age, they *should make efforts* to adopt the necessary measures for ensuring the stable employment of older persons until age 65 via the introduction or improvement of continued employment systems, and they *should take measures* to assist those who do leave to find alternative work.

There have been no attempts to introduce age discrimination legislation. However, under a new provision in the Employment Measures Law that took effect in late 2001, employers are *requested to make efforts* to give equal opportunities regardless of age when recruiting, and a set of relevant guidelines were issued. While it seems there was some initial decrease in the use of job advertisements containing age limits, the guidelines permitted numerous exemptions. Thus, firms with a mandatory retirement system may legitimately set an age limit for recruitment on the grounds that substantial training is required in the post, while those with a seniority wage system are often exempted if they cannot hire an older person at a lower wage because of their working rules. Data from 2002 show 44% of unemployed people aged 45-54, and nearly 55% of those aged 55 and older, claiming that the principal reason for their failing to find work was that 'I'm not in the age group qualified to apply for the job' (MHLW, 2003, p 38).

Official reports make frequent reference to how active labour market policy interventions directed at older people have been strengthened (MHLW, various years; OECD, 2004). For many years, the government has operated wage subsidy schemes to promote the hiring of 'difficult to employ persons' – such as the elderly and the disabled – and to these have been added subsidies to employers hiring middle-aged or elderly employees in regions of high unemployment. In addition, there exists a subsidy for people taking on new work after leaving a job at 60 that compensates for a part of the fall in wages they experience – a measure that covered nearly one in 20 of those working as employees by the year 2001. However, there appears to be no evaluation of the impact of many of these measures.

Commentators also point to how employers appear to be making some gradual changes to their employment practices. In particular, reference is made to the way in which employers claim to be planning to reduce the weight given to seniority in determining pay. The results of a survey carried out in the late 1990s, which is relatively typical of those cited, are shown in Figure 4.6. However, what is to be noted is that employers are expecting greater changes to be made to wage

Figure 4.6: Employers' intentions with respect to modifying wage systems

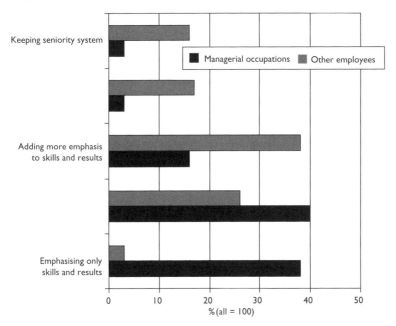

Source: JIL (2000)

structures for managerial grade employees than they are to those for regular employees – junior white-collar and blue-collar workers – who make up some five sixths of the male labour force in the critical 45- to 54-year age group.

As far as blue-collar workers are concerned, wage adjustment through the use of employment extension schemes might be more practical. The downward adjustments associated with part-time and temporary employment are substantial. Non-standard workers have rates of pay dramatically lower than regular workers and are usually ineligible for many fringe benefits, including participation in the second-tier pension (Casey, 2004; OECD, 2005, ch 6).

As well as suggestions that some consideration is being given to modifying wage systems, there are suggestions that consideration is being given to modifying promotion systems. Some employers are giving less weight to seniority in determining promotion and more to performance. The result is what are termed 'out of turn' promotions. In about a third of workplaces, this is claimed to be an 'everyday' or 'frequent' occurrence (JIL, 2000). Of course, where such promotions do occur, employers might experience declines in motivation among those older employees who have been passed over. Thus, they often also claim to have taken some kind of compensatory action to reassure the older people concerned. This action might or might not be cosmetic, and older employees' reported acceptance of their situation might be more or less real.

However, it is not only to their wage and promotion structures that employers need to look. In Japan, as in most other countries, firms allot a disproportionate share of training resources to younger people. This could, of itself, discourage older workers from retraining, and might also make them unproductive workers (Seike, 1994). Employers in Japan seem as preoccupied as employers elsewhere with a traditional view of older persons and feel they cannot hire them because 'they lose their vocational ability and flexibility as they grow older' (Wanatabe, 1992). The need to accommodate an ageing workforce, and the need to extend working life, means that resorting to traditional measures for dealing with older workers – temporary extensions, downgrading and transfers – will no longer be adequate. Retraining middle-aged and older workers will become inevitable. Yet the evidence to date is that no substantial training provision is made for older workers – except for helping them cover correspondence course fees. As an increasing number of them try to enhance their professional and technical competencies, some employers encourage middle-aged and older workers to acquire formal qualifications. However, most leave the decision to engage in such training to the workers themselves (Kawakita, 1996).

Conclusion

Japan has often been suggested to be a special case. According to some commentators, the country has a distinct, perhaps unique, culture that means that there is little transferability of its experiences or practices. According to others, especially those interested in 'bridge jobs', it is a country from which others can learn. Such bridge jobs, either part-time or less demanding, and often less well paid, are taken by older people after leaving their 'career jobs', and before retiring completely (Ruhm, 1991). This chapter argues that Japan is, indeed, a special case, although not as special as at first might appear. However, it also argues that Japan is unlikely to be special for much longer. There is little that Japan does that cannot be emulated, and the conditions that allowed it to be special are disappearing. At the same time, Japan is facing problems faced by many other industrialised countries. Thus, if there is something to be learnt, it is not necessarily to be learnt from Japan; on the contrary, it could be that there is something that Japan may learn from other countries. On the other hand, few other countries have yet developed policies and practices that improve the 'employability' of older people. All of them, and Japan as well, should be searching vigorously for them.

Notes

[1] Almost all the data in this article refer to men. The employment rates of older women are also high in Japan, although in both Sweden and the US they are at least as high, if not higher.

[2] The Japanese public pension has two tiers – a basic, flat-rate tier and an earnings-related tier – worth, respectively, some 18% and some 30% of gross average earnings. The basic pension has, since the early 1950s, been available only at 65, but the full earnings-related pension may be drawn at 60. Those who ceased working completely at 60 were at one time eligible for a supplement to the earnings-related pension that was the equivalent of the basic pension. However, this supplement was phased out gradually after 1994 and ceased applying at all after 2000 (Casey, 2004).

[3] By 2003, people aged 65 and over made up 47% of the agricultural workforce. Since 1996, the overall agricultural workforce had fallen

by nearly 20%, but the number of people aged 65 and over working in agriculture had fallen by only 5%.

References

Araki, T. (1995) 'Modification of working conditions through dismissals? A comparative analysis of the SAS case', *Japan Labor Bulletin*, vol 34, no 8, pp 5-8.

Casey, B. (2004) *The Japanese Retirement Income System: A Special Case?*, Global Briefing Series, Boston, MA: Centre for Retirement Research, Boston College (www.bc.edu/centers/crr/gib_4.shtml).

Ibson, D. (2001) 'Reinventing the Japanese way of doing business: interview with Carlos Ghosn', *Financial Times*, 23 July.

JIL (2000) *White Paper on Labour 2000*, Tokyo: Japan Institute of Labour.

Kawakita, T. (1996) 'Japanese in-house training and development', *Japan Labor Bulletin*, vol 35, no 4, pp 5-8.

Koike, K. (1997) *Human Resource Development*, Japanese Economy and Labor Series, No 2, Tokyo: Japan Institute of Labour.

Lazear, E. (1979) 'Why is there mandatory retirement?', *Journal of Political Economy*, vol 87, pp 1261-84.

Lincoln, E. (2001) *Arthritic Japan: The Slow Pace of Economic Reform*, Washington, DC: Brookings Institution Press.

Management and Co-ordination Agency, Statistics Bureau (2000a) *Report on the Special Survey of the Labour Force, February 2000*, Labour Force Series No 65.

Management and Co-ordination Agency, Statistics Bureau (2000b) *Annual Report on the Labour Force Survey: 2000*.

Matsuzuka, Y. (2002) *Changes in the Permanent Employment System in Japan between 1982 and 1997*, New York, NY: Routledge.

MHLW (Ministry of Health, Labour and Welfare (various years), *Annual Report on Health, Labour and Welfare*, Tokyo: MHLW.

OECD (Organisation for Economic Co-operation and Development) (1996) *Economic Survey 1995–1996: Japan*, Paris: OECD.

OECD (2000) *Economic Survey 1999–2000: Japan*, Paris: OECD.

OECD (2004) *Ageing and Employment Policies – Japan*, Paris: OECD.

OECD (2005) *Economic Survey 2005: Japan*, Paris: OECD.

Osawa, M. and Kingston, J. (1996) 'Flexibility and inspiration: restructuring the Japanese labour market', *Japan Labor Bulletin*, vol 35, no 1, pp 4-8.

Rebick, M. (1995) 'Rewards in the afterlife: late career job placements as incentives in the Japanese firm', *Journal of the Japanese and International Economies*, vol 9, no 1, pp 1-28.

Ruhm, C. (1991) 'Career employment and job stopping', *Industrial Relations*, vol 30, no 2, pp 193-208.

Sano, Y. (1997) 'Performance-based compensation: individual, group and corporate level', in Y. Sano, M. Morishima and A. Seike (eds) *Frontiers of Japanese Human Resource Practices*, Tokyo: Japan Institute of Labour.

Sato, A. (1994) 'Employment adjustment of middle-aged and older white-collar workers', *Japan Labor Bulletin*, vol 33, no 2, pp 5-8.

Sato, A. (1996) 'Keeping employees employed: shukko and tenseki job transfers – formation of a labor market within corporate groups', *Japan Labor Bulletin*, vol 35, no 12, pp 5-8.

Sato, A. (2000) 'Are Japan's small firms "ageless"', *Japan Labor Bulletin*, vol 39, no 5, pp 5-8.

Seike, A. (1994) 'The employment of older people in Japan and policies to promote it', *Japan Labor Bulletin*, vol 33, no 12, pp 5-8.

TDB (Teikoku Databank) (various issues) Teikoku Databank bankruptcy reports (www.tdb.co.jp/english).

Wanatabe, M. (1992) 'Employment of older persons and need for support systems', *Japan Labor Bulletin*, vol 31, no 10, pp 5-8.

Yahata, S. (1995) 'Ongoing price reduction and employment adjustment in the Japanese distribution sector', *Japan Labor Bulletin*, vol 34, no 5, pp 5-8.

Yamada, A (2000) 'Wage reduction after quitting the career job: implications for social policy', *Quarterly Journal of Social Security Research* (Kikan Shakai Hosho Kenkyu), vol 35, 4, pp 377-94.

Yomiuri Shimbun (2001) 'More employees at major firms applying for early retirement', *Yomiuri Shimbun/Daily Yomiuri*, 14 August.

This article was originally published in *The Geneva Papers* (Casey, B. [2005] 'The employment of older people: can we learn from Japan?', *The Geneva Papers*, vol 30, no 4, pp 620-37). It is reproduced here with the kind permission of the publishers, Palgrave Macmillan.

FIVE

Moving older people into jobs: Incapacity Benefit, Labour's reforms and the job shortfall in the UK regions

Christina Beatty and Steve Fothergill

Introduction

More than any of its predecessors, the current Labour government in the UK is committed to raising employment among older workers. Through advice and active support, backed up in some cases by financial incentives, the aim is to increase the number of over-50s in work and reduce dependency on welfare benefits. Since Labour was elected in 1997, the schemes targeted at older workers have proliferated, and further major reform is still planned.

This chapter[1] casts a critical eye over these initiatives. Its central thesis is that although the new initiatives have undoubtedly proved helpful to many individuals, they fail to take account of the profound regional and local differences in the availability of jobs. Indeed, it is in the areas where older workers living on benefits are most numerous that the government's new initiatives seem least relevant.

The chapter begins by outlining the key features of the government's initiatives to help older people into jobs. The description is intentionally brief because much fuller versions can be found elsewhere, not least in departmental publications (see in particular DWP, 2002, 2004, 2006). The factors influencing the effectiveness of the initiatives are then explored. Particularly full consideration is given to the pattern of employment and unemployment across the country, including estimates of the job shortfall affecting older workers in each region.

The government's own figures show that in 2006 a total of 8.8 million people in the UK were aged between 50 and state pension age (currently 60 for women and 65 for men) (DWP, 2006). Of these, nearly 30% (2.6 million) were not working; 1.3 milllion were claiming incapacity benefits, another 140,000 were claiming unemployment benefits, and a further 250,000 were dependent partners of benefit claimants. It is the Labour government's stated aim to move around one million of these older men and women into work.

Labour's reforms: the story so far

Jobcentre Plus lies at the heart of Labour's reforms. It affects all jobseekers and benefit claimants of working age but is of particular relevance to the over-50s because so many of them are claimants. Jobcentre Plus is the product of a merger between the Employment Service and the parts of the Benefits Agency dealing with working-age benefits. It was foreshadowed by the announcement as far back as 1998 that the government intended to introduce a 'single work-focused gateway' to benefits. This took tangible form in the ONE pilots that ran from 1999 onwards. Jobcentre Plus itself went live in 2002, with the aim of having the new offices up and running in all parts of the country by 2006.

The new, combined offices are at the core of the vision. When individuals of working age first make a benefit claim, they are now asked to discuss not only their benefits but also what they might do to move into work. This applies not only to the unemployed claiming Jobseeker's Allowance (JSA) but also to people registering for other benefits such as Incapacity Benefit (IB) and Income Support. In these initial interviews, the intention is to offer guidance on moving into work and claimants are directed towards the appropriate services on offer. Each individual is also given a nominated caseworker with whom they can meet periodically to review progress.

The significance of these changes for the over-50s lies in the number of older jobless people who are on benefits other than JSA. Above all, incapacity benefits have become the repository for very large numbers of jobless older workers. These benefits comprise IB itself, National Insurance (NI) credits for incapacity (for those with a poor NI contributions history, who are normally then entitled to Income Support with a disability premium) and Severe Disablement Allowance (for those with a poor NI record but with a high level of disability).

As noted, 1.3 million men and women over 50 claim these incapacity benefits. Unlike JSA, IB is not means-tested, except for post-2001 claimants with substantial income from a company or personal pension. Also, Income Support with a disability premium is worth more than Income Support on its own. For many men and women, being out of work on incapacity benefits is therefore financially more attractive than being unemployed on JSA. Access to incapacity benefits is dependent on claimants having an important degree of ill health or disability and is granted initially by family doctors, then later by doctors working on behalf of Jobcentre Plus. To qualify for incapacity benefits, an individual does not necessarily have to be incapable of all possible work in all possible circumstances.

With the introduction of Jobcentre Plus, new incapacity claimants are for the first time required to participate in a work-focused interview. The existing stock of incapacity claimants also has the option of making use of the job search and training advice provided by Jobcentre Plus, though their engagement is voluntary. This is an important change because the contact between incapacity claimants and the employment services had hitherto been negligible. Once they had satisfied the medical criteria to qualify for IB, they by and large disappeared from official view until called in for periodic medical re assessment. Indeed, incapacity benefits often proved to be a one-way ticket: it was easy to slip on to them, but very difficult to move off again. Labour ministers have famously pointed out that once a claimant has been on Incapacity Benefit for two years, they are more likely to reach pension age or die than move back into work.

New Deal 50+ is a less far reaching reform. It is one of the family of New Deal programmes introduced by Labour since 1997 and was first announced in 1999, with a national roll-out following during 2000. New Deal 50+ is open to people over 50 who have been out of work for more than six months and who are claiming JSA, IB, Severe Disablement Allowance or Income Support. It is also open to the dependent partners of these claimants. Like the other New Deals, there is a heavy emphasis on personal advice and job search help. Financial help with the cost of training is also available, now up to £1,500 per person. Participation in New Deal 50+ has so far been entirely voluntary, unlike the corresponding programmes for younger people.

The other programme that is particularly relevant to the over-50s is the New Deal for Disabled People. This is because of the considerable overlap between older people without jobs and those on incapacity benefits. New Deal for Disabled People aims to assist men and women who have a long-standing impairment to find work. Like New Deal 50+, participation has so far been voluntary. It provides a Personal Adviser Service, aimed as in the other New Deals at providing support on job seeking and training opportunities. Claimants of incapacity benefits can access the services of New Deal for Disabled People at any time – they do not have to wait until after a six-month qualifying period.

Labour's reforms: the next steps

Mid-way through Labour's second term (2001-05), it was apparent that the initial round of reforms had not always delivered the return to work that the government had intended. In particular, the numbers claiming incapacity benefits were showing a stubborn reluctance to fall, even in the context of a national labour market that was tighter than at any time for more than 20 years. This realisation prompted a new round of reform, set out in particular in a Green Paper published in February 2006 (DWP, 2006).

The Green Paper sets out major reforms to incapacity benefits. The name will change. The government takes the view that 'Incapacity Benefit' sends the wrong signals about people's ability to work, so in 2008 the present benefits will be replaced by Employment and Support Allowance. For the first time, this will introduce an important element of conditionality into incapacity benefits: all but the most severely ill claimants will in future have to agree to a 'return-to-work plan'. This may involve rehabilitation, retraining, voluntary work or formal job search. Failure to comply with the plan will result in a progressive reduction in benefits, to the level payable under JSA.

The other key element of the new reforms involves rolling out the Pathways to Work initiative to cover the whole country. Pathways to Work was piloted in a number of areas in late 2003, and by 2006 had been extended to cover nearly a third of the country. It requires the majority of new incapacity claimants to attend a series of compulsory work-focused interviews during the first six months of their claim. These route claimants to appropriate support, including enhanced services to deliver physical and mental rehabilitation. A return-to-work premium, worth £40 a week, is also available for the first year for those entering low-paid employment. The government takes the view that the results of the Pathways to Work pilots are encouraging: the share of new claimants leaving incapacity benefits within six months is up eight percentage points compared with non-Pathways areas (DWP, 2006).

These new reforms to incapacity benefits have mostly been welcomed, with quite wide acceptance that, as with JSA at present, entitlement to benefit should be linked to action by the claimant aimed at returning to work. The significance of these new reforms to the over-50s is that very large numbers will eventually become caught up in the changes.

From the point of view of the over-50s, the other significant reform in the Green Paper is that long-term claimant unemployed people aged 50-59 will in future be required to take up the additional jobseeking support available through New Deal 25+, whereas previously this engagement had been entirely voluntary. The number of long-term unemployed claimants aged over 50 is, however, far outweighed by the number of incapacity claimants.

The determinants of success

The first thing to note about these initiatives is that they should not be seen in isolation. They are really part of a much wider effort to create the conditions in which men and women in their 50s and 60s can engage with the labour market.

Central to these efforts is the creation of a stable and healthy macroeconomic framework. So far, the Labour government has been exceptionally successful in this respect and has maintained steady, if rather unspectacular, economic growth, leading to a reduction in claimant unemployment to below one million. A strong economy generates demand for labour and makes it easier for most groups to find work, including the over-50s. Sustained economic growth undoubtedly underpins the modest recent reduction in economic inactivity among 50- to 64-year-old men – the reversal of a long-established upward trend.

The government is also keen to 'make work pay' so that it is worthwhile for people to move off benefits. The establishment of a national minimum wage is part of this strategy. So too is the introduction of a growing range of in-work tax credits. Detailed reforms to IB rules, in particular, mean that IB claimants who move into employment can already return to their previous (usually higher) rate of benefit if in the first 12 months the job does not work out. This removes an important financial disincentive to looking for work for many over-50s.

The point is simply that the extent to which the over-50s move into work does not depend simply on the success or failure of Jobcentre Plus, the New Deals or IB reform. Putting aside these wider considerations, and assuming that the Department for Work and Pensions (DWP) can actually deliver all that the government is now promising – and that is a tall order in the context of planned cuts in staff – the extent to which these interventions can be expected to make a difference depends on two factors:

- whether there is willingness and ability on the part of the non-employed over-50s to move into jobs;
- whether there are actually jobs for these people to move into, out in the labour market.

Regarding **willingness and ability to work**, it is possible to draw fairly firm conclusions about older men. Our own research, including a recent book (Alcock et al, 2003), is helpful here. This has involved interviews with well over 1,000 non-employed men aged 50-64, spread across a range of locations in Britain. It is among men of working age that economic inactivity has risen until recently, and it is among men of working age that full-time engagement with the labour market was once the norm. Nearly 800,000 of the 1.3 million over-50s who claim incapacity benefits are men.

Table 5.1 refers to what we call the older 'detached male workforce'. These are men aged 50-64 who are economically inactive or have been unemployed for most or all of the previous six months. Part-time workers are also included on the basis that they too are detached from conventional full-time employment, though of course there is nothing inherently wrong with part-time work if that is what people choose for themselves. The table shows how all these men describe themselves. What is noticeable is that among this group, which is a key target for the government's welfare-to-work initiatives, the men who see themselves as 'retired from paid work altogether' make up barely 30%. Those who describe themselves as 'long-term sick or disabled' are distinctly more numerous and outweigh the 'unemployed' by well over two to one. The obvious implication is that with so relatively few men seeing themselves as retired, there should in theory be fertile territory for the government's back-to-work initiatives.

There is, of course, variation within the 50- to 64-year-old group. A man who is 63 or 64 is unlikely to share the same aspirations as one in his early 50s, or to see himself in the same way. Figures 5.1 and 5.2 make this point but do not undermine the general observation that

Table 5.1: Self-declared status of detached 50- to 64-year-old men

	% of survey respondents
Long-term sick or disabled	38
Retired from paid work altogether	31
Unemployed	15
In part-time employment	9
Full-time carer	3
Looking after family and home	1
Other	2
	100

Source: Sheffield Hallam surveys (see Alcock et al, 2003)

Figure 5.1: Early retirement among older detached men

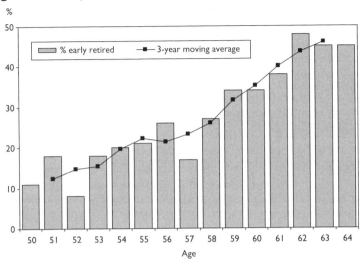

Source: Sheffield Hallam surveys (see Alcock et al, 2003)

Figure 5.2: Share of older detached men who would like a full-time job

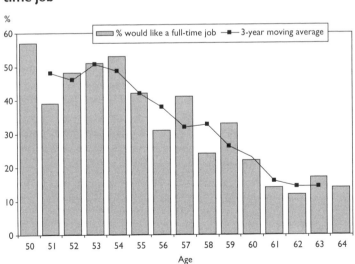

Source: Sheffield Hallam surveys (see Alcock et al, 2003)

among older men there is significant potential for labour market re-engagement. Figure 5.1 shows the share of detached male workforce that describes itself as retired. This rises with age, as might be expected, but never reaches 50%, even for men in their early 60s. Figure 5.2 shows the share of these men who say they would like a full-time job. Across the whole 50-64 age group this averages 30%. Just under half of the men in their early 50s say they would like a full-time job, and the proportion declines steadily thereafter but is still around 15% for men in their early 60s.

Wanting a job is, of course, not the same as actually looking for one, and the evidence points to a high level of disillusionment. A third of the 50- to 64-year-old men in our surveys said that they looked for a full-time job after their last job ended, but only 12% were still looking when we interviewed them. The active jobseekers included just 2% of the men on IB.

Neither is wanting a job the same as being in a reasonable position to secure one. Table 5.2 uses the same survey data to examine a number of aspects of employability. A clear majority of the men formerly worked in manual occupations – a segment of the labour market that has been in gradual decline. Nearly 40% of the total have no formal qualifications

Table 5.2: Selected characteristics of detached 50- to 64-year-old men

	% of survey respondents
Usual occupation	
Professional	5
Other white-collar	39
Manual	57
Qualifications	
Degree	12
Craft apprenticeship	22
No formal qualifications	39
Time since last full-time job	
Less than two years	20
Five years or more	49
Health	
'Can't do any work'	13
Some health limitation	46
No limitation	40

Source: Sheffield Hallam surveys (see Alcock et al, 2003)

at all, and nearly half have not worked full-time for at least five years. Health is also a problem – while only about one in eight say they cannot do any work at all, almost half report health limitations on the work they are able to do.

These are personal characteristics that are likely to disadvantage many older men in the eyes of potential employers and they emphasise the importance of practical support if many are ever to return to paid employment. If older men without jobs are to compete on equal terms with younger, better-qualified and healthier workers, they will often need intensive guidance, access to appropriate training and supportive employers.

Closer examination of the data suggests that there are actually two rather different groups of older men who have dropped out early from full-time employment. One comprises middle-class professionals and other white-collar workers, for whom detachment mostly takes the form of early retirement. They tend to leave voluntarily from jobs that they have usually held for a very long time, and in doing so begin to draw on accumulated pension rights. Nearly all no longer want a full-time job, though a few do look for work before reconciling themselves to retirement, and a sizeable minority maintain contact with the labour market through part-time work. Overall, this group draws little if at all on the benefits system.

The other group includes just about all manual workers. These men are much more likely to have fallen out of work because of redundancy or ill health. Fewer of these men have a pension. Accordingly, they tend to be more dependent on the benefits system, above all on IB. Many of these former manual workers would still like a job, but hardly any think there is a realistic chance of getting one.

This is a division among 50- to 64-year-old men that DWP research has tended to confirm (Barham, 2002). There is some overlap between the two groups. Quite large numbers of former manual workers do have a pension (not necessarily a generous one), though hardly any of the middle-class professionals are without a pension of some sort. IB is also widely claimed across the social spectrum, even though it is more common among manual workers. In numerical terms, it is the world of the manual worker that is more common – roughly a 60–40 split in its favour.

The verdict on willingness and ability to work among older men is therefore that plenty would welcome the opportunity to re-engage with paid employment, including full-time employment, but many find themselves facing personal obstacles associated with poor skills or ill health that would make re-engagement difficult.

For women over 50, the situation regarding willingness and ability to work is more uncertain, and not simply because the evidence is more patchy. For many women, there is the added complication of domestic roles, sometimes looking after children, grandchildren or ageing parents. Even if they are fit and able to take up paid work, and have appropriate qualifications, older women may not always want to do so because employment conflicts with their other responsibilities. What the statistics tell us is that economic activity rates among women have been rising, albeit more slowly in recent years. Also, successive cohorts of women are more likely to be economically active than their predecessors – so tomorrow's 50- to 64-year-olds are more likely to look for work than today's. The increase in the state pension age for women, from 2010 onwards, will presumably accentuate this trend. On the other hand, the statistics also show that since 1997 the continuing growth in the stock of incapacity claimants – around 200,000 – has nearly all been among women and, as with men, older women are particularly likely to be incapacity claimants. The reasons why the number of women on incapacity benefits has continued rising, while the number of men has stabilised, are not at all well understood.

Turning to the other determinant of success – the **availability of jobs** – serious questions begin to appear. There are two issues here. One is about the way the labour market works, which is actually a debate about economic theory. The other is about the true state of the contemporary UK labour market, which is really a debate about regional differences.

Starting with the economic theory, it needs to be emphasised that Jobcentre Plus, the New Deals and IB reform are all 'supply-side' measures, that is, they are intended to boost the quantity and quality of the labour supplied to the marketplace. They do not in themselves increase the demand for that labour. Some economists say this does not matter because supply will generate its own demand. This is because normal competitive market pressures tend to bring demand and supply into balance through the adjustment of wage levels. In this view, the government should therefore not worry unduly about where all these extra workers over 50 are going to find jobs.

The alternative view, rooted in the Keynesian economic tradition, is that the demand for labour depends on the demand for goods and services. In this view, the mechanisms that are supposed to balance labour demand and supply, through the adjustment of wage levels, operate so slowly or imperfectly as to be irrelevant in all but the very long run. An additional supply of labour that is not matched by a commensurate boost to labour demand will therefore lead to extra unemployment. In the case of initiatives to raise labour force participation among the over-50s, the extra unemployment will not all fall on this group, because there will be displacement involving younger workers, but the extra labour supply will one way or another lead to extra unemployment for someone.

It is perhaps wrong to set up these two views as irreconcilable opposites. In some circumstances that even Keynesians would accept, an additional supply of trained labour can lead directly to additional employment. This is likely when firms' output is constrained by a shortage of labour. There are also circumstances where an additional supply of labour might trigger lower interest rates, which in turn would tend to boost labour demand. This is likely when interest rates are set primarily by the need to curb wage inflation. Some of these rather specific circumstances can currently be observed in the UK. In parts of southern England, the economy is operating at, or close to, full employment and firms there are sometimes constrained by the availability of labour. More generally, the Bank of England's interest rate policy involves keeping a close eye on inflationary pressures generated in that part of the country. So there might be a good case for arguing that bringing forth extra labour supply from among the ranks of the over-50s is likely to facilitate higher output rather than cause unemployment.

This logic is seductive but flawed. The problem is that it founders on the deeply divided regional geography of the UK. In simple terms, the vast reserve of over-50s who might be lured back into the labour market is disproportionately concentrated in the wrong places. It is to these regional differences that we now turn.

The geography of joblessness

There is a widely held view that the UK economy is not far off full employment and that residual unemployment is attributable mainly to a shortage of skills and motivation on the part of the unemployed themselves. The notion that full employment is just around the corner is buttressed by claimant unemployment figures that in the early 2000s have been lower than at any time since the 1970s and point to only modest regional differences.

While there has unquestionably been significant improvement in the labour market since the early 1990s, the view that the unemployment problem is all but solved is wrong. It is based on a misunderstanding of what has happened in the labour markets where job destruction was so widespread in the 1980s and early 1990s. This is a conclusion we have reached through a number of studies, beginning in the coalfields where there was an apparently inexplicable fall in claimant unemployment despite the closure of most or all of the mines (Beatty and Fothergill, 1996; Beatty et al, 2005). Our conclusions are shared by other commentators who, like ourselves, have started by looking not at national figures but instead at what is actually going on in local and regional labour markets (see Green and Owen, 1998; Mackay, 1999; Turok and Edge, 1999; Webster, 2002).

In brief, what has happened in the areas badly affected by job losses in the 1980s and '90s is that exceptionally large numbers of jobless people have been diverted away from unemployment-related benefits on to other benefits or out of the benefits system altogether. These shifts have been the principal adjustments in response to job loss. Their effect has been to mask the scale of unemployment because only JSA claimants are included in the monthly unemployment claimant count. If jobless men and women also give up looking for work – and most incapacity claimants do – they also drop out of the wider International Labour Organization measure of unemployment derived from the Labour Force Survey, which only counts those actually looking for work and available for work. Subsequent job creation has reduced claimant unemployment but, as noted earlier, it has largely failed to dent the stock of marginalised men and women on incapacity benefits.

To illustrate this point, Figures 5.3 to 5.6 show the proportion of men aged 50-64 and women aged 50-59 who are incapacity claimants. Because of the way that the social security system works, none of these people are included in the claimant unemployment figures. Two points need to be noted.

The first is the astonishingly high proportion of over-50s who are incapacity claimants in some districts. At the very peak, 44% of all 50- to 64-year-old men in the Easington district of County Durham are out of work and claiming incapacity benefits. It is not just small former mining districts like Easington that display very high levels – in Glasgow the proportion of 50- to 64-year-old men receiving these benefits is 36%, in Liverpool it is 33% and in Manchester 31%. Overall, in no fewer than 74 districts the proportion exceeds 20% of all 50- to 64-year-old men. In 31 districts, the proportion of 50- to 59-year-old women on these benefits also exceeds 20%.

The other point is the geographical distribution of these claimants. In much of South Wales, Merseyside, the North East and Clydeside, the figures are especially high. What these areas have in common is that they all experienced large-scale job losses in the 1980s and '90s, especially from traditional industries, and for many years they have all

Figure 5.3: Male incapacity claimants aged 50–64, Scotland, November 2005

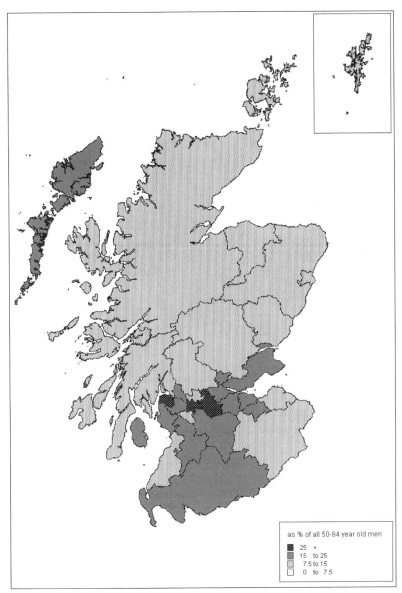

Source: DWP, ONS

Figure 5.4: Male incapacity claimants aged 50–64, England and Wales, November 2005

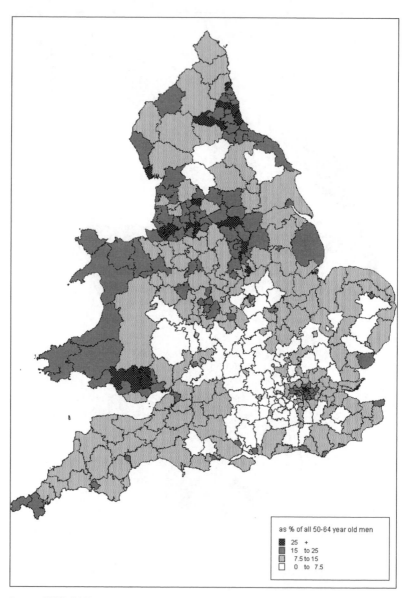

Source: DWP, ONS

Figure 5.5: Female incapacity claimants aged 50–59, Scotland, November 2005

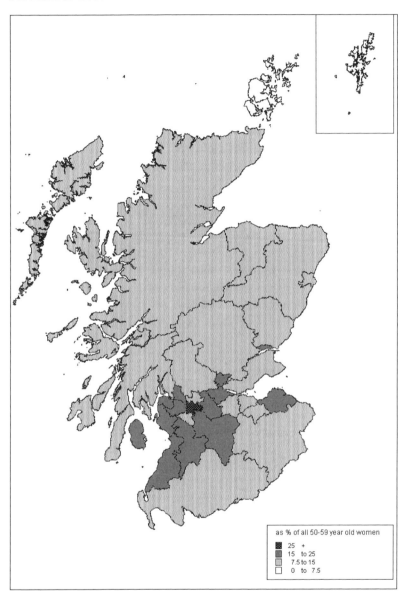

as % of all 50-59 year old women

- 25 +
- 15 to 25
- 7.5 to 15
- 0 to 7.5

Source: DWP, ONS

Figure 5.6: Female incapacity claimants aged 50–59, England and Wales, November 2005

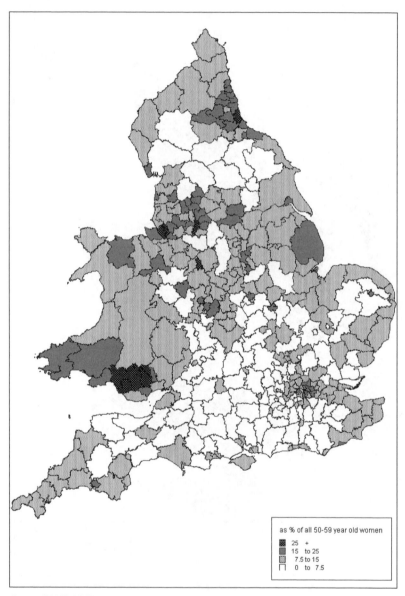

Source: DWP, ONS

faced significant unemployment problems. Conversely, in nearly all of the south and east outside London the proportion of older men and women claiming incapacity benefits is much lower, usually below 10%.

This is not to suggest that the exceptionally high level of incapacity claimants in some areas is evidence of fraud or malingering. All these people will have had to secure the appropriate medical certification. Equally, it is not the intention to deny that there are higher underlying levels of sickness and disability in some places than in others. However, the geographical pattern is exactly what could be expected as a result of the diversion of men and women on to incapacity benefits in areas where jobs are harder to find. It is also impossible to explain away the fourfold increase in the number of incapacity claimants in Britain as a whole over the past 30 years in terms of health factors alone.

Over the past 10 years we have developed and refined methods of estimating 'hidden unemployment' around the country – that is, unemployment that is excluded from the official claimant count (see, in particular, Beatty et al, 2002; Beatty and Fothergill, 2005). Our methods draw heavily on comparisons with what has already been shown to be possible in terms of the numbers on incapacity benefits in the areas closest to full employment, and take account of underlying differences in health.

This is not the place to explain in full either the methods or the detailed results (see Beatty and Fothergill, 2005). What we estimate are the numbers that *could reasonably be expected to have been in work in a genuinely fully employed economy*. This is not the same as the number of active jobseekers, which is much less because so many people give up looking for work because they think there is nothing appropriate available for them. Our estimates have also been cross-checked against the results of other methods, and against survey data, and shown to be robust.

The important point is the general pattern that emerges. As a general rule, the higher the rate of claimant unemployment, the greater the extent of hidden unemployment, especially on incapacity benefits. London is the important exception – the capital appears to have surprisingly low hidden unemployment in relation to its quite high claimant unemployment. On the whole, however, it is in the older industrial areas of the North, Scotland and Wales that the scale of hidden unemployment is greatest. In contrast, large parts of southern England outside London have not only very low claimant unemployment but also relatively little hidden unemployment. In total, we have estimated that in August 2003 around 1.1 million out of the headline total of 2.7 million incapacity claimants across Britain as a whole were 'hidden unemployed' in the sense that they could reasonably be expected to have been in work in a genuinely fully employed economy (Beatty and Fothergill, 2005). This figure is remarkably close to the government's own target of a one million reduction in incapacity claimant numbers by 2016 (DWP, 2006).

All this has strayed a long way from assessing the prospects of returning over-50s to work but let us spell out its significance. The point is that the very large numbers of marginalised over-50s tend not to be located in the southern and eastern parts of Britain where the economy is close to full employment and where there is therefore likely to be a ready demand for their labour. In the older industrial areas of northern England, Wales and Scotland, the economy is often still a long way from full employment. Trying to encourage more older workers in these areas to join the workforce is merely likely to compound the existing scramble for the jobs that are available. In these areas, older workers may even resist labour market reattachment because they know that where there is strong competition for jobs they are unlikely to be employers' first choice.

The job shortfall for older workers

This regional analysis can be taken one step further. Table 5.3 shows the employment rate among 50- to 64-year-olds in each UK region in spring 2006. For women, the employment rate is lower than for men, reflecting traditionally lower levels of labour force participation and women's earlier state pension age. However, among both men and women there is a clear regional hierarchy. The gap between the highest and lowest regions – 15% for men and 16% for women – is especially large.

The South East has the highest employment rates among older workers. As officially defined since 1996, this region comprises the nine counties to the west and south of London, in an arc from Oxfordshire to Kent. This is the part of Britain where large areas could be described as being at, or close to, full employment. Employment rates in the South East therefore serve as a useful guide to what might in theory be achievable in a fully employed economy elsewhere in the country. Table 5.4 shows the additional jobs that would be required to raise the employment rate for 50- to 64-year-olds in every region up to the levels already prevailing in the South East. This gives a simple but robust estimate of the 'job shortfall' among older workers.

Table 5.4 points to a total job shortfall in 2006 of approaching 600,000, of which women account for just over half. Whichever way

Table 5.3: Employment rate among 50- to 64-year-olds by region, spring 2006

Men	%	Women	%
South East	77	South East	63
East Midlands	75	Eastern	62
Eastern	75	South West	60
South West	75	West Midlands	60
West Midlands	74	London	59
London	73	East Midlands	59
Yorkshire and the Humber	72	Yorkshire and the Humber	56
Scotland	69	Scotland	54
North West	66	North West	54
Wales	66	North East	51
Northern Ireland	64	Wales	50
North East	62	Northern Ireland	47
United Kingdom	**72**	**United Kingdom**	**58**

Source: Labour Force Survey.

this figure is viewed, it represents a substantial shortfall in jobs. However, the last time we made the same calculation, using data for 2002, the shortfall appeared to be considerably greater – 775,000 in all (Beatty and Fothergill, 2002). This would suggest that between 2002 and 2006 the job shortfall for older workers in the UK fell by around a quarter – an encouraging trend in such a short space of time. What this reflects is a measure of convergence between the regions: during the first half of the present decade, employment among older workers has grown faster away from the South East of England. Whether this trend will be sustained remains questionable, and it could reflect no more than the different timing of the economic cycle across the UK regions.

Table 5.4: Estimated job shortfall among older workers,* UK, spring 2006

	Men	Women	Total
50- to 54-year-olds	115,000	120,000	235,000
55- to 59-year-olds	85,000	75,000	160,000
60- to 64-year-olds	75,000	120,000	195,000
50- to 64-year-olds	**275,000**	**315,000**	**590,000**

* Based on raising the employment rate in all regions to the level in the South East.

Source: Authors' estimates

Furthermore, the job shortfall figures in Table 5.4 may be inherently conservative because they implicitly assume that employment rates among older workers can be pushed no higher than those currently found in the South East. In practice, if labour force participation among women continues to rise, it should in due course prove possible for women's employment rates to move still higher. Raising older women's employment rate in every region from the current level in the South East up to, for example, the current national average for older men – that is, from 63% to 72% – would generate a requirement for another 250,000 jobs for 50- to 59-year-olds and a further 220,000 jobs for 60- to 64-year-olds. That would bring the total job shortfall for 50- to 64-year-olds to just under 1.1 million.

Finally, Table 5.5 shows the distribution of the estimated job shortfall across the regions. As in Table 5.4 earlier, the figures here represent the extra jobs for older workers that would be required to raise their employment rate to the level currently found in the South East. The figures underline the points made earlier about the divided nature of the UK's regional economy:

Table 5.5: Estimated job shortfall among 50- to 64-year-olds by region,* spring 2006

	Job shortfall	% increase needed in jobs held by 50- to 64-year-olds
North East	70,000	27
Northern Ireland	40,000	26
Wales	75,000	23
North West	130,000	18
Scotland	85,000	17
Yorks and Humber	55,000	9
London	45,000	6
West Midlands	30,000	5
East Midlands	20,000	4
South West	25,000	4
Eastern	15,000	2
South East	0	0
UK	**590,000**	9

* Based on raising the employment rate among 50- to 64-year-olds to the level in the South East.

Source: Authors' estimates

- The five regions in the south and east of Britain (London, South East, South West, Eastern and East Midlands), which together cover about half the UK population, account for less than a fifth of the job shortfall among older workers.
- The seven regions in the north and west, with the other half of the UK population, account for more than four fifths of the job shortfall for older workers.

To put it another way, the intensity of the job shortfall for older workers is at least *four times greater* away from the strong economies of southern and eastern England. As Table 5.5 also shows, to raise the employment rate among older workers in the North East up to the level in the South East would require a 27% increase in the number of jobs held by 50- to 64-year-olds. In Northern Ireland, a 26% increase would be required, and in Wales a 23% increase.

Conclusion

A balanced conclusion on Labour's reforms would be that expectations should not be raised too high. There is logic in linking the benefits and employment services so that men and women who would like to return to work do not become parked on benefits. There is also logic in trying to tailor services to the needs of the individual. Many over-50s will no doubt welcome this fresh approach. But we should not necessarily expect a huge impact on overall levels of employment. In the parts of the country where near full employment is a reality, the over-50s who are supported in their efforts to find work do stand a good chance of getting jobs. In the rest of the country, where the majority of the marginalised over-50s are to be found, it is a different story. In these areas, there is still a sizeable job shortfall. More people actively engaged in these labour markets may simply mean more people chasing each vacancy. Where the over-50s find work in northern Britain, they will often do so at the expense of other jobseekers.

Substantial progress in increasing employment among the over-50s requires a different approach. It needs the economic growth of the past 10 years to be sustained – indeed, this has already delivered the first increases in employment among older men for many years. While the Labour government is unquestionably committed to stable economic growth, whether it can continue to deliver on this front is questionable. It is hard to see big increases in consumer spending and rising debt continuing to drive economic growth to the same extent as in Labour's first ten years in office, and public finances limit the scope for further increases in public sector employment. Meanwhile, UK manufacturing remains in the doldrums. Since 2005, claimant unemployment in the UK has once again been on the increase.

Above all, however, substantial progress in moving the over-50s into work needs a serious assault on the regional problems that currently disfigure the UK. This means a stronger regional economic policy designed to deliver job creation in the areas where it is needed most. Despite the creation of Regional Development Agencies across England, the Labour government's regional policy falls a long way short of providing the generous and geographically targeted assistance that would be needed to make a major difference (Anyadike-Danes et al, 2001). In the coming years, regional development across northern Britain will also take a big hit from a reduction in EU aid as funding is switched to the new member states of central and eastern Europe.

We should hardly be surprised that after two decades of job destruction in Britain's older industrial areas, very large numbers of older workers in these places have become marginalised. We should also not fool ourselves that balance can be restored in these local labour markets without a massive injection of new jobs to replace those that have gone.

Note

[1] This is a revised and updated version of a chapter first published in October 2002, under the same title, by the Third Age Employment Network (Beatty and Fothergill, 2002).

References

Alcock, P., Beatty, C., Fothergill, S., Macmillan, R. and Yeandle, S. (2003) *Work to Welfare: How Men become Detached from the Labour Market*, Cambridge: Cambridge University Press.

Anayadike-Danes, M. et al (2001) *Labour's New Regional Policy: An Assessment*, London: Regional Studies Association.

Barham, C. (2002) 'Patterns of economic inactivity among older men', *Labour Market Trends*, vol 110, no 2, pp 69-78.

Beatty, C. and Fothergill, S. (1996) 'Labour market adjustment in areas of chronic industrial decline', *Regional Studies*, vol 30, no 7, pp 627-40.

Beatty, C. and Fothergill, S. (2002) *Moving Older People into Jobs*, London: Third Age Employment Network.

Beatty, C. and Fothergill, S. (2005) 'The diversion from "unemployment" to "sickness" across UK regions and districts', *Regional Studies*, vol 39, no 7, pp 837-54.

Beatty, C., Fothergill, S., Gore, T. and Green, A. (2002) *The Real Level of Unemployment 2002*, Sheffield: Centre for Regional Economic and Social Research, Sheffield Hallam University.

Beatty, C., Fothergill, S. and Powell, R. (2005) *Twenty Years On: Has the Economy of the UK Coalfields Recovered?*, Sheffield: Centre for Regional Economic and Social Research, Sheffield Hallam University (and forthcoming in *Environment and Planning A*).

DWP (Department for Work and Pensions) (2002) *Helping People into Employment*, London: DWP.

DWP (2004) *Building on New Deal: Local Solution Meeting Individual Needs*, London: DWP.

DWP (2006) *A New Deal for Welfare: Empowering People to Work*, London: DWP.

Green, A. and Owen, D. (1998) *Where are the Jobless? Changing Unemployment and Non-employment in Cities and Regions*, Bristol: The Policy Press.

Mackay, R. (1999) 'Work and nonwork: a more difficult labour market', *Environment and Planning A*, vol 31, no 11, pp 1919-34.

Turok, I. and Edge, N. (1999) *The Jobs Gap in Britain's Cities: Employment Loss and Labour Market Consequences*, York: Joseph Rowntree Foundation.

Webster, D. (2002) 'Unemployment: how official statistics distort analysis and policy, and why', *Radical Statistics*, vol 79/80, pp 96-127.

SIX

Women's knowledge of, and attitudes to, pensions

Sue Ward

Introduction

There is a school of thought that claims that women do not know much about pensions, do not understand them, and therefore do not join schemes or pay large sums out of their wages into personal pensions. If women understood pensions rather better, this argument goes, everything would be fine. This view was epitomised in the Department for Work and Pensions' (DWP) 2002 Pensions Green Paper, which had a concluding section on women and pensions, tacked on rather as an afterthought. It went through a reasonably sound analysis of women's pension position, and its roots in their employment position and caring roles, and then concluded with one single action point:

> The Government is committed to improving pensions information for everyone, but this is particularly important for women. Proposals in this Green Paper to promote informed choice, such as individualised pension forecasting, will help women. *We propose to look at how best to ensure that women are aware of their pension position and the choices they face. We would welcome views.* (DWP, 2002, p 121, emphasis in original)

This chapter is based on a literature review carried out in 2004 for the Equal Opportunities Commission (EOC).[1] That project was not a direct response to the DWP Green Paper, or to its approach to women's pensions issues, but it lay in the background. The project took the form of a literature search of readily available publications, taking 1995 as a fairly arbitrary starting point, because so much had changed in the decade after that. This was not a totally rigid criterion, however. For example, Field and Prior's 1996 report for the then Department of Social Security (DSS), *Women and Pensions*, was based on fieldwork in

1994-95, but was simply too central to the concerns of the review to omit. Nor was the research confined to academic literature or official publications. It includes a fair amount of material, though mostly rather superficial, from bodies such as the Association of British Insurers and other organisations that commission opinion polls and questions in omnibus market research surveys. Some searches were also carried out for useful non-UK material, in particular from Australia and the US, though these would not claim to be universal.

In some areas, such as attitudes to the purchase of annuities at retirement, information is scarce. To simplify a complex legal position, up until April 2006 anyone with a personal or stakeholder pension had to use at least 75% of their fund to buy an annuity from an insurance company, by the date of their 75th birthday at the latest. (It is now possible to set up an alternatively secured pension or ASP instead, though the Treasury, having discovered that it has created a loophole, is now seeking to close it, so it is not clear how long this position will last.) When selling an annuity, an insurance company is exchanging a cash sum for a flow of income that (in general) will continue until the death of the individual or, in the case of a joint annuity, of the survivor in a couple. Because women's average life expectancy is longer than men's, a woman will be paid a smaller annuity for the same cash sum than a man of the same age (Curry and O'Connell, 2004). It would be interesting to know how women (and men) felt about these points, but although there has been plenty of anecdotal evidence and press and political discussion around this issue, research evidence is very limited.

In other areas, although some general material may be available, there is little analysis by gender, as opposed to other factors such as age, occupation or income. For some topics, it has been necessary to include research that does not analyse by gender, or does so only to a marginal extent. This ensures that there is at least some coverage of public attitudes in general (male and female) on these topics.

Summary of areas covered

This chapter first considers what women (and men) know about pensions – state, occupational and private. Particular concerns in the research were to find out whether, for women with children, lack of pension provision affects the decision to work/return to work; and to what extent women think they are covered by state pensions when absent from the labour market.

The chapter then covers the level of planning for retirement that is undertaken, and the question of who takes responsibility for budgeting, saving and pensions planning in the household. It goes on to consider what persuades women to make either short- or long-term savings, what advice they seek, and what barriers they find to making such savings. It also considers the question of whether women are able or willing to continue pension contributions while absent from the labour market, and evidence on how people would react if compelled to pay more into a pension. It then examines how confident people are in the arrangements they themselves have made with pensions, pensions provided by the government, by the providers of private pensions, and by their employers.

Subsequent sections consider the age until which women would like to work, when they expect to retire, and whether or not they are aware of the coming change in state pension age. Given recent improvements in the financial return for deferring state pension, views on this are also explored. The final section looks at women's attitudes towards state pensions, and in particular whether they might be willing to pay more towards a better level of state benefit, and considers women's views on whether they should be compelled to pay more towards pensions.

Knowledge and understanding of pensions

This topic should be treated with caution. Mortimer et al (2000) compiled an in-house report for the (then) DSS that stressed how little either sex knows about pensions, and therefore how unreliable the answers to many survey questions are. (The author's experience, from many years of working within pensions, is that even people in senior positions and of mature age often understand very little, and make some remarkably strange decisions.)

The fault lies only partly with the individuals. Quite rightly, respondents to in-depth interviews and participants of focus groups are critical of the complexity and jargon-ridden nature of the pensions system, which makes knowledge and understanding difficult (Peggs and Davies, 2001).

It is to be regretted that no research has been undertaken by the DWP or anyone else to investigate the scandal over personal pensions mis-selling between 1988 and 1994. For example, little is known about the sales techniques that persuaded members of the Teachers' Pension Scheme and the Mineworkers' Scheme to go from a secure pension based on their earnings to one with high charges and no guarantees of what they would get. Even a fairly low level of understanding of the differences between the two types of pension arrangement would show that this action was not rational.

Bearing this in mind, the findings of the various studies that informed the EOC literature review suggest that women are more likely than men to say that they have little knowledge of pensions (Mayhew, 2001, 2003; Peggs and Davies, 2001; Mori, 2002). Most but not all women knew about the state basic pension, personal pensions and occupational schemes, while fewer knew about the additional earnings-related element of state pensions (formerly called the state earnings related pension scheme or SERPS, but reformed in 2002 and rebranded as the state second pension or S2P). Very few knew about appropriate personal pensions (APPs) (Field and Prior, 1996). When the level of knowledge and understanding was tested by specific questions, there were many misunderstandings and mistakes (Garman and Hawkes, 1995; Evason and Spence, 2002), but not a lot of difference between men and women and some evidence of male over-confidence.

To some extent, the level of knowledge can be linked with the *individual's* pension provision. Mayhew (2003) found that people with pension provision (more usually men than women) were more likely to report good pension knowledge, though this did not account for the whole of the difference (and nor does it show, of course, which way causation runs).

Women had very little knowledge of aspects of state benefits particularly relevant to them, such as the contribution conditions for state pensions, home responsibilities protection (the arrangements for protecting state pension rights during periods when women are not working due to caring responsibilities) or the reduced rate national insurance contributions (NICs) still being paid by some married women (Field and Prior, 1996; Evason and Spence, 2002). The government itself has recently recognised how important these National Insurance rules are, in restricting the numbers of women receiving a full state pension, and is now planning wholesale changes (DWP, 2006).

Some women's lack of knowledge about pensions seems to stem from a view that pensions are a male responsibility (Hedges, 1998). Women may be very unclear about their pension position in the event of a breakdown of their relationship or the death of their partner (Hedges, 1998; Peggs and Davies, 2001; Evason and Spence, 2002). Little is known about women's understanding of their pensions position if they leave the labour market to have children. However, the lack of knowledge of state pensions (Field and Prior, 1996; Hedges, 1998; Evason and Spence, 2002) means that most people are not in a position to be influenced by the state benefit rules discussed earlier, since they do not know of their existence. There is little research on public attitudes to annuities, but what there is suggests considerable ignorance among both men and women. Annuities are a mystery to most people (FSA, 2001) and highly unpopular (Gardner and Wadsworth, 2004), mainly because they are seen as inflexible. Although there is no direct evidence, in the face of the ignorance about the workings of annuities, it is highly unlikely that many people are sufficiently well informed to have concerns about the fact that women have to save more in order to receive the same annuity as men.

Interest/engagement with pensions

Hawkes and Garman (1995) found that more men than women said that they had given thought, or a lot of thought, to their income in retirement, and Anderson et al (2000) found that this was especially true of married men compared with married women. (How far this translates into action is covered in a later section.) However, at least as strong as the gender difference, and possibly outweighing it, are the other factors that come into play:

- age: older people are more likely to have thought about retirement than younger people, and there is also some evidence of a cohort effect, that is, of generations thinking differently;
- being married or partnered: those with a spouse or partner are more likely to have given thought to retirement than those without;
- employment position: those in work are more likely to have given thought to retirement than those not in work;
- income: people on higher incomes are more likely to have given thought to retirement than those on lower incomes;
- socioeconomic class: those in 'career jobs' are more likely to have given thought to retirement than those in the 'working class';
- existence of private pensions: those with such pensions are more likely to have given thought to retirement than those without; and
- sense of control over their lives: those with this were more likely to have given thought to retirement than those without.

Indeed, for those on the lowest incomes and in the lowest social groups, 'taking life as it comes' is not an irrational response to a situation over which they have very little control. People may feel angry and frustrated about their situation, and push it to the back of their minds as a method of coping (Hawkes and Garman, 1995; Field and Prior,

1996; Wood, 1999; Anderson et al, 2000; Mayhew, 2001, 2003; Evason and Spence, 2002; King, 2003).

The same is true about planning for the future (mentioned earlier). However, women seem to be more optimistic that they will be 'comfortable' or 'all right' in retirement, even when they have given less thought to it (Anderson et al, 2000; Evason and Spence, 2002).

Women are more likely than men to be relying on their spouse's or partner's income in retirement (Field and Prior, 1996; Thomas et al, 1999; King, 2003, Mayhew, 2003). However, there is evidence that women feel they have been 'conditioned' to this (Barnes et al, 2004) and that a declining proportion of women subscribe to views of traditional gender roles with man as the 'breadwinner', with some evidence of a 'cohort' effect (Field and Prior, 1996; Mintel, 1998; Crompton et al, 2003). Despite expecting to rely on their husbands' incomes in retirement, a considerable proportion of women, when asked how much they knew about the details of the arrangements their husband or partner had for a pension or retirement income, said they knew little or nothing (Field and Prior, 1996; Evason and Spence, 2002). Where financial decisions were taken by one person in a couple, it was more likely to be the man than the woman who took responsibility, although the woman might not be entirely happy about this (Field and Prior, 1996; Peggs and Davies, 2001; Evason and Spence, 2002). However, there were also views that women were more likely to be prudent than men and to be better money managers. Where money was short, they might be given the responsibility for this reason (Snape and Molloy, 1999; Rake and Jayatilaka, 2002; King, 2003).

Propensity to make pension and other savings

Again, a note of caution. There does seem to be a certain lack of rigorous definition among researchers and within government about the distinction between 'savings' and 'budgeting'. If people are going on holiday in six months' time, they will work out what spending money they would wish to take, and set it aside over those six months: that could be defined as prudent budgeting. The same applies to setting aside money over the year in a Christmas club, or buying stamps at the post office for a TV licence. It is not *saving* in the sense of putting money aside 'for a rainy day' or for a long-term goal like a comfortable retirement. However, surveys and reports often lump all these things under one umbrella term, and blur definitions between 'savings' and 'investment', where respondents might give different answers depending on the term used.

Overall, although there is a considerable amount of research in this area, disappointingly little of it is broken down by gender. What there is suggests that affordability is the main issue in terms of both pensions and savings more generally.

For people on lower incomes, there is a tendency (or a need) to 'take each day as it comes' (Field and Prior, 1996; Purcell et al, 1999; Wood, 1999; Rake and Jayatilaka, 2002; LGPC, 2003). However, there are people who will continue to save if at all possible, whatever their circumstances; those working part-time and still managing to save are likely to be in that category (RAKM, 2003). For pensions more specifically, there is also a feeling among many women that employment is temporary and that conditions may change, and concerns about not understanding schemes or a lack of communication (Garman and Hawkes 1995; Field and Prior, 1996; Peggs and Davies, 2001; Evason and Spence, 2002).

However, the evidence is that where the option of joining a scheme is offered, women are slightly more likely than men to join (Evason and Spence, 2002). This is borne out by other statistical evidence (Mayhew, 2003), that where men and women work full-time, there is no difference between the proportions with a private pension. Men are rather more likely than women to say that they are happy with their other arrangements and are therefore not inclined to join an occupational scheme (Garman and Hawkes, 1995). Employers' encouragement or compulsion, and the fact that an employer makes a contribution to the pension scheme, are significant for both sexes but slightly more so for women (Peggs and Davies, 2001; Mori, 2002; Vidler, 2002).

Women's 'persistency' – that is, propensity to continue paying into a personal pension – is lower than men's, mainly because of the effect of life events. Leaving work to have children is significant for women but not for men. Changes in earnings or becoming unemployed are significant for men but not for women (Smith, 2004). Hawkes and Garman (1995) found that fewer women than men pay additional voluntary contributions (AVCs). There is some evidence that it was specifically married women with children who were less likely to make *additional* contributions to their pension (Loretto and White, 2003).

Where additional contributions were being paid, Hawkes and Garman (1995) found that women were more likely than men to say that a reason for paying them was to make up for a period when no contributions were being paid towards their pension, and conversely less likely to say that it was to increase the value of their pension.

There was only limited evidence that women were not joining a pension scheme because they expected to rely on their husband's pension (Field and Prior, 1996; Peggs and Davies, 2001). For those on low incomes, maximising income over the short term took preference over saving, and if compelled to pay more into a pension, they would need to go without. For those on higher incomes, it would be a question of reordering priorities (Thomas et al, 1999).

In terms of savings behaviour generally, there is some evidence that women have a stronger preference for avoiding debt than men (CIS Research, 2004), and that women have more cautious financial attitudes, although also at times lacking knowledge and confidence in their own abilities (Alcon, 1999; Anthes and Most, 2000; FSA, 2001)

Confidence in pension provision

People tend to be reasonably confident in the arrangements they have made, although many women do not believe their occupational or personal pension will be enough to live on (Hawkes and Garman, 1995; Field and Prior, 1996; Evason and Spence, 2002; Mori, 2002; Mayhew, 2003). Men find it easier than women to guess how their private pension will compare with their earnings before retirement, though this becomes easier as they get closer to retirement (Field and Prior, 1996). Both men and women find it easier to guess their occupational pension income than their personal pension income.

With regard to state basic pension, this confidence may be partly based on ignorance. Views tend to change when the true position is explained to those participating in surveys (Evason and Spence, 2002). Very few women expect to receive any SERPS pension (Field and Prior, 1996). Men in general are rather more confident than women about receiving the benefits they have been paying for (Garman and Hawkes, 1995; Mori, 2002). Divorcees and the legally separated tend to be least confident about what they will be receiving from non-state pensions, while single women are most likely to believe that non-state pensions will be enough to live on (Field and Prior, 1996).

There is a general feeling of distrust of both government and insurance companies, although there is no evidence of any difference between men and women in this (Thomas et al, 1999; Evason and Spence, 2002; Mori, 2002). The distrust of insurers is based on experience of, or having heard about, mis-selling and a feeling that insurers talk jargon; distrust of government is based on a feeling of 'not knowing where the money has gone', since NICs do not seem to be providing the expected pension. There is some scepticism about whether the state pension will still exist by the time younger people reach retirement age (Field and Prior, 1996). Recent evidence, not broken down by gender, suggests that such scepticism has increased; for example, qualitative research for the Department for Work and Pensions (Hall et al, 2006) found that there were strong doubts among some young respondents (aged 20-34) about the future of the state pension.

Retirement age

Both men and women's earlier expectations about when they are going to retire are not borne out in practice, especially for men (Disney et al, 1998; Humphrey et al, 2003). People change their minds about retirement, or have their minds changed for them by external events. This means that basing policy on people's predictions about what they intend to do is of limited value.

However, according to research by Humphrey et al (2003) and Mayhew (2003), more women than men expect to retire below their employer's fixed age of retirement, while men are more likely to expect to retire before their state pension age (Humphrey et al, 2003; Mayhew, 2003). This is probably because these ages differ between the sexes; many women have employers' retirement ages of 65 and a state pension age of 60, while many men will have state pension age of 65 and employers' retirement ages of 60, or between 60 and 65.

Of those expecting to go before state retirement age, 'family' factors predominate for women, such as wanting to spend more time with their partners or family, or caring needs. For men, financial factors, such as being offered an early retirement package, predominate. For both, however, 'pull' factors are more important than 'push' factors (Humphrey et al, 2003). Retiring at the same time as one's spouse/partner was more likely to be a reason for women retiring, either early or late, than for men (Humphrey et al, 2003). Gradual retirement is attractive, and more men than women intend to reduce their hours gradually before retirement (Humphrey et al, 2003) – though for many this may be more of an aspiration than an intention.

Women's retirement intentions do not seem to be affected by the planned changes in state retirement age, from 60 to 65 by 2020 (Mayhew, 2003). Those planning to retire later divided broadly into those with interesting and stimulating work and those who felt they could not afford to retire; 'working-class' people were more likely to be in the second group, while those in professional, creative and entrepreneurial occupations were more likely to be in the first. Barnes et al (2004) found that these distinctions seemed to outweigh gender differences. There was, however, a group of women whose plans had been upset by divorce or other changes, who found they had to work even if it meant moving to a different field. Hedges (1998), however, found that financial factors were keeping more women than men at work, while more men than women quoted a wish to keep fit and active, or because they would not know what to do after stopping work. Mori (2002) found no-one *wanting* to work on after retirement age, but some people resigned to the fact that they might have to.

There is no direct evidence on attitudes to deferring state pension. However, one can infer from the comments earlier that those deferring their retirement because of 'interest' might consider the idea of not drawing their state pension in the meantime, and having a larger amount when they did so. For those deferring for financial reasons, the 'bird in the hand' of having a larger income while still at work seems more likely to be attractive.

State pensions and compulsion

Social security spending tends not to be a very high priority when people are asked whether they favour higher government spending, and it has fallen below that for health and education in recent years (Hills, 2002; Crompton et al, 2003; Sefton, 2003). Where responses have been analysed by gender, differences of view between men and women appear marginal. Pensioners are consistently given much higher priority in opinion surveys for increased spending than other groups of social security clients (Hills, 2002). Few people see NICs as anything other than a tax (Stafford, 1998; Thomas et al, 1999).

There is general support for the idea of the state providing enough for people to live on as a pension, though a significant minority, especially among younger people, consider it should be up to the individual or the employer to provide this (Sefton, 2003). Men are more likely than women to say that the pension should provide some disposable income rather than simply covering living expenses (Mori, 2002). In detailed discussions, women clearly want the state to take a bigger role and provide a bigger pension (Evason and Spence, 2002).

However, when asked whether they would pay increased NICs to this end, there were views that this would only be acceptable if greater benefits were *guaranteed*, or that people were paying enough already (Evason and Spence, 2002). Thomas et al (1999) found that compulsion to pay a greater amount might be acceptable under some fairly strict conditions, including independence from government interference and transparency of charges and benefits. It was also considered that people would need additional incentives.

The alternative strategy of increased means testing was not popular because of the disincentive effects, and a feeling that people should 'get what they have paid for', although there was also support for the idea of redistribution towards the poorest (Stafford, 1998; Evason and Spence, 2002). The bulk of the research considered was carried out before the introduction of the pension credit. Sadly but rather predictably, a more recent DWP research report (Talbot et al, 2005) on the take-up of pension credit has very limited analysis by gender. It would have been useful to know what proportion of the 35% of non-recipients who said that nothing would induce them to apply for pension credit were women, and what proportion were men, but this information is not available.

It is worth pointing out here that a lack of clarity about the effects of saving on means-tested benefits is inherent to the system, not the result of confusion or lack of knowledge among individuals. The government-sponsored Pensions Commission (2004) demonstrated that for anyone in or near the ambit of the pension credit, the question of what rate of return they will get on their pension savings is almost impossible to answer. For anyone within the ambit of pension credit who is also part of a couple, it is truly impossible. Pension saving is done as an individual but the pension credit is calculated on the basis of being part of a couple, so that changes in one's own pension arrangements can be negated, or reinforced, by changes in one's partner's position, about which one may not even know (Pensions Commission, 2004, figure 6.23).

Conclusion

This conclusion draws together a number of points from the discussion. First, little is known about attitudes to, and knowledge of, pensions, and there have been many missed opportunities to gather information, or to analyse what information there is by gender. Second, the DWP's 2002 analysis (quoted earlier), suggesting that the essence of the problem for women is a lack of understanding of pensions and that the solution therefore lies in additional information, is far too simplistic and bears little relation to the real issues. Third, there are differences by gender in a number of areas. However, they are frequently outweighed by other differences, such as income and employment position, and what they often reflect is the greater uncertainty of many women's lives, and the difficulty of planning ahead, rather than anything 'inherent' to either men or women. Fourth, the complications of our pensions system are such that it is exceedingly difficult for anyone to say what it is 'right' for any individual, especially a lower-paid one, to do. For the half or more of the population who may be eligible for pension credit, to say that they understand and are confident in their plans probably means they do not understand their situation.

Reform proposals in the government's 2006 Pensions White Paper, *Security in Retirement* (DWP, 2006), take a number of these concerns on board, and if carried through, the reforms will improve the position of many women so far as state benefits are concerned. They are by no means perfect, but do provide a basis on which to build.

Note
[1] The views expressed in this chapter are solely those of the author and in no way reflect EOC policy.

References

Alcon, A. (1999) 'Financial planning and the mature woman', *Journal of Financial Planning*, February (www.fpanet.org).

Anderson, M., Li, Y., Bechhofer, F., McCrone, D. and Stewart, R. (2000) 'Sooner rather than later? Younger and middle-aged adults preparing for retirement', *Ageing and Society*, vol 20, no 4, pp 445-66.

Anthes, W.L. and Most, B.W. (2000) 'Frozen in the headlights; the dynamics of money and women', *Journal of Financial Planning*, September (www.fpanet.org).

Barnes, H., Parry, J. and Taylor, R. (2004) *Working After State Pension Age; Qualitative Research*, Department for Work and Pensions Research Report 208, London: Corporate Document Services.

CIS (Co-operative Insurance Society) Research (2004) 'Three quarters would rather save than borrow says CIS Research', CIS news release, 24 May, Manchester.

Crompton, R., Brockmann, M. and Wiggins, R.D. (2003) 'A woman's place ... Employment and family life for men and women', in A. Park et al (eds) *British Social Attitudes; The 20th Report*, London: Sage Publications.

Curry, C. and O'Connell, A. (2004) *An Analysis of Unisex Annuity Rates*, EOC Working Paper Series no 16, Manchester: Equal Opportunities Commission.

Disney, R., Grundy, E. and Johnson, P. (eds) (1998) *The Dynamics of Retirement; Analyses of the Retirement Surveys*, London: The Stationery Office.

DWP (Department for Work and Pensions) (2002) *Simplicity, Security and Choice; Working and Saving for Retirement*, Cm 5672, EOC Working Paper Series no 16, London: The Stationery Office.

DWP (2006) *Security in Retirement; Towards a New Pensions System*, Cm 6841, London: The Stationery Office.

Evason, E. and Spence, L. (2002) *Women and Pensions*, Belfast: Equality Commission for Northern Ireland.

Field, J. and Prior, G. (1996) *Women and Pensions*, DSS Research Report 49, London: HMSO.

FSA (Financial Services Agency) (2001) *Consumer Panel Annual Survey Report 2000*, London: FSA.

Gardner, J. and Wadsworth, M. (2004) *Who would Buy an Annuity? An Empirical Investigation*, Technical Report RM.UK.12, London: Watson Wyatt LLP.

Hall, S., Pettigrew, N. and Harvey, P. (2006) *Public Attitudes to Personal Accounts; Report of a Qualitative Study*, Department for Work and Pensions Research Report 370, London: Corporate Document Services.

Hawkes, C. and Garman, A. (1995) *Perceptions of Non-state Pensions*, DSS Social Research Branch In-house Report 8, London: HMSO.

Hedges, A. (1998) *Pensions and Retirement Planning*, DSS Research Report 83, London: Corporate Document Services.

Hills, J. (2002) 'Following or leading public opinion? Social security policy and public attitudes since 1987', *Fiscal Studies*, vol 23, no 4, pp 539-58.

Humphrey, A., Costigan, P., Pickering, K., Stratford, N. and Barnes, M. (2003) *Factors Affecting the Labour Market Participation of Older Workers*, Department for Work and Pensions Research Report 200, London: Corporate Document Services.

King, J. (2003) *No Nest Egg; Research into Attitudes of Younger Consumers to Saving for Retirement*, London: National Consumer Council.

LGPC (Local Government Pensions Committee) (2003) *Draft Response to Retirement Benefit Package Options Discussion Paper*, London: LGPC (available at www.lge.gov.uk/lge/aio/55710).

Loretto, W. and White, P. (2003) *Early Retirement: Entitlement or Banishment?* Unpublished draft paper (phil.white@ed.ac.uk).

Mayhew, V. (2001) *Pensions 2000; Public Attitudes to Pensions and Saving for Retirement*, Department for Work and Pensions Research Report 130, London: Corporate Document Services.

Mayhew, V. (2003) *Pensions 2002; Public Attitudes to Pensions and Saving for Retirement*, Department for Work and Pensions Research Report 193, London: Corporate Document Services.

Mintel (1998) *Women and Finance Report*, London: Mintel.

Mori (2002) *Attitudes towards Income in Retirement for Age Concern*, London: Mori.

Mortimer L., Farrant, G., and Turner, R. (2000) *Asking about Pensions: A Review and Test of Survey Questions*, London: DSS Social Research Branch.

Peggs, K. and Davies, M (2001) 'Women and pensions; perspectives, motivation, choices', in J. Ginn, D. Street and S. Arber (eds) *Women, Work and Pensions*, Buckingham: Open University Press.

Pensions Commission (2004) *Pensions; Challenges and Choices; The First Report of the Pensions Commission*, London: The Stationery Office.

Purcell, K., McKnight, A. and Simm, C. (1999) *The Lower Earnings Limit in Practice; Part Time Employment in Hotels and Catering*, Manchester: Equal Opportunities Commission.

Rake, K. and Jayatilaka, G. (2002) *Home Truths: An Analysis of Financial Decision-making within the Home*, London: Fawcett Society.

RAKM (Research Analysis and Knowledge Management) (2003) *Savings Ratio*, London: IFA Promotion.

Sefton, T. (2003) 'What we want from the welfare state', in A. Park et al (eds) *British Social Attitudes; the 20th Report*, London: Sage Publications.

Smith, S. (2004) *Stopping Short; Why do so many Consumers Stop Contributing to Long-term Savings Policies?*, FSA Occasional Paper (www.fsa.gov.uk/pubs).

Snape, D. and Molloy, D. (1999) *Relying on the State, Relying on Each Other*, London: HMSO.

Stafford, B. (1998), *National Insurance and the Contributory Principle*, London: DSS Social Research Branch.

Talbot, C., Adelman, A. and Lilly, R. (2005) *Encouraging Take-up, Awareness and Attitudes to Pension Credit*, Research Report 234, London: Department for Work and Pensions (www.dwp.gov.uk/asd/asd5).

Thomas A., Pettigrew N. and Tovey, P. (1999) *Increasing Compulsory Pension Provision; Attitudes of the General Public and the Self Employed*, DSS Social Research Branch In-house Report 48, London: DSS Social Research Branch.

Vidler, G. (2002) *What Makes People Save?*, London: Association of British Insurers.

Wood, C. (1999) *Pensions for All*, London: AMP.

SEVEN

Sustaining working lives: the challenge of retention

Donald Hirsch

Older workers, choice and sustainability

A long-term rise in early exit from working life might be interpreted in one of three ways. One is that people are taking a positive choice to increase their lifetime leisure. A second is that they face distorted financial incentives to retire or claim invalidity benefits rather than carry on working, and do not have to face the true economic cost of a decision to leave work. A third is that people lack sufficient opportunity and capacity to carry on working, regardless of their preferences and the economic consequences.

Up until about 10 years ago, early retirement was seen largely in positive terms, with declining older worker participation being interpreted as people enjoying the fruits of prosperity – the first of the explanations listed above. The concern to reverse this culture during the past decade has owed much to the economic imperative, in particular the feared consequences of falling labour participation combined with lengthening life expectancy. As a result, much of the public debate has focused on the second factor, retirement incentives, and on the case for making individuals bear the real cost of retiring earlier while offering them improved rewards for retiring later.

At the same time, it is recognised that financial considerations may influence but do not determine retirement behaviour. The findings of the Joseph Rowntree Foundation's Transitions after 50 programme of research (summarised in Hirsch, 2003) gave strong support for the third explanation – that workforce exit is more about whether people are able to carry on working than about whether they think it is financially worthwhile. This has profound implications for policy responses. To prolong working lives, we need to think about how to improve opportunities for older workers to remain in their jobs. This chapter explores how policy makers, employers and individuals might approach the issue of job retention, and suggests that the most effective responses move beyond a focus on the immediate circumstances surrounding retirement, to consider how working lives need to change to make them more sustainable.

Rescue, retention and disadvantage in working life

How can choices and opportunities for older workers be improved? Those who are experiencing difficulties in the labour market can be helped directly in a number of ways. For example, government employment services and other measures designed to help disadvantaged groups in the labour market can help people to become 'work ready' and to look for work.

However, the evidence suggests that the problem will not be solved only by attempting to reconnect non-working older people with the labour market. A key reason to think about retention of older workers is that 'rescuing' those who have dropped out of work is so difficult. Once someone has stopped work after the age of about 45, their chances of ever working again are remarkably low: panel evidence suggests, for example, that only a small minority of men of this age will return to work once they have become economically inactive (Campbell, 1999). While intensive help in re-entering employment may raise prospects at the margins, the best hope of improving choices and opportunities in work is clearly through 'retention' rather than 'return'.

A key problem with retention policies is that it is harder to target people who are 'at risk' of losing their jobs than people who have already done so. One approach is to identify some of the immediate causes of older workers falling out of work, including employer discrimination (addressed by age discrimination legislation) and ill health (which can be addressed by helping older workers on temporary sick leave to return to work before they are retired for health reasons). However, if responses are confined to such immediate causes of premature exit from the labour market, they will not address some of the underlying causes of the problem. The labour market difficulties that older workers experience tend to result from a complex set of factors that have developed in the course of their working lives. These can include:

- poor job quality, which makes many workers, particularly those in lower-paid jobs, feel negative about work and pleased to stop it as early as possible;
- long-term problems with health and stress, which can build up over the course of a working life and eventually lead employees

to feel that they have no option but to stop work for the sake of their health, or to be forced to do so by their employers;

- a lack of attention to learning and self-development in the course of people's working lives. Not everyone is able to progress through coherent career pathways, and many workers have not acquired the skills to adapt as work changes around them;
- competing priorities in people's lives, such as caring for parents, partners and grandchildren, which may become difficult to reconcile with work unless it is flexibly structured to enable people to balance home and work priorities;
- limited options for changing roles and working status as one's situation changes throughout working life, so that too often the choice is between continuing to do exactly the same job or retiring completely, rather than being able to work in new ways, including part-time work or self-employment.

Thus, a strategy to improve the position of older workers and to give them more options about how they make the transition to retirement needs to rest on creating more *sustainable working lives*.

A framework for addressing sustainability in policy and practice

The improvement of working lives is a huge agenda, which has been pursued at least since reformers and trade unions started campaigning for better working conditions in the 19th century. This chapter aims more specifically to suggest a framework for change that could make working lives more sustainable by helping people to continue to play a productive and rewarding role in the labour market as they get older.

It suggests that government, employers and individual workers need to think about how to improve sustainability in three main ways:

- by ensuring that workers are able to plan their futures better, and to prepare for them through learning and career development;
- by ensuring that work is structured in a way that gives sufficient flexibility for people to balance priorities in their lives inside and outside work;
- by paying attention to features of work that promote workers' health and sense of fulfilment and satisfaction with their working lives.

In all three of these areas, progress requires a productive partnership between employers and employees in which they share responsibility for improving sustainability.

This discussion follows on from the Joseph Rowntree Foundation's Transitions after 50 research, which has been particularly concerned with the most disadvantaged groups in society. These are the groups least likely to think of their jobs as 'careers', least likely to feel that their skills are valued by their employers, least likely to be able to find alternative job pathways if their existing roles become redundant and most likely to suffer long-term ill health before reaching state pension age.

The following framework is not intended as an alternative to measures that address the immediate difficulties of older workers in the labour market, on which considerable attention has been focused in recent years (see, for example, Cabinet Office, Performance and Innovation Unit, 2000; DWP, 2002). Its suggestion of a longer-term perspective, concerned with how we might reduce the incidence of such difficulties by changing working lives, is complementary to such measures. However, in this, as in so many areas, if we only look at remediation rather than prevention, we can expect only to alleviate the symptoms, rather than address their underlying causes.

The discussion that follows is supported by a set of working papers, published on the Joseph Rowntree Foundation (JRF) website (Hirsch, 2005). The present chapter is adapted from the first of these papers.

Personal and career development, guidance and learning

'Working life' has a very different meaning for different groups of people. For some, it is a developing narrative, in which an individual can progress and develop, with each chapter bringing new experiences that help sustain interest and enthusiasm. Others see it as a recurrent, routine means of earning a living, by carrying out a more or less standardised set of tasks, which remain largely the same after any initial period of induction or training. While these are simplified caricatures, many people in lower-earning and lower-status jobs tend towards the latter view, while professionals and managers are more likely to think in terms of having a 'career' as well as a job.

Continuous career development, in its widest sense, is an important ingredient in job sustainability, for two main reasons: first, it can help sustain *motivation*; second, it can help sustain *capacity*. Finnish research on 'work ability', described below, underlines the importance of motivational characteristics alongside people's competencies in influencing whether they continue in work beyond a particular age. The JRF's own research (for example, Barnes et al, 2002; Arthur, 2003) found that many people leaving work early dislike their jobs because they do not feel that they are leading anywhere, and feel undervalued by their employers. In-work learning and career development can both increase workers' capacity to meet new work demands and make them feel more positive about work itself.

In this context, learning and career guidance are things that can be of value to all workers throughout their working lives, rather than being restricted to a minority and concentrated around the time of initial entry into work. As part of JRF's work in this area, Geoff Ford of The Age and Employment Network has produced a valuable overview of how policies can better promote a continuation of learning and guidance into later working life (Ford, 2005).

Reforms to policy and practice could have a number of objectives:

Promote learning in later life

Despite widespread calls for an ethos of 'lifelong learning', education and training remain heavily weighted to younger age groups. This is true even within adult learning: people are much more likely to take 'mature' courses and receive training earlier than later in their adult lives. Public programmes continue to discriminate in this way (Ford, 2005). Employers are a long way from accepting that investment in people in their 40s and 50s can potentially bring strong returns, given that someone of this age is likely to spend longer in the future with their present employer than someone in their 20s, who is more likely to change jobs (see Macaulay, 2003). One necessary change is to improve provision for workers who lack the most basic skills, but another is to move beyond a 'deficit' model of older worker skills. The disadvantages faced by older workers in the labour market are much more wide-ranging than the lack of basic competencies. In order to progress, they need to be able to build continually on their skills, and in some cases will have to learn to negotiate new roles. Thus, a third-age learning strategy requires much more than a basic skills agenda.

Promote learning as an ongoing part of everyone's working life

Efforts to avoid age bias in the provision of adult learning opportunities can do only a limited amount to make jobs sustainable as long as many workers neither expect nor receive any work-related training at any age. Older workers who have never received any training from their employers find it difficult, when their skills become redundant, to start acquiring a learning ethos, or to believe that employers or the government have suddenly become interested in their personal development. Thus, a huge culture shift is needed in the ways in which employers train and develop all their workers. At the same time, individuals will need to think in new ways about their own development: career-long learning requires them not only to be passive recipients of periodic skill upgrading but also to learn to manage the development of their own 'human capital'.

Promote guidance among older adults

Until recently, the concept of career guidance was largely limited to the counselling of young people around the time that they leave school. Over the past few years, the government has promoted the provision of guidance to adults, in particular through the establishment of local information, advice and guidance partnerships. However, this has had limited impact, particularly on older adults, due to low take-up and an emphasis on information and low-level advice rather than deeper, potentially life-changing guidance activity. Sound guidance can potentially help individuals to take greater control of their working lives, for example by identifying their own skill needs and negotiating new roles. There have been a range of promising local initiatives in this area, and government, employers and local organisations need to learn from 'what works' (see Mitton and Hull, forthcoming).

Extend the concept of career

A 'career' is typically conceived of by professional workers as comprising a sequence of linked roles of ascending responsibility and status in a particular field over the course of a working lifetime. But many people in lower-status jobs do not find themselves in a work structure that lends itself to the idea of an ordered progression, and nor do they necessarily encounter personnel departments encouraging them to do so. An alternative way of thinking about 'career' is as a sequence of events relating to people's lives inside and outside work. These include movements in and out of different jobs, personal self-development and managing the relationship between one's work and the rest of one's life. It is important in this context for public policy to be supportive of career paths that do not always lead to paid work, valuing other contributions that people can make. This can be especially important for disabled people and others who are not necessarily able to access permanent paid employment, but who can make other contributions of value. There is scope for the development of guidance services at multiple levels, ranging from good information to intensive guidance, appropriate for different people at different times of their lives. The challenge for policy and practice is to ensure that those services are accessible where they are needed, including in workplaces and in communities. This implies a partnership between government and employers to improve what is currently a very minimal framework of provision.

Characteristics of work 1: time, flexibility and work–life balance

Recent research has consistently shown that many people in their 50s and 60s, both those who remain in work and those who have left it, have encountered difficulties reconciling work with the rest of their lives, and would welcome greater work flexibility (see, for example, Hirsch, 2003; McNair et al, 2004). For example, a strikingly large number of respondents across surveys express interest in the idea of working part-time for some period before retirement.

Part of this phenomenon can be attributed to the intuitively powerful idea that a 'cliff-edge' retirement, by which people move instantly from a full-time career job to no paid work, is unsatisfactory for many people, particularly those who are relatively fit yet still wish to scale down their working lives. However, deeper analysis of the research suggests that older workers have a wide range of diverse needs and preferences, more complex than simply a desire for 'bridge jobs' in between career jobs and retirement. As Sue Yeandle (2005) points out, different people acquire a number of new needs and perspectives as their lives change as they get older, including:

- new responsibilities outside work, for example caring for older family members or for grandchildren;
- new perspectives on work and life, causing people to reassess work–life balance;
- changing capacities in terms of the pace of working life, for example in terms of capacity to respond to stress, which in some cases may be tied up with long-term illness or disability.

These changes will produce different requirements for different people – whether, for example, to work more flexibly, for fewer hours or in different kinds of jobs, or to take a career break. None of these needs is unique to older workers, and nor should one stereotype all older workers as being suited to a particular kind of work pattern. Rather, we can conclude that flexibility to change one's working pattern to suit changing life situations is an important ingredient for sustaining working lives (see Chapter Nine).

If we accept this conclusion, the rationale for taking work–life balance seriously extends greatly. Much policy debate and action promoting a balance between home and working life has focused on the needs of parents, especially mothers, seeking a balance between the responsibility of bringing up children and the demands and opportunities of the working world. This is starting to be extended to take account of other caring responsibilities, most particularly in the proposal to extend the right to have a request for flexible working to be considered by one's employer, from parents of children up to the age of five to anyone with caring responsibilities. Yet to maximise the degree to which working life becomes more sustainable by being more flexible would require employers to address the nature of work generally, rather than just thinking about the needs of specific sub-groups. The problem with the latter approach is that people's need for work–life balance arises from such diverse circumstances that it is in practice impossible to identify entitled groups fairly, and indeed to do so may cause resentment among those excluded.

Thus, a framework for policy and practice needs to ask what changes in the way work is structured can help work and other priorities to be balanced throughout everyone's working lives. This cannot be brought about just by legislating for some new entitlements – it will require long-term cultural change, some of which is arguably already under way with the recognition by many employers of the wider needs of their workers. However, particular reforms to policy and practice could have a number of objectives, including the following:

Extend policies for work–life balance to people other than parents

In particular, this could apply to the presumption that people need flexibility in their working lives. Since 2002, parents with children aged under six or disabled children aged under 18 have the right to request a flexible working pattern and their employers have a duty to consider their applications seriously. Now that employers have had the chance to experience the consequences of such a duty, it would be appropriate to consider extending it to requests from all employees. The government's current commitment to extend it just to people with caring responsibilities raises difficult questions about both judging and justifying the eligibility of those in various circumstances. A different approach is to presume that anybody requesting such flexibility has an equal right to have their case considered in the light of the character of their job.

Systematically improve options for part-time work in the transition to retirement

Judging by responses to surveys (see, for example, McNair et al, 2004), such a measure would help a number of people to extend the length of their working lives. A first step has, after a long delay, been taken in 2006 by the Inland Revenue in removing the rule that prevents people from drawing a part-time pension in a scheme run by an employer for whom they are still working. But should the government be just permissive or actively encouraging of part-time work during this transition? The overall effect that this would have on the labour supply is at present far from clear. In Sweden and Finland, the public pension systems are supportive of part-time working. In Sweden, for example, part-time pensions have been available for older people in different forms for the past 40 years. In both countries, the evidence suggests that the direct net effect on labour supply could potentially be negative. For example in Sweden, as more older people took advantage of part-time pensions in the 1990s the employment rate did not rise, suggesting that many people used part-time work as an alternative to full-time work rather than retiring (OECD, 2003, pp 60-1). However, this is not necessarily an argument against having such pensions. It may well be that the effect at one point in time of introducing such a policy would be to cause many people to shift from full- to part-time work, yet in the longer term if this improved job sustainability and caused individuals to remain in the workforce longer, overall labour supply would be higher than otherwise. Moreover, even if the net effect in these terms were neutral, there could be a social benefit, just as there is with tax credits that allow parents to work part-time, in terms of releasing the individuals concerned to do unpaid activities including caring, as well as being potentially beneficial for their health. Finally, it should be noted that the Scandinavian partial pensions have been extremely generous, creating in some cases a strong disincentive to work full-time; Sweden has now switched to a system where a pro-rata percentage of pension can be taken early, which is less likely to distort unduly decisions about working among those happy to continue full-time.

Develop options for more flexible working lives

Flexibility in the way that people structure working time is most commonly considered in terms of the working day or the working week. But what about the working lifetime? The career break is now a well-established feature of many women's working lives, linked most commonly to bearing and looking after young children. Yet might it also play a role in helping to sustain working lives that have to end at a later age than we have become used to? A paper by Linda Boyes and Jim McCormick (2005) specifically considers whether 'contributory sabbaticals' might help sustain 'work ability', by helping to overcome some of the factors contributing to workforce withdrawal. At first glance, such a proposal seems fraught with difficulties. For example, if it is to be partly or wholly funded by the individual, how could anyone but the most privileged workers afford it? And might employers not see it simply as a further difficulty under which workers that they have grown to rely on disappear for six months or a year? Such objections start to look less intractable if such sabbaticals have the long-term effect of prolonging working lives, and if they are programmed well in advance and paid for over a long period. Certainly at the financial level, working to 65 with one or two six-month breaks should be more viable, for example, than working to 55 or 60 in continuous employment. The development of new working patterns of this kind is unlikely to happen overnight, but if in the coming decades we expect working lives gradually to lengthen, we should consider whether the development of career breaks should be part of this long-term change.

Support the needs of carers at work

People with caring responsibilities can find it particularly difficult to balance work and other commitments. The evidence shows that some leave work because of the pressure of caring, but also that many remain in work while caring (Mooney and Statham, 2002). Among the latter, many suffer severe pressure and stress in their lives, which can reduce the long-term sustainability of work, or conversely reduce the amount of unpaid care that people are able to give.

As set out in Marilyn Howard's (2005) review for JRF, carers face a series of surmountable barriers to remaining in paid employment while caring. These include in particular the lack of opportunities to work flexibly, a lack of supportive services and the absence of a work culture that gives sympathy and legitimacy to the position of being a working carer – in some cases resulting in a reluctance to disclose this status. Change is required both at a general level (not specific to carers) and at a specific level (responding to carers' needs). For example, carers are not the only group who need flexibility in work, but they are likely to need a particular type of flexibility based on the often unpredictable nature of demands on their time outside work. Efforts to change the culture of workplaces need to address employers' and co-workers' understanding and acceptance of such carer-specific needs.

Characteristics of work 2: control, job quality and health

The quality of people's working lives is a fundamental ingredient for work sustainability. People who dislike their jobs, and those suffering physical or mental damage from work, are less likely to continue their working careers, either through choice or because their employability declines.

This relationship between job sustainability and the nature of work came across strongly in qualitative studies in JRF's research programme, showing the strong influence of negative work experiences in relation to early departure from the labour force. The relationship is confirmed in systematic Finnish research on 'work ability'. Longitudinal analysis in the 1980s and 1990s studied the determinants of the work motivation, prospects and competence of Finns in their late 50s, which was found also to be correlated with productivity. The strongest predictors of future work ability among workers in their 40s and 50s concerned work demands and the work environment, followed by aspects of work organisation. Poor physical aspects of the work environment were important, but so were a number of mental and psychological factors. Workers who enjoyed the most control over their work and the least ambiguity in roles were less likely to face difficulties later on (Tuomi et al, 2001).

The importance of psychological as well as social influences on people's working lives is underlined by the changing character of incapacity benefit (IB) recipients. Today, a third of people receiving IB have mental health problems, and the numbers are rising as new claimants are more likely to have such problems than existing claimants. The fact that there is also a trend towards more female claimants, and more from white-collar and public sector jobs, illustrates the extent to which work-related health difficulties are no longer primarily experienced by manual workers in heavy industry.

Some commentators attribute these trends to an intensification of work, contributing to stress. Research confirms that new pressures have negative long-term effects on workers (see, for example, Burchell et al, 1999), but these are not just caused by higher pressure to perform and long-hours cultures. Crucially, they are also linked to a sense of a loss of control. In the 1980s, it was thought that the decline of process-oriented manufacturing industries would result in greater flexibility and control over working lives. However, information technology has made it possible to exercise a highly detailed form of supervisory control over workers in service industries, as exemplified by call centres, where every keystroke and action can be monitored. A very big challenge is to develop jobs that have meaning and allow autonomous action in this new, performance-oriented environment.

This is a vast agenda, and it is unrealistic to expect that the imperative of extending working lives will in itself create a reorganisation of work. However, in some respects it can make a contribution. Again, Finland provides a good example. As described in Box 7.1, issues raised by problems faced by older workers can stimulate a wide debate about how companies operate, which contributes to changes in working practices. The Finnish use of statutory instruments to oblige employers to participate in these efforts contrasts starkly with the voluntary approach adopted by the UK, for example, in announcing recently a strategy for the health and well-being of working-age people (HM Government, 2005).

However, the contrast between statutory and voluntary methods is not the most crucial difference between the approaches of the UK and Finland. The UK strategy consists largely of promoting health awareness in and out of work, raising the profile of occupational health and building links between community and work-based healthcare and promotion. The Finnish strategy goes further by encouraging the development of organisations in ways that create healthy ways of working. Employers and inspectors are encouraged to consider matters such as working hours, which are not mentioned in the UK strategy.

Box 7.1: Finland's programme on ageing workers*

Finland identified a serious problem of changing demography and falling older worker participation earlier than most countries, and has run a coordinated and high-profile programme to improve things for older workers. A principal focus was the Older Workers Programme (1998–2002), a joint initiative of the Ministries of Social Affairs, Labour and Education, which also involved local authorities, the Social Insurance Institution, the Institute of Occupational Health and pension companies.

The research on the multiple influences on 'work ability', mentioned earlier, encouraged Finns to address the whole work environment rather than isolated features such as accident prevention. Moreover, even though an important aspect of the strategy is to adapt employment services to the needs of older people, it pays just as much attention to improving retention as to aiding re-employment.

The tools for doing so are numerous. They include:

- An Occupational Health Care Act, putting a duty on employers to have systematic approaches to care for their workers, in collaboration with other authorities including health and education services, addressing such issues as working hours, rest periods, shift work and overtime.
- A network of occupational health inspectors responsible both for ensuring compliance with the law and for provision of expert advice, and now required to take account of ageing issues as a central aspect of good practice. This is also a priority for the Finnish Institute of Occupational Health, which is involved in a training programme to support organisational development that addresses both the physical and mental well-being of workers as they grow older.
- Action by the Ministry of Education to ensure that older workers systematically receive information on training and other learning opportunities open to them, along with an initiative to make adult education more tailored to individual adults' needs, under a programme in which 40 educational institutions provide vocational education to adults.

Results of the programme, according to the Finnish authorities, have been to make workplace health promotion more common, to affect the ways in which organisations are managed and to increase the training provided for employees and employees' means to influence management.

* For a good description, see Ministry of Social Affairs and Health (2002).

In the UK, reforms to policy and practice could have the following objectives:

Redefine occupational health to aim at creating health-promoting workplaces

A first step is to think more widely about occupational health. Health and safety at work tends to be thought of primarily in terms of avoiding hazards. It may be possible to think about it more proactively, in terms of what creates a health-promoting workplace. This would mean moving away from a purely regulatory approach to health and safety, and encouraging managers to think about how the whole working environment affects the long-term health of workers. It would also mean moving beyond the conceptualisation of the occupational health professional as, typically, a nurse focused on trouble-shooting difficulties as they arise, towards occupational health advisers who look at the whole work environment. At the same time, a health-promoting workplace needs to engage managers and employees as well as health professionals. At best, it involves a dialogue between workers and employers, potentially with the help of trade unions, about how to work well. One example of how this approach has been applied at local level is through the Sandwell Work Well project and the follow-up Wellbeing at Work project (for further information, see www.ohstrategy.net/Database/project_search_browse_display/display_single_project_from_browse.php?Project_ID=46). Such initiatives take a broad view of healthy working, linked to organisational development and to worker learning as well as to specific physical aspects of the work environment.

Develop specific initiatives to address health needs of older workers

The Health Development Agency's Midlife programme has been looking at ways of developing support for the health of workers in their 50s and early 60s. At the end of 2003, it reported on its evaluation of eight pilot projects with this objective, and drew lessons from them, in its report *The Gap Years: Rediscovering Midlife as the Route to Healthy Active Ageing* (Bowers et al, 2003). This study illustrated a wide range of methods of getting individuals and organisations to become actively involved in the promotion of mid-life health, involving partnerships between different agencies. It emphasised that no single model is appropriate in all cases, but an underlying theme was that better knowledge and understanding is often the starting point. This is why an initial step is often to offer health checks or audits of individuals or organisations, and also explains why one of the most promising forms of partnership is between employers and primary healthcare organisations. Such partnerships can build links between the promotion of preventative healthcare and a 'preventative' approach to premature job exit. These two missions overlap but are not identical, since health prevention is not limited to the context of work, while preventative approaches to job exit may include features such as personal skill development and guidance as well as health matters.

Create more flexibility about how people work at different stages of their lives

A striking theme that emerged from JRF's Transitions after 50 research was a lack of systematic attempts by employers to look at how people's work advantages and limitations change in the course of their lives, and thus how they might be redeployed as they grow older. For example, in the health service, there appears to be no strategy by employers to retain older nurses by shifting them away from more physically demanding jobs where appropriate (Watson et al, 2003). In devising strategies to improve job retention, employers may need to start thinking about worker needs long before they reach a stage where they no longer want to do a standard full-time job. Reducing undue stress or excessive physical strain at an earlier stage may be an important factor in prolonging their capacity for work. Research has shown that those who have made satisfactory job changes are indeed more likely to want to stay in work (McNair et al, 2004).

Conclusion: sustaining working lives, changing work, changing workers

This chapter has suggested a framework for thinking about change that improves the sustainability of working lives, by paying greater attention to how workers develop their skills, make career choices, remain healthy and are able to access a flexible range of work opportunities compatible with other life demands and priorities.

An ambitious agenda for the future would be for government, employers and individual workers to move in these directions by adapting their approaches to work and to working life. Public policy can be influential, but the most important determinants of sustainability will be the ways in which employers and individuals behave, and the attitudes that underlie these behaviours.

On the one hand, it is in employers' collective interest to ensure that work is designed in ways that nurture workers as a resource, rather than treating them as expendable. This means paying more attention to worker development throughout people's careers, rather than just tackling the failings of older workers when they run into difficulties. On the other hand, it requires workers to take more control and responsibility for their working lives, and not expect working roles and opportunities to be automatically handed down to them by a benevolent lifelong employer. Both sides need therefore to take some responsibility for outcomes, and improving working lives needs to become more of a partnership between employers and employees.

This chapter has in particular identified two ways in which thinking will need to change in order to support this process. The first is the extension of the concept of 'career', from a neatly planned sequence of professional progression for well-educated workers to a way of thinking about lifetime job opportunities for everybody. Central to this will be having the information and guidance required to make good decisions, and having the generic skills required to negotiate and regulate one's own working life. This requires above all a new way for individuals to think about their own futures and about what kinds of skills they need to acquire.

The second fundamental change required is in approaches to workplace well-being. A 'health-promoting workplace' needs to address some of the underlying causes of stress and other forms of ill health related to how we conduct our working lives. This means moving beyond traditional notions of occupational health, to address the ways in which work is organised. While this poses a particular challenge for employers, workers themselves also need to be closely involved in this dialogue.

A change of culture that stops treating older workers as an expendable resource, and starts considering how to nurture our skills and well-being as we get older, may require many years. Widespread recognition of the desirability of this objective has been an important first step in this culture change. Further progress will require concerted efforts among all stakeholders. The underlying objective must be to move towards an extension of working lives that is rooted in positive opportunities, rather than a reluctant acceptance that we must 'work till we drop'.

References

Arthur, S. (2003) *Money, Choice and Control: The Financial Circumstances of Early Retirement*, Bristol: The Policy Press for Joseph Rowntree Foundation.

Barnes, H., Parry, J, and Lakey, J. (2002) *Forging a New Future: The Experiences and Expectations of People Leaving Paid Work over 50*, Bristol: The Policy Press.

Bowers, H., Secker, J., Llanes, M. and Webb, D. (2003) *The Gap Years: Rediscovering Midlife as the Route to Healthy Active Ageing*, London: NHS Health Development Agency.

Boyes, L. and McCormick, J. (2005) 'Experiences of work and sustaining workability' (www.jrf.org.uk/bookshop/ebooks/experiencesofworkandsustainingworkability.pdf).

Burchell, B., Day, D., Hudson, M., Ladipo, D., Mankelow, R., Nolan, J.P., Reed, H., Wichert, I.C. and Wilkinson, F. (1999) *Job Insecurity and Work Intensification: Flexibility and the Changing Boundaries of Work*, York: York Publishing Services.

Cabinet Office, Performance and Innovation Unit (2000) *Winning the Generation Game: Improving Opportunities for People aged 50–65 in Work and Community Activity*, London: The Stationery Office.

Campbell, N. (1999) *The Decline of Employment among Older People in Britain*, CASEpaper 19, London: LSE/STICERD.

DWP (Department for Work and Pensions) (2002) *Simplicity, Security and Choice: Working and Saving for Retirement*, London: The Stationery Office.

Ford, G. (2005) *Am I Still Needed? Guidance and Learning for Older Adults*, Derby: Centre for Guidance Studies, University of Derby (summary available online at www.jrf.org.uk/bookshop/ebooks/guidanceandlearningforolderadults.pdf).

Hirsch, D. (2003) *Crossroads after 50: Improving Choices in Work and Retirement*, York: Joseph Rowntree Foundation.

Hirsch, D. (ed) (2005) 'Sustaining working lives: a framework for policy and practice' (www.jrf.org.uk/bookshop/details.asp?pubID=682).

HM Government (2005) *Health, Work and Well-being – Caring for our Future*, London: Department for Work and Pensions.

Howard, M. (2005) 'Support for working carers' (www.jrf.org.uk/bookshop/ebooks/supportforworkingcarers.pdf).

Macaulay, C. (2003) 'Job mobility and job tenure in the UK', *Labour Market Trends*, vol 111, no 11, pp 541-50.

McNair, S., Flynn, M., Owen, L., Humphreys, C. and Woodfield, S. (2004) *Changing Work in Later Life: A Study of Job Transition*, Guildford: Centre for Research into the Older Workforce, University of Surrey.

Ministry of Social Affairs and Health (2002) *The Many Faces of the National Programme on Ageing Workers*, Helsinki: Ministry of Social Affairs and Health (www.stm.fi/english/tao/publicat/manyfaces/themanyfaces.pdf).

Mitton, L. and Hull, C. (forthcoming) 'The information, advice and guidance needs of older workers', *Social Policy and Society*.

Mooney, A. and Statham, J. (2002) *The Pivot Generation: Informal Care and Work after Fifty*, Bristol: The Policy Press.

OECD (Organisation for Economic Co-operation and Development) (2003) *Ageing and Employment Policies – Sweden*, Paris: OECD.

Tuomi, K., Huuhtanen, P., Nykyri, E. and Ilmarinen, J. (2001) 'Promotion of work ability, the quality of work and retirement', *Occupational Medicine*, vol 51, no 5, pp 318-24.

Watson, R., Manthorpe, J. and Andrews, J. (2003) *Nurses over 50: Options, Decisions and Outcomes*, Bristol: The Policy Press.

Yeandle, S. (2005) 'Older workers and work-life balance' (www.jrf.org.uk/bookshop/ebooks/olderworkersandworklifebalance.pdf).

EIGHT

Healthy work for older workers: work design and management factors

Amanda Griffiths

Introduction

Much of the recent concern in Britain in relation to the reducing ratio of employed to retired people has centred on national-level policy and economic issues such as retirement, state pension age and the burden on welfare and healthcare systems. For some time now, it has been suggested that one of the more straightforward, and least unpopular, ways of reducing the associated fiscal deficits would be to encourage people to stay in the labour force for longer than has been typical in recent decades (Griffiths, 1997; Miles, 1997). Sustaining the productivity of retained older workers may play a role in maintaining the economy's and individual organisations' competitive edge. However, it is important that any proposed increased involvement in work for older workers should be framed by appropriate expectations. Over-extending working capacity may have negative consequences for both individual employees and their employing organisations. It may also impact negatively on health and quality of life on employees' eventual exit from the workforce.

It is recognised that work can be a source of much satisfaction. It can provide purpose, meaning and challenge, a vehicle for learning, creativity and growth, opportunities to use skills and to demonstrate expertise, to exert control and to achieve success (Csikszentmihalyi, 1997). Many people report that work plays a significant part in their lives, providing psychological and social as well as material benefits. It is recognised that, by and large, work is better for health than unemployment (Waddell and Burton, 2006) providing, of course, that it is 'healthy work'.

Unhealthy work has traditionally been thought of in terms of exposure to physical hazards and inadequate attention to safety. Recognition of the importance of the more intangible aspects of work and their effects on individual health, both psychological and physical, began to emerge in the 19th century with the Industrial Revolution. In 1845, Engels was one of the first to voice concern in *The Condition of the Working Class in England* (Engels, 1987). He described the physical and psychological health problems suffered by workers from many trades and suggested their origins lay in the design and management of work and its associated physical environments. The question of how workplace management policies and practices affect employees' physical and psychological well-being has continued to attract attention ever since. It featured in novels in the late 19th and early 20th centuries, for example in the writings of Flaubert, Svevo, Kafka and Orwell (Barling and Griffiths, 2003). However, a considerable period of time elapsed before the effects on health of the nature and organisation of work were subject to serious scientific attention. More substantial investigations into the nature of the relationship between health and work from a psychological perspective began to emerge in publications from northern Europe and the United States in the mid-20th century. Some 50 years on, the central assertions of this field of study such as the importance of employee control, participation and support in determining health, have become visible in government legislation and advice for employers in several European, Australasian and North American countries. Data from many countries show that the major contemporary challenges to health at work continue to be those associated with the way work is designed and managed. This is particularly true for mental health (Cox et al, 2004). In Britain, work-related stress (conceptualised as a response to poor work design and management among other factors) is currently thought to be responsible for more lost working time than all other categories of work-related illness (Jones et al, 2006). However, important for the purposes of this chapter is that the majority of such research has been conducted with 'age-free' models. They take no account of the varying interests, priorities, lifestyles and needs of workers as they age. As a result, these data cannot contribute to a better understanding of the relationships between work design, health and age. It is proposed here that the relationship between work design and health may vary with age and that this area should be subject to a more rigorous and appropriate analysis.

There are many relevant questions about work design and organisation with regard to older workers. Are older workers subject to discrimination and, if so, how does this affect them? Do managers have an informed understanding of older workers' needs and abilities? What are the facts about the performance and health of workers as they age? Do older workers differ from their younger colleagues in those aspects of work that they experience as challenging or 'stressful'? Does the experience of stress at work impact on retirement decisions? How can we take advantage of older workers' strengths without disadvantaging them in terms of their weaknesses? How can we design work to be more appealing to older workers and persuade them to remain in, or return to, work? What are the training implications of this knowledge for today's managers? Can effective interventions in work design and management be implemented such that working life is extended? These are among the many potential 'push' and 'pull' factors that require exploration in attempts to understand working life for older workers and to influence their participation in the labour force. This chapter focuses on these work design and management factors, in particular on the relationships between work performance and age, between work-related health and age, and between work-related stress and age. It will explore what remains to be done in order to harness the potential, and protect the health, of older workers. While many interpret a desire to keep workers working for longer as concerning those over the ages of 60 or 65, there remains considerable scope for encouraging the substantial proportion of workers who retire at 50 or 55 to remain in the labour force. Making work a more attractive and less stressful experience may be a significant factor.

Work performance and age

Most reviews and meta-analyses in the scientific literature make clear that there is no consistent effect of age on work performance (eg Rhodes 1983; Waldman and Avolio 1986; McEvoy and Cascio, 1989; Warr, 1994; Salthouse and Maurer, 1996; Griffiths, 1997; Benjamin and Wilson, 2005). Overall, older workers perform as well as younger workers. Furthermore, there are many positive findings with regard to older workers. For example, older workers demonstrate less turnover and more positive work values than younger workers (Rhodes, 1983; Warr, 1994). They also exhibit more positive attitudes to safety and fewer occupational injuries (Siu et al, 2003), although there is some evidence that it is tenure (time on the job) that should be examined here rather than age per se (Breslin and Smith, 2006). It is frequently reported that older workers are better at 'customer relations' than their younger colleagues. There are many methodological challenges in this type of research; for example, the interpretation of performance measures is not straightforward. Some research has identified increases in performance with age when using objective measures, but decreases when using supervisor ratings. This may be because supervisors' reports reflect a general bias against older workers (Waldman and Avolio, 1986). Even enlightened human resource policies can be stifled by stereotypical attitudes and discriminatory practices of supervisors and managers (Taylor and Walker, 1994; Walker, 1997).

Despite the equitable overall picture with regard to work performance and age, studies have shown that age bias can lead to discriminatory actions at work, and has been linked to decreases in self-efficacy, job satisfaction, organisational commitment, job involvement and performance among older workers (Rupp et al, 2006). Considerable evidence exists to suggest that older workers have often been misunderstood, ignored, and vulnerable to the effects of age-related stereotyping. Although age stereotypes tend to be multidimensional, with the possibility of both positive and negative aspects, attitudes are generally more negative towards older adults than towards younger adults (Kite et al, 2005). Evidence suggests that these negative beliefs about older workers are associated with discriminatory attitudes that may in turn influence employment decisions (Warr and Pennington, 1993; Chiu et al, 2001) as well as individual well-being. For example, younger job applicants and workers have been found to be perceived and evaluated more positively than older applicants and workers (Gordon and Arvey, 2004). Assumptions that chronological age is the most important determinant of health or that older workers are more likely than younger workers to be absent from work due to illness may both be influential factors in employment decisions. In fact, although older workers as a group may suffer more from 'genuine' health problems that require a period of certified sick leave, they do not, overall, take more sickness absence (Benjamin and Wilson, 2005). They are less likely to take the short-term, uncertified absences demonstrated more commonly by younger workers. In summary, the literature suggests that many common myths and stereotypes about older workers' decreased performance and availability for work are not accurate.

However, the evidence from epidemiological and laboratory-based studies paints a slightly less favourable picture of older people's performance. Such studies reveal age-related declines in cognitive abilities such as working memory capacity, attentional capacity, novel problem-solving and information processing speed. Age-related deterioration is also documented in motor-response generation, selecting target information from complex displays, visual and auditory abilities, balance, joint mobility, aerobic capacity and endurance (Kowalski-Trakofler et al, 2005). There is great individual variation in the extent of such declines. We should be cautious about the relevance of some of this research to our interest in older workers for two reasons. First, much of it is laboratory-based, uses abstracted tasks and may therefore not be ecologically valid (that is, not relevant to actual jobs in real organisations). Second, a considerable proportion of the research into age-related declines in abilities, particularly in cognitive abilities, focuses on adults over the age of 65, and who are therefore not traditionally of working age.

Nonetheless, these different positions may be reconciled. It could be that older workers cope with any age-related deficits such that they are not expressed in performance at work (Griffiths, 1997). Recent models of ageing and work propose that certain mediating factors can operate in a compensatory way and that chronological age should be viewed simply as one dimension along which these mediating factors exert their influence, rather than a predictor in itself. Factors that might underpin the relationship between chronological age, work performance and behaviour might function at three levels: individual, organisational and societal. At the individual level, for example, experience, job knowledge, abilities, skills, disposition, motivation may operate (Salthouse and Maurer, 1996; Kanfer and Ackerman, 2004). There is evidence that older workers adopt different problem-solving tactics (such as superior anticipation and more economical search strategies) than younger workers doing the same tasks (Warr, 1994). Other mediating variables may reflect organisational policies and practice: for example, age awareness programmes, supervisor and peer attitudes, management style, the physical work environment and equipment, health promotion, workplace adjustments, and learning and development opportunities (Griffiths 1997). To take the latter example, is well established that older workers engage in fewer training and professional development activities than younger workers, they get less support for such activities from supervisors, they have different preferred learning styles although training provision rarely reflects this, and they are more anxious about training. All of which could lead to underachievement in rapidly changing jobs. Research has shown that prior experience of development activities, a belief in the need for development, belief in one's ability to learn and develop skills, social support for development (from work and outside work), job involvement and career insight may all be operational in predicting involvement in development activities (Maurer et al, 2003). Applying the precautionary principle, employers could counter the risk that declines in older adults' abilities may affect performance not only by offering training but also by offering support and reducing age-inappropriate demands. Changes to shift systems, for example, can provide benefits for all workers, but can be particularly beneficial for older workers (Harma et al, 2006).

A further level of exploration for the relationship between age and work performance might be provided by examining global markets, the wider employment context and worker protection (Quinlan, 2004a, 2004b; Johnstone et al, 2005). In the Britain, and in other developed countries, there has been a decline in manufacturing and a recent export of some service sector work to developing countries. The way work is designed and organised has changed substantially over the past 20 years. There has been a fall in permanent jobs, and a growth in contingent or 'precarious' work such as temporary, agency, fixed–contract and subcontracted jobs. There has also been an increase in part–time work, home–based work, telework, multiple job–holding and unpaid overtime. These changes might make it increasingly difficult for vulnerable workers (for example, people with disabilities, immigrant workers, young and older workers) to gain or maintain employment, and such employment may entail inferior and unhealthy working conditions. These recent transformations in work design and management have also been accompanied by changes in worker protection; for example, a decline in union density and collective bargaining, some erosion in workers' compensation and public health infrastructure, and cutbacks in both disability and unemployment benefits – again contexts which are unlikely to favour vulnerable workers (Quinlan, 2005).

Work-related health and age

Surveys indicate that the prevalence of self–reported poor health, of chronic illness, cancer, cardiovascular and respiratory conditions have either remained constant over recent years or have increased. A similar picture emerges for rates of general practitioner referrals, hospital admissions and numbers of people unable to work (Dunnell and Dix, 2000). Overall, survival (life expectancy) has improved but the number of years of healthy life (healthy life expectancy) has not. Widescale social inequalities in ill health persist. A substantial proportion, probably about a third, of working people over the age of 50, suffer from a chronic illness. They need sympathetic management in order to sustain productivity and employability, as do people with multiple chronic health conditions: the latter group generally demonstrate a markedly lower probability of maintaining employment (Wilson, 2001).

Incapacity benefit figures in Britain reveal how many people of working age (who have worked for a specified period and meet certain contribution conditions) are unavailable for work because of ill health.

For example, in 1997, the two most prevalent types of claim, with each category representing a quarter of all claims, were (i) mental and behavioural disorders (which would include what could be described as 'stress-related' symptoms), and (ii) diseases of the musculoskeletal system and connective tissue (Social Security Statistics 1997). This pattern of reasons for being a beneficiary of incapacity benefit has remained largely the same since, except that numbers in the former category now outstrip those in the latter. In 2005 nearly a third of all beneficiaries of incapacity benefit fell into the diagnosis group of 'mental and behavioural disorders' (DWP, 2005). But these figures do not tell us about the work-relatedness of these illnesses – whether they are caused or made worse by work – only that people who have worked in the past now suffer them and are deemed unavailable for work. There are two other potential sources of useful information on the health of working-age people: national surveys of occupational ill health and data on early ill-health retirements. Examples are described below.

A stratified random sample of people in Britain who work or who have worked have been asked, as part of successive Labour Force Surveys, whether they have suffered in the last 12 months from 'any illness, disability or other physical problem' that they think was caused or made worse by their work (Hodgson et al, 1993; Jones et al, 1998, 2006). In some surveys, respondents' general practitioners have been contacted about the work-related nature of their patients' conditions, and by and large their views have tended to concur with those of their patients. Respondents are asked about the nature of their illness, the job they considered to have caused it (or made it worse) and how many working days were lost. There are other surveillance schemes such as the Occupational Disease Intelligence Network (ODIN) where specialist doctors report on the incidence of work-related ill health. In 2004/05 an estimated 12.8 million working days were lost for reasons of work-related stress, depression or anxiety, and an estimated 11.6 million days for work-related musculoskeletal disorders (Jones et al, 2006). These were by far the two largest categories of work-related ill health. Overall, older workers are more likely to report work-related stress, depression and anxiety than younger workers (HSE, 2002). This is an interesting statistic for those concerned with factors influencing early retirement decisions and may be partly explained by cumulative exposure to workplace hazards. Although there is limited research in this area, poor work design and management have been found to be more powerful predictors of early retirement than challenging physical work environments (Kloimüller et al, 1997). The Whitehall II study suggests that job satisfaction, together with employment grade and self-perceived health, are independent predictors of early retirement in British civil servants (Mein et al, 2000).

In Britain, there are no definitive, centralised records on early ill-health retirements. However, one can piece together from disparate sources a picture that suggests they are common. According to the General Household Survey, the number of early ill-health retirements rose by 66% between 1972 and 1996 (ONS, 1997). A survey of over 50,000 employees taking retirement from a cross-section of blue-chip employers in the UK revealed that 14% retired early on the grounds of ill health (Income Data Services, 1998). A survey commissioned by the Department for Work and Pensions (Disney et al, 1998) suggested that 30% of early retirements were caused by ill health. There is wide variation in rates of early retirement due to ill health within and between organisations (Poole et al, 2005). Interpreting any trends in such data in relation to actual differences in the health of the working population is not straightforward. Part of any increase may be attributable to people's changing perceptions of health and to changes in corporate objectives and pension scheme policies and practices. Some indication of the reasons for early ill-health retirement are revealed by various surveys over the years. A survey of nearly 2,000 NHS employees who retired early on the grounds of ill health revealed the main diagnostic categories to be musculoskeletal, psychiatric and cardiovascular (Pattani et al, 2001). Similar patterns were revealed in an earlier study (Poole, 1997). A third of the respondents in Pattani et al's study considered that their ill health was caused by work, although there was some disagreement with their managers about this. Of course, such discrepancies are difficult to resolve. Evidence from epidemiological studies using broad-brush measures, suggests that work design, work organisation and work climate are among the factors that contribute to the social gradient in health (Ferrie, 2004).

In summary, work design and management factors remain relatively unexplored in the quest to understand the relationship between ageing, work and health. It is established that the largest causes of work-related ill health among the working population of Britain today are minor psychiatric disorders (commonly labelled stress, anxiety or depression) and musculoskeletal disorders. It is established that these disorders, responsible for a large proportion of work incapacity and early ill-health retirements among older workers, are known to be strongly associated with the way work is designed and managed (Bongers et al, 1993; Moon and Sauter, 1996; Theorell and Karasek, 1996). Clearly, we need to examine why work design and management may be less than optimal for older workers, to identify effective interventions to reduce the experience of work-related stress and associated ill-health outcomes in this group and to facilitate rehabilitation and redeployment where necessary. An exploration of the concept of work-related stress may be one way forward.

Work-related stress and age

One of the main pathways by which work design and management are thought to affect health has commonly been referred to as the experience of 'stress' (Cox, 1993). More recently this has been defined as 'the adverse reaction people have to excessive pressures or other types of demand placed on them' (HSE, 2005). It begins as a psychological mechanism involving workers' perceptions and appraisals of their working conditions and the meanings they ascribe to them (Cox, 1993). These appraisal processes are fundamental in understanding any relationship between working conditions and health outcomes (Dewe, 1992).

A large body of published research from the past 25 years has identified in broad terms the characteristics of work design and management that can be detrimental for many people. Reviews suggest that they traditionally concern difficulties with workload, work pace, working hours, organisational culture, participation and control, interpersonal relationships, career development, role-related issues and the home–work interface (for example Cox, 1993; Cox et al, 2000). Research has demonstrated that it is feasible for employers to adopt a risk assessment approach to identify such risk factors for work stress and to design and implement interventions intended to improve the situation (for example, Cox et al, 2002, 2003; Randall et al, 2005; Griffiths et al, 2003, 2006). The Health and Safety Executive has developed a population-based, preventative approach for employers to manage work-related stress called 'Management Standards' (Cousins et al, 2004; Cox, 2004; MacKay et al, 2004). It aims to help employers move from less desirable to more desirable states by identifying problems in key areas of work design that, if not managed properly, are known to be associated with poor health and well-being, lower productivity and increased sickness absence (HSE, 2005). It provides a toolkit to assess employees' reports about key primary sources of stress: work demands, control, support, relationships, role and change. There are other systems produced by unions, insurance companies, employers' and employees' representative bodies, researchers, consultants, and international bodies such as the World Health Organization, International Labour Office and the European Commission. By and large, they use similar taxonomies of workplace stressors. It might be argued that the rapidly changing world of work requires that we be aware of the possibilities of new risk factors: lack of feedback, unsuitable or non-existent appraisal mechanisms, not feeling 'valued', poor communication with senior management, inappropriate target-setting, a lack of dignity, organisational justice or fairness may reflect contemporary concerns.

Such strategies for the prevention and management of work-related stress, and the original research on which they are based, do not consider age as a variable in its own right. Age, when it has been considered, has usually been treated as a potential confound, and has been partialled out statistically or simply ignored. It has consequently been assumed that what is bad (that is, a stressor) for one age group is bad for all, that older and younger workers think about their work in similar ways, make judgements about it in much the same way, and that models based on a full age range will be meaningful. This assumption could be challenged. The big picture that is available from the scientific literature concerning harmful aspects of work design and management may be masking age-related differences. Key to our concerns for older workers is that there may be specific characteristics of work design and management that are experienced as particularly problematic by older workers and therefore are likely to be particularly stressful for them. In a study of manual workers aged 16–63 (all doing the same job), the older members of the group reported concerns about contextual issues such as management systems and procedures and the knock-on effects of work on home life. Younger workers' concerns, in comparison, appeared more immediate and focused on task content (Griffiths, 1999a). In another study, older workers experienced particular problems with lack of recognition, devaluing behaviours of supervisors and colleagues, and disappointment with management: again, all contextual issues (Kloimüller et al, 1997). The pioneering longitudinal studies conducted by the Finnish Institute of Occupational Health (for example, Ilmarinen et al, 1991; Ilmarinen, 1999) have suggested that, for older workers, certain aspects of work design and management are significantly associated with decreasing 'work ability' – notably role conflict, fear of making mistakes or of failure, lack of influence over one's work, lack of professional development and lack of feedback and appreciation. The role of the supervisor seems particularly critical in predicting continued work ability, notably in being well informed about ageing, demonstrating a positive attitude and employing team-based management strategies (Ilmarinen, 1995).

Conclusion

In conclusion, it has been suggested that people may need to stay at work for longer than has traditionally been the case in recent decades. The key questions to be asked are: (i) what will persuade older workers to stay at work?, and (ii) how do we ensure that they remain healthy and productive? This chapter has argued that specific actions may be required. This is not to deny the significance of attempts to draw older, economically inactive people back into the labour force, nor the value of rehabilitation following extended periods of sick leave, nor the importance of recognising the needs of employees with long-term health conditions. However, experience suggests that rehabilitation and return to work are complex issues. Preventative actions might counter age bias and discrimination, and accommodate the particular needs of older workers. Work should be designed and adjusted to suit their abilities. Most age-related deteriorations (in people of working age) may be variously countered by interventions including the introduction of state-of-the-art technologies, equal access to learning and development opportunities, age-appropriate training systems, flexible and individual work designs, support from well-informed management and colleagues, and health promotion activities. The 1995 Disability Discrimination Act already provides workers with a right to reasonable adjustments according to their needs.

On a more positive front, employers could capitalise on older workers' job knowledge, make more use of them as mentors, encourage horizontal as well as vertical mobility, and allow greater flexibility. Age awareness programmes are important for all sections of the workforce, but especially for supervisors and managers. Above all, because many of the origins of stress are local and context-specific, employers need to consult their older employees when considering work design and management issues. The strengths and weaknesses of relying solely on context-free definitions of what is 'good' and 'bad', based on broad-brush measures of work design, may become clear with time (Griffiths, 1999b).

In addition, it may be useful to explore broader policy developments with regard to occupational health issues. The infrastructure and expertise available to employers with regard to managing occupational health, preventing work stress and facilitating the employment of older workers varies considerably across Europe (Griffiths, 2003). The British approach does not oblige employers to have links to professional occupational health and safety schemes. Employers are required to do their own risk assessments and to self-regulate, employing competent persons where they considerate it appropriate. Finland, as another example, obliges all employers to arrange occupational health care and requires them to monitor their employees' well-being throughout all stages of their working careers. Locally delivered, comprehensive advice on workplace health matters is provided for its entire working population: those in large enterprises, small enterprises, entrepreneurs and self-employed persons such as farmers. Expertly staffed and approved occupational health care units are located in municipal health centres, private medical centres and in units belonging to larger organisations. These professionals focus on prevention, visit workplaces, provide information and guidance, carry out risk assessments, suggest improvements, monitor employee health and working capacity, and monitor and support disabled employees. Identifying known risk factors for stress is specified in legislation as among their responsibilities. Accompanying this focus on occupational health in general, has been a long-term and effective national programme on ageing workers in Finland that focuses on extending productive working life and preventing disability at work (Ministry of Social Affairs and Health, 2003).

As yet, many traditionally managed organisations may not represent optimal systems for an age diverse workforce. Once steps are taken to remove current barriers to older workers' full participation, improved opportunities for extending healthy working life may emerge. There is currently little indication that work is designed and managed with reference to age. However, there is only a small evidence base upon which policy makers and managers can base their actions; a multidisciplinary and co-ordinated forward strategy involving research, practice and education is required.

References

Barling, J. and Griffiths, A. (2003) 'A history of occupational health psychology', in J.C. Quick and L. Tetrick (eds) *Handbook of Occupational Health Psychology*, Washington: American Psychological Association, pp 19-33.

Benjamin, K. and Wilson, S. (2005) *Facts and misconceptions about age, health status and employability*, Report HSL/2005/20 (Buxton: Health & Safety Laboratory).

Breslin, F. and Smith, P. (2006) 'Trial by fire: A multivariate examination of the relation between job tenure and work injuries', *Occupational and Environmental Medicine*, vol 63 , no 1, pp 27-32.

Bongers, P., de Winter, R., Kompier, M. and Hildebrandt, V. (1993) 'Psychosocial factors at work and musculoskeletal disease', *Scandinavian Journal of Work, Environment and Health*, vol 19, no 5, pp 297-312.

Chiu, W., Chan, A., Snape, E. and Redman, T. (2001) 'Age stereotypes and discriminatory attitudes towards older workers: an East–West comparison', *Human Relations*, vol 54, no 5, pp 629-61.

Cousins, R., Mackay, C., Clarke, S., Kelly, C., Kelly, P. and McCaig, R. (2004) '"Management Standards": work-related stress in the UK: Practical development', *Work and Stress*, vol 18, no 2, pp 113-36.

Cox, T. (1993) *Stress research and stress management: Putting theory to work*, Sudbury: HSE Books.

Cox, T. (2003) 'Work stress: Nature, history and challenges', *Science in Parliament*, vol 60, no 1, pp 10-11.

Cox, T. (2004) 'Work-related stress, risk management and management standards', *Work & Stress*, vol 18, no 2, pp 89-90.

Cox, T. Griffiths, A. and Rial González, E. (2000) *Research on work-related stress*, Luxembourg: Office for Official Publications of the European Communities, European Agency for Safety & Health at Work.

Cox, T., Griffiths, A. and Randall, R. (2003) 'A risk management approach to the prevention of work stress', in M.J. Schabracq, J.A.M. Winnnubst and C.L. Cooper (eds) *Handbook of Work and Health Psychology*, 2nd edn, Chichester: Wiley & Sons, pp 191-206.

Cox, T., Randall, R. and Griffiths, A. (2002). *Interventions to control stress at work in hospital-based staff*, Sudbury: HSE Books.

Cox. T., Leka, S., Ivanov, I. and Kortum, E. (2004) 'Work, employment and mental health in Europe', *Work & Stress*, vol 18, no 2, pp 179-85.

Csikszentmihalyi, M. (1997). *Living Well: The Psychology of Everyday Life*, London: Weidenfeld & Nicholson.

Dewe, P. (1992) 'Applying the concept of appraisal to work stressors: some exploratory analyses', *Human Relations*, vol 45, no 2, pp 143-64.

Disney, R., Grundy, E. and Johnson, P. (1998) *The Dynamics of Retirement: Analyses of the Retirement Surveys,* Department for Work and Pensions Research Report No 72, London: The Stationery Office.

Dunnell, K. and Dix, D. (2000) 'Are we looking forward to a longer and healthier retirement?' *Health Statistics Quarterly 06,* pp 18-25.

DWP (Department for Work and Pensions) (2005) *Incapacity Benefit and Severe Disablement Allowance Quarterly Summary Statistics: February 2005* (www.dwp.gov.uk).

Engels, F. (1987) *The Condition of the Working class in England*, London: Penguin Books.

Ferrie, J. (2004) *Work Stress and Health: The Whitehall II study*, London: Cabinet Office and Council of Civil Service Unions.

Gordon, R. and Arvey, R. (2004) 'Age bias in laboratory and field settings: A meta-analytic investigation', *Journal of Applied Social Psychology*, vol 34, no 3, pp 468-92.

Griffiths, A. (1997) 'Ageing, health and productivity; A challenge for the new millennium' *Work & Stress*, vol 11, no 3, pp 197-214.

Griffiths, A. (1999a) 'Work design and management: the older worker', *Experimental Ageing Research*, vol 25, no 4, pp 411-20.

Griffiths, A. (1999b) 'Organizational interventions: Facing the limits of the natural science paradigm', *Scandinavian Journal of Work, Environment and Health* vol 25, no 6, pp 589-96.

Griffiths, A. (2003) 'Actions at the workplace to prevent work stress', *Science in Parliament*, vol 60, no 1, pp 12-13.

Griffiths, A., Randall, R., Santos, A. and Cox, T. (2003) 'Senior nurses: Interventions to reduce work stress', in M. Dollard, A. Winefield and H. Winefield (eds) *Occupational stress in the service professions*, London: Taylor & Francis, pp 169-91.

Griffiths, A., Cox, T., Karanika, M, Khan, S. and Tomás, J.M. (2006) 'Work design and management in the manufacturing sector: Development and Validation of the Work Organisation Assessment Questionnaire' *Occupational and Environmental Medicine*, vol 63, no 10, pp 669-75.

Harma, M., Taria, H., Irja, K., Mikael, S., Jussi, V., Anne, B. and Pertti, M. (2006) 'A controlled intervention study on the effects of a very rapidly forward rotating shift system on sleep-wakefulness and well-being among young and elderly shift workers', *International Journal of Psychophysiology*, vol 59, no 1, pp 70-9.

Hodgson, J., Jones, J., Elliott, R. and Osman, J. (1993) *Self-reported work-related illness,* Sudbury: HSE Books.

HSE (Health and Safety Executive) (2002) 'Occupational ill-health age statistics', Information Sheet 2/02/EMSU, www.hse.gov.uk/statistics.

HSE (2005) *Tackling stress: The management standards approach*, Sudbury: HSE Books, www.hse.gov.uk/stress/standards.

Ilmarinen, J. (1995) 'A new concept for productive aging at work', in A.C. Bittner and P.C. Champney (eds) *Advances in industrial ergonomics and safety VII. Proceedings of the Xth Annual International Industrial Ergonomics and Safety Conference, Washington, USA*, London: Taylor & Francis.

Ilmarinen, J. (1999) *Ageing workers in the European Union: Status and promotion of work ability, employability and employment,* Helsinki: Finnish Institute of Occupational Health.

Ilmarinen, J., Tuomi, K., Eskelinen, L., Nygård, C.-H., Huuhtanen, P. and Klockars, M. (1991) 'Summary and recommendations of a project involving cross-sectional and follow-up studies on the aging worker in Finnish municipal occupations, 1981-1985', *Scandinavian Journal of Work, Environment and Health*, vol 17 (Supplement 1), pp 135-41.

IDS (Income Data Services) (1998) *IDS Pensions Service Bulletin 115*, May, London: IDS.

Johnstone, R., Quinlan, M. and Walters, D. (2005) 'Statutory OHS workplace arrangements and the modern labour market', *Journal of Industrial Relations*, vol 47, no 11, pp 93-116.

Jones, J., Hodgson, J., Clegg, T. and Elliott, R. (1998) *Self-reported work-related illness in 1995*, Sudbury: HSE Books.

Jones, J., Huxtable, C. and Hodgson, J. (2006) Self-reported illness in 2004/5: Results from the Labour Force Survey. Health & Safety Executive (www.hse.gov.uk/statistics/swi/swi0405).

Kanfer, R. and Ackerman, P. (2004) Aging, adult development, and work motivation, *Academy of Management Review*, vol 29, no 3, pp 440-58.

Kite, M., Stockdale, G., Whitley, B., and Johnson, B. (2005) Attitudes toward younger and older adults: An updated meta-analytic Review. *Journal of Social Issues*, vol 6, no 2, pp 241-66.

Kowalski-Trakofler, K., Steiner, L. and Schwerha, D. (2005) Safety considerations for the aging workforce, *Safety Science*, vol 43, no 10, pp 779-93.

Kempe, P.T. (1994) 'Social policy and perspectives: conclusion', in J. Snel and R. Cremer (eds) *Work and aging: A European perspective*, London: Taylor & Francis, pp 393-5.

Kloimüller, I., Karazman, R. and Geissler, H. (1997) 'How do stress impacts change with aging in the profession of bus drivers? Results from a questionnaire survey on "health and competition" among bus drivers in a public transport system in 1996', in P. Seppälä, T. Luopajarvi, C-H. Nygård, and M. Mattila (eds) *From experience to innovation: Volume V, Proceedings of the 13th Triennial Congress, International Ergonomics Association*, Helsinki: Finnish Institute of Occupational Health, pp 454-6.

Mackay, C., Cousins, R., Kelly, P., Lee, S. and McCaig, R. (2004) 'Management Standards' and work-related stress in the UK: policy background and science', *Work & Stress*, vol 18, no 2, pp 91-112.

Maurer, T., Weiss, E. and Barbeite, F. (2003) 'A model of involvement in work-related learning and development activity: the effects of individual, situational, motivational, and age variables', *Journal of Applied Psychology*, vol 88, no 4, pp 707-24.

McEvoy, G. and Cascio, W. (1989) 'Cumulative evidence on the relationship between employee age and job performance', *Journal of Applied Psychology*, vol 74, no 1, pp 11-17.

Mein, G., Martikainen, P., Stansfeld, S., Brunner, E., Fuhrer, R. and Marmot, M. (2000) 'Predictors of early retirement in British civil servants', *Age and Ageing*, vol 29, no 6, pp 529-36.

Miles, D. (1997) 'Financial markets, ageing and social welfare', *Fiscal Studies*, vol 18, no 2, pp 161-88.

Ministry of Social Affairs and Health (2003) *Trends in social protection in Finland 2003*, Helsinki: Publications of the Ministry of Social Affairs and Health, p 17.

Moon, S. and Sauter, S. (1996) *Psychosocial aspects of musculoskeletal disorders in office work*, London: Taylor & Francis.

ONS (Office for National Statistics) (1997) *Living in Britain – preliminary results from the 1996 General Household Survey*, London: ONS.

Pattani, S., Constantinovici, N. and Williams, S. (2001) 'Who retires early from the NHS because of ill health and what does it cost? a national cross sectional study', *British Medical Journal*, vol 322, pp 208-9.

Poole, C. (1997) 'Retirement on grounds of ill-health: cross sectional survey in six organisations in United Kingdom', *British Medical Journal*, vol 314, pp 929-32.

Poole, C., Bass, C., Sorrell, J., Thompson, M., Harrison, J., Archer, A. and Association of Local Authority Medicals Advisers (2005) 'Ill-health retirement: national rates and updated guidance for occupational physicians', *Occupational Medicine*, vol 55, no 5, pp 345-8.

Quinlan, M. (2004a) 'Workers' compensation and the challenges posed by changing patterns of work', *Policy and Practice in Safety and Health*, vol 2, no 1, pp 25-52.

Quinlan, M. (2004b) 'Flexible work and organisational arrangements: regulatory problems and responses', in L. Bluff, N. Gunningham and R. Johnstone (eds) *OHS Regulation in the 21st Century*, Sydney: Federation Press, pp 120-45.

Quinlan, M. (2005) 'The hidden epidemic of injuries and illness associated with the global expansion of precarious employment', in C. Mayhew and C. Peterson (eds) *Occupational health and safety: International influences and the new epidemics*, New York, NY: Baywood, pp 53-74.

Randall, R. Griffiths, A. and Cox, T. (2005) 'Evaluating organizational stress-management interventions using adapted study designs', *European Journal of Work and Organizational Psychology*, vol 14, no 1, 23-41.

Rhodes, S. (1983) 'Age-related differences in work attitudes and behaviour: a review and conceptual analysis', *Psychological Bulletin*, vol 93, no 2, pp 328-67.

Rupp, D., Vodanovich, S. and Credé, M. (2006) 'Age bias in the workplace: the impact of ageism and causal attributions', *Journal of Applied Social Psychology*, vol 36, no 6, pp 1337-64.

Salthouse, T. and Maurer, T. (1996) 'Aging, job performance, and career development', in J. Birren and K. Schaie (eds) *Handbook of the psychology of aging*, San Diego, CA: Academic Press, pp 353-64.

Siu, O., Phillips, D. and Leung, T. (2003) 'Age differences in safety attitudes and safety performance in Hong Kong construction workers', *Journal of Safety Research*, vol 34, no 2, pp 199-205.

Social Security Statistics (1997) London: The Stationary Office.

Taylor, P.E. and Walker, A. (1994) 'The ageing workforce - employers' attitudes towards older people', *Work, Employment and Society*, vol 8, no 4, pp 569-91.

Theorell, T. and Karasek, R. (1996) 'Current issues relating to psychosocial job strain and cardiovascular disease research', *Journal of Occupational Health Psychology*, vol 1, no 1, pp 9-26.

Waddell, G. and Burton, A.K (2006) *Is work good for your health and well being?*, London: The Stationary Office.

Waldman, D. and Avolio, B. (1986) ;A meta-analysis of age differences in job performance;, *Journal of Applied Psychology*, vol 71, no 1, pp 33-38.

Walker, A. (1997) *Combating age barriers in employment: European research report*, Dublin: European Foundation for the Improvement of Living and Working Conditions.

Warr, P. (1994) 'Age and job performance', in J. Snel and R. Cremer (eds) *Work and aging: A European perspective*, London: Taylor & Francis, pp 309-22.

Warr, P. and Pennington, J. (1993) *Views about age discrimination and older workers*, London: Institute of Personnel Management.

Wilson, S. (2001) 'Work and the accommodation of chronic illness: a re-examination of the health-labour supply relationship', *Applied Economics*, vol 33, no 9, pp 1139-56.

NINE

Flexible work and older workers

Wendy Loretto, Sarah Vickerstaff and Phil White

Introduction

In the context of the UK government's aim to extend working lives and encourage people to retire later, the availability of flexible working arrangements, such as part-time work, temporary work or self-employment, has been flagged as important (PIU, 2000; DWP, 2002a, p 98; Phillipson and Smith, 2005, pp 49-53; see also Chapter Seven of this volume).[1] The UK government has taken various steps to prolong working lives, including the establishment of an Extending Working Life group within the Department for Work and Pensions (DWP); regulations to combat age discrimination in the workplace, with effect from October 2006; the raising of women's state pension age (SPA) from 60 to 65 by 2020; and the opportunity for people to defer receipt of their state pension (Whiting, 2005, p 286). The White Paper on pensions reform published in May 2006 also proposes further raising the state pension age to an eventual 68 by 2050 (DWP, 2006b, p 113).

It is hypothesised that increasing flexible work options could have an impact on activity rates of older workers in three main ways:

- by providing opportunities for older workers to downshift at the end of their working careers and hence delay full retirement;
- by providing 'bridge jobs' between career occupation and full retirement;
- by encouraging those not currently in work because of unemployment, caring responsibilities or health issues to return to the labour market.

Hitherto, relatively little has been known about the existing patterns of flexible working among older workers or about the aspirations and motivations of older workers with respect to flexible work options. This chapter addresses these issues, drawing on work undertaken for the Equal Opportunities Commission (see Loretto et al, 2005).

The chapter is in five sections. The first sets the scene with an analysis of the January to March 2006 Labour Force Survey (LFS) to provide a picture of the existing patterns of employment among older workers (defined as those aged 50+). The second section continues this analysis of the LFS to consider the current patterns of flexible working and in particular, the gender differences in these. The third reviews existing research, which considers the kinds of flexible work options that older workers need and what informs their needs. The fourth examines the issue from the employers' perspective, to investigate the extent to which organisations are likely to increase the range of flexible working options available. The fifth concludes by exploring what might happen if flexible work was more widely available and whether this would provide advantages or disadvantages for older workers.

Economic activity status among older men and women in Great Britain

According to LFS estimates, 47% of men aged 50+ and 32% of women aged 50+ in Great Britain class themselves as *economically active*, the vast majority of these being in employment (ILO definitions). These rates equate to 4.09 million men and 3.3 million women in employment. However, these figures mask a sharp decline in economic activity with age. A more detailed analysis by age group and gender is presented in Table 9.1.

As can be seen from Table 9.1, the sharpest declines in employment rates occur at age 65 for men and 60 for women. These are the ages at which men and women, if they qualify, are entitled to start claiming the state pension. This supports other work (see Loretto et al, 2005) that

Table 9.1: Economic activity status of women and men aged 50+ (GB)

Age	% in employment		% ILO unemployed		% inactive	
	Women	Men	Women	Men	Women	Men
50-54	75	85	2	3	22	12
55-59	62	76	1	3	36	21
60-64	33	53	1	2	67	45
65-69	11	20	*	1	89	80
70+	2	5	*	*	98	95
Total (50+)	31	45	1	2	67	53

* Less than 0.5% (numbers too small to be statistically reliable).

Source: Labour Force Survey, Jan-Mar 2006 (weighted). Authors' analysis

has suggested that SPA is perceived by many as the de facto retirement age. Nevertheless, there is also a significant drop in the proportions of men and women in their late 50s who are working.

Up until the later 50s, employment rates are very similar to those for the 'prime working-age' population (88% for men aged 25-49 and 75% for women aged 25-49). For men, the trend for declining labour market participation of the over-50s appears to have begun in the mid-1970s and accelerated in the 1980s and 1990s, especially through periods of recession (Loretto et al, 2000a, p 281). It is more difficult to discern trends over time among women, as any decline in employment tends to be masked by the general increase in women's labour market participation. Although recent labour market analysis (Hotopp, 2005) suggests that the employment rates of men and women aged over 50 have begun to rise again, they still lag behind those for the 'prime-age' workforce. In terms of gender differences, the figures show that women's employment as a proportion of men's employment declines with age after the age of 50 and particularly after the age of 60.

Employment by industry and by occupation

Where older workers are employed, and at what levels, is significant in relation to flexible work opportunities, as some sectors and occupations have a history of part-time and varied hours contracts whereas others are more traditional. The distribution of older men and women across the various industries reflects the well-established gender segregation seen in the workforce as a whole. Thus, for example, 24% of older female workers, but only 6% of older male workers, are in health and social work; on the other hand, 19% of older male workers, compared with 7% of older female workers, are in manufacturing. Associated with these figures is the finding that older women are twice as likely as older men to work in the public sector (38% of women aged 50+ work in the public sector compared with 18% of men aged 50+). When compared with employment patterns for the rest of the workforce (aged 16-49), for most sectors gender segregation is more marked among the older workforce.

Employment by occupation also shows traditional gender differences. Only 11% of older women class themselves as managers or senior officials, compared with 20% of older men. Nearly a quarter (24%) of all working females aged 50+ hold administrative and secretarial jobs. This dwarfs the 4% of men who hold such positions. Men, on the other hand, are markedly more likely to work in skilled trades occupations or as process, plant and machine operatives.

A comparison of these figures with the occupational spread of the workforce aged 25–49 reveals only a few differences. Twenty per cent of women aged 16–49 work in administrative and secretarial occupations, compared with nearly 25% of older women. Younger workers are proportionately more likely to be working in personal service and sales and customer service occupations. These patterns provide evidence of two distinct types of difference: older women's employment differs from that of older men; and older women's employment differs from that of younger women.

Flexible working among older women and men

Part-time working

Part-time working represents the most popular form of flexible working: LFS (2006) figures show that half of all older female workers work part-time, compared with two fifths of those aged 25–49. Older male workers are also more likely to work part-time than younger male workers (see Table 9.2).

Table 9.2 also shows that the incidence of part-time work increases across the age groups. As with other aspects of employment, established gendered patterns of working continue into the older age groups; that is, older women in all age groups are more likely than their male equivalents to work part-time. Nevertheless, part-time working is markedly more prevalent among both sexes after their respective SPAs. For those in their 70s who are still working, part-time work is by far the norm.

Table 9.2: Employment of older workers in part-time work

Age	Women		Men	
	N (000s)	% of all in employment in that age group	N (000s)	% of all in employment in that age group
25–49	3,052	40	388	5
50–54	535	40	82	6
55–59	573	48	153	11
60–64	343	67	178	22
65–69	125	84	147	59
70+	64	84	85	70
Total (50+)	1,640	50	646	16

Source: Labour Force Survey, Jan-Mar 2006 (weighted). Authors' analysis

A comparison of the situation 12 years ago indicates that there has been a substantial increase in the proportion of older men who are working part-time as opposed to full-time. Using 1994 LFS data, Dex and McCulloch (1995, p 44) found that 15% of men aged 60-64 who were working worked on a part-time basis. The figure in 2006 was 22%. Direct comparisons for women are not possible as Dex and McCulloch's analysis focused on individuals of working age only, and used different age bands. Nevertheless, they recorded that 52% of working women aged 50-59 worked on a part-time basis. As can be seen from the figures in Table 9.2, the proportion in 2006 is somewhat lower. Using LFS data from 1986 to 2003, Francesconi and Gosling (2005) showed that there has been no upward trend in part-time working among women aged 23-59. Their analysis also indicated that, for men in the same age group, there had been a substantial increase in both the absolute numbers of men working part-time and in the proportion of working men who are part-timers.

Reasons for working part-time

According to LFS figures, 84% of men and 92% of women over 50 say they are working part-time because they do not want a full-time job. For men in particular, there is a steady increase in the proportion of 'voluntary' part-time working across the age groups. For example, 64% of men aged 50-54 are voluntary part-timers, compared with 98% of those aged 70+ who are in employment. This in turn means that there is a significant proportion of men in their 50s who are working part-time for other reasons. Once again, using the 50-54 age group as an illustrative example, it can be seen that 21% of men say they work part-time because they cannot find a full-time job, and 12% do so because of illness or disability. The situation for women varies little across the age groups. For all age groups, over 90% of women work part-time because they do not want a full-time job. The reasons for such a strong response were investigated further in the authors' analysis of LFS data from 2004[2] (Loretto et al, 2005, pp 17-18).

According to responses obtained in the spring 2004 LFS, men in all age categories are markedly more likely than their female colleagues to offer financial reasons for working part-time rather than full-time, notably that they are 'financially secure and work because they want to'; and that they 'earn enough working part-time'. So, for example, in total 35% of older men work part-time because they are financially secure, compared with only 18% of women. In contrast, women are more than three times as likely as men to say they work part-time to 'spend more time with family' – 21% of women and only 6% of men give this reason. The gender differences in this respect are apparent across all age groups. Women are four times more likely than men to say they work part-time because their 'domestic commitments prevent them working full-time': 17% of women and 4% of men provide this reason. Numbers are too small (among men) to provide a breakdown by age group.

The 2004 LFS further explored those reasons for part-time working that are linked to caring commitments. Our analysis of these is limited to women, as the numbers of men are too small to make any reliable pronouncements for most of the categories. Women are markedly more likely than men to say they work part-time because of childcare responsibilities: 239,000 women aged 50 and above provide this reason, whereas the numbers of men are too small to be statistically reliable (that is, below 10,000 in total). Nearly 77,000 women and over 13,000 men work part-time because they also care for an incapacitated adult. These figures suggest that parenting, and especially grandparenting,[3] is more prevalent than caring for adults among female part-time workers aged 50 and above.

The reasons for working part-time are consistent with existing research findings, while also providing additional detail. Fredman (2004, p 302) has asserted that most men who work part-time are under the age of 25 or over 55. Women, however, work part-time at all stages of the lifecycle. Others have maintained that male workers are more likely to choose part-time work when approaching retirement age (Dex and McCulloch, 1995, p 68) or when suffering from ill health (Wareing, 1992). Analysis of the second wave of the English Longitudinal Study of Ageing (ELSA) indicates that up to SPA (65 for men, 60 for women) women are more likely to go from full-time work to part-time work than from full-time to not working, whereas men are more likely to move from full-time working to not working than from full-time to part-time work (Emmerson and Tetlow, 2006, Table 3A.2)

Non-permanent working

Figures from the January to March 2006 LFS show that, overall, 96% of jobs held by older male employees and 95% of those occupied by older female employees[4] are on a permanent basis. This is virtually identical to the proportion of 25- to 49-year-olds who work in permanent jobs. The largest increase in non-permanent/temporary jobs takes place after SPA, and so happens some five years earlier for women than men. Apart from that, the gender differences are not particularly marked.

Further analysis of the types of temporary work undertaken reveals age differences, but again shows little variation between men and women. For men and women in their 50s, the most common form of temporary work is a contract for a fixed period, or a fixed task. For example, 56% of women aged 50-54 and 54% of men aged 55-59 working on a temporary contract define their work in this way. This remains the most prevalent form of temporary working for both sexes, until after age 65, where casual working is more common.

Reasons for working in a temporary job

Further analysis of 2006 LFS data reveals that gender differences are nevertheless apparent in the reasons provided for working in a temporary job. Men in all age groups from 50 to 70+ are more likely than women to say that they are working on a temporary contract because they could not find a permanent job. As an illustration, 36% of men aged 50-54 say they cannot find a permanent job, compared with 26% of women in that age group who are working on a temporary contract. In contrast, women in all age groups are more likely than men to be voluntarily working in temporary jobs (for example, 28% of female temporary workers aged 50-54, compared with 23% of men of the same age; or 60% of female temporary employees aged 60-64, compared with 41% of men in that age group).

There are associations between permanency and full-time working, and between temporary jobs and part-time working. Those employees working full-time are also significantly ($p<0.001$) more likely to be employed on permanent contracts than those working part-time. Or, to express it in another way, part-time work accounts for 29% of permanent, and 60% of nonpermanent, jobs among the over-50s.

Self-employment

Older men and women are more likely than their younger counterparts to be self-employed, with the incidence of self-employment increasing with age. For all age groups, men are more likely than women to be self-employed (Table 9.3).

Other research has shown that, in the UK, the self-employed are those most likely to continue working beyond SPA (Smeaton and McKay, 2003, p 30; Barnes et al, 2004, p 33). Moreover, there is some evidence that the death rate of businesses run by older people is lower than for the rest of the business population. However, it has also been shown

Table 9.3: Employment of older workers in self-employment

Ages	Women		Men	
	N (000s)	% of all in employment in that age group	N (000s)	% of all in employment in that age group
25–49	631	8	1,444	17
50+	364	11	1,004	25

Source: Labour Force Survey, Jan-Mar 2006 (weighted). Authors' analysis

that the UK is lagging behind other countries in the proportion of self-employed aged 45 to SPA (Hart et al, 2004, p 5).

Although our analysis supports previous findings that men are more likely than women to be self-employed, the figures in Table 9.3 do show a relatively high proportion of women aged 50+ to be self-employed. Drawing on LFS data from 1995-2001, Hart et al (2004, p 7) found that self-employment among women peaked in the 40- to 44-year-old age bracket and declined among 'Third Agers'. Importantly, the cut-off for their analysis was 59 years old. However, our analysis, which includes older age groups, suggests that self-employment among women *and* men aged 60 and above is much higher than for those aged 25 to 49.[5]

Homeworking

Data from the 2006 LFS show that around 12% of older women (409,000) and 22% of older men (906,000) work mainly from home. These proportions are higher than for the 'prime-agers': 9% of women aged 25-49 and 15% of men aged 25-49 work mainly from home. Within the category of homeworking, women are most likely to work in their own home, whereas the largest proportion of men state that they work in different places, using home as their base. Over half of the men (52%) work on their own account, while women are more likely to work for an outside firm or organisation than to work for themselves. This reflects the gender differences in self-employment already discussed. LFS 2004 data show that 70% of male homeworkers aged 50+ and 64% of female homeworkers aged 50+ use a phone and computer in their work. Furthermore, the vast majority of these (86% of the men and 78% of the women) could not carry out their work without a phone and computer.

Other forms of flexible work

The January–March 2006 LFS does not record other forms of flexible work; the analysis here relies on LFS data from spring 2004 when the survey asked about a variety of working arrangements within the respondent's main job. The prevalence of these is shown in Table 9.4.

The first observation is that the majority of men and women over 50 are not employed under any of these working arrangements: 84% of men and 74% of women say that none of these apply to their job. These proportions are virtually identical to the under-50s. They also show that women are more likely than men to work flexibly. Moreover, there are substantial differences in the type of flexible working arrangement experienced by workers aged 50+. Women are more likely to undertake term-time working and job sharing (81% of term-time workers are women, as are 86% of job sharers), whereas men are more likely to work shorter weeks (67% of those working a nine-day fortnight and 78% of those working a four-and-a-half day week are men). In addition, there is a small minority (characterised by twice as many men as women) who do not know if they work flexibly.

Table 9.4: Employment of older workers in flexible work

	Women		Men	
	N (000s)	% of all in employment in that age group	N (000s)	% of all in employment in that age group
Flexitime	310	10	304	8
Annualised hours contract	140	5	140	4
Term-time working	248	8	57	2
Job sharing	40	1	*	0
Nine-day fortnight	*	0	13	0
Four-and-a-half day week	15	1	55	2
Zero-hours contract	*	0	17	1
Any of these (50+)	768	26	592	16
None of these (50+)	2,218	74	3,099	84
None of these (16–49)	6,450	75	8,143	85

* Numbers too small to be statistically reliable.

Source: Labour Force Survey, Spring 2004 (weighted). Authors' analysis

Number of days per week usually worked

In agreement with the predominance of 'standard' working already seen, it appears that the modal number of days per week worked by men and women aged 50+ is five. Nearly two thirds (66%; n = 2.34 million) of men aged over 50 who work do so on five days per week, compared with 56% (n = 1.65 million) of women aged 50+. However, the numbers working five days per week do decline across the age groups. As an illustration, 70% of men and 62% of women aged 50-54 usually work five days per week, compared with 34% of men and 27% of women aged 70+.

The full-time/part-time split between men and women is seen through the next most common number of days worked. For men, the next most common categories are six and seven days per week. However, it should be noted that only 12% of men say they usually work six days, while 8% claim that they do so seven days per week. Women, on the other hand, are more likely to work three (13%) or four (12%) days per week. Having examined existing patterns of flexible work among those 50+, we now consider what older workers might want.

Do older workers want to work flexibly?

The empirical analysis shows that, with the exception of women and part-time working, relatively few older workers in the UK engage in flexible working. Most work on a permanent contract and only a small minority have access to temporal flexibility within their jobs. Most work for five days per week. As with the workforce as a whole, flexible working among the over-50s is gendered: women are more likely than men to work part-time; and men are more likely to be self-employed or to work from home.

However, this analysis provides restricted insight into the reasons behind the figures. For example, the extent to which many women 'choose' to work part-time or on non-permanent contracts is heavily constrained by commitments to family and gendered employment across the life course. We examine these issues later in this section. First, we believe that there is an even more fundamental issue to be addressed.

Lying behind current government exhortations to delay retirement and work for longer are two largely unanswered questions: do older workers want to carry on working, and, if so, how? And do employers want to carry on employing them? Here we will primarily address the former question. For the purposes of this discussion we can divide older workers into three groups: those who have 'retired' from a career job and may seek further employment in a new field; those still in employment who may wish to modify their work pattern so as to retire gradually; and those currently outside the labour market because of unemployment, caring responsibilities, ill health or a combination of these factors.

Research on older workers' aspirations presents a contradictory picture. Some commentators argue that expectations about retirement are rising and that retirement is seen as 'deserved reward' for a hard working life (Meadows, 2003, p vii; see also Scales and Scase, 2000; Phillipson 2002). While recent survey work has found that attitudes towards work among 50- to 69-year-olds are positive, those in work wanted to carry on working and half of those who were retired would have worked for longer if there had been part-time or flexible work options available (CROW, 2004; McNair et al, 2004). Over half of the survey respondents also said that they might like to continue working after retiring from their main job but an overwhelming majority of these would prefer part-time work. This is borne out by the analysis of LFS data, which provides some evidence that the incidence of flexible working increases among those past the respective SPAs of 60 for women and 65 for men.

These reported differences in attitudes to work are perhaps less surprising if we remember that older workers are not a homogenous group. In addition to individual preferences, older workers are differentiated by gender, skills and education, work history, domestic circumstances, health and location. Professionals and those in managerial occupations are more likely to have an occupational or private pension and a history of earnings, which maximises their financial choices with regard to retirement timing. Those with inadequate or non-existent private pensions and a weaker earnings history may need to continue working, whether they want to or not, while also being more vulnerable to redundancy. For many of those outside the labour market, access to any kind of suitable employment is contingent on their own circumstances and the local labour market. Notwithstanding these distinctions within the older population, flexible work, most notably part-time options, seem to offer desirable possibilities for different groups.

Research suggests that many older workers in relatively secure employment would welcome more flexible work options at the end of their working lives. Opportunities for gradual retirement can be achieved either by a change in working pattern with the existing employer or by bridge employment. Qualitative studies of retirement transitions confirm broad support for individuals to have the choice to downsize or downscale with their current employer in the years before full retirement if they want to (Barnes et al, 2002, p vi;Vickerstaff et al, 2004, pp 30–5).

Research on bridge employment shows that older workers with more advantaged work histories, in terms of income and skills, are more likely to enter flexible employment on leaving full-time careers and are, unsurprisingly, better placed to obtain higher quality flexible employment (Lissenburgh and Smeaton, 2003, p 30). Analysis of ELSA also suggests that those moving from full-time to part-time work before SPA are more likely to be receiving some income from a private pension than those who remain full-time (Emmerson and Tetlow, 2006, p 49).

Evidence suggests that those who combine employment and caring would welcome a range of flexible working options. In particular, they would appreciate better access to flexible working hours; the opportunity to reduce working hours if necessary; the right to time off for caring responsibilities; and the ability to work from home where feasible (Mooney et al, 2002; Howard, 2004).

For those outside the labour market, it has been calculated that among the 2.7 million people aged between 50 and the SPA who are not currently in work, between 700,000 and a million would like some form of employment (NAO, 2004, p 3). For those who wanted to work in the future, over half would consider part–time rather than full–time work (Humphrey et al, 2003, p 106). The reasons for unemployment among older workers are highly gendered. For men in their 50s, the main factors behind economic inactivity are health afflictions and early retirement. Those suffering from poor health are most likely not to be seeking work and many are receiving incapacity benefit (IB). Those who have retired early are more likely to be financially secure and have chosen to retire from well-paid jobs with an occupational pension (Humphrey et al, 2003, p 108). Although health is a significant factor for women also, another main reason for inactivity among women over 50 is 'keeping home' or other caring responsibilities, although the numbers giving this reason are declining (Scales and Scase, 2000, p 17; Barham, 2002a, 2002b, 2003; Humphrey et al, 2003, p 9). (For fuller discussion of inactivity rates, see Chapter Five of this volume.)

Looking after the home and family accounts for nearly a quarter of female labour market inactivity in the age range 50–59 (Humphrey et al, 2003, p 100). Evandrou and Glaser found that one in five mid-life women who were faced with taking up caring responsibilities either worked fewer hours or stopped work altogether (2003, pp 586-87;

2004, pp 782-3). Those working part-time, among whom women predominate, are more likely to provide care and are more likely to reduce the hours they work to accommodate caring responsibilities (Mooney et al, 2002, p 11; Henz, 2004, pp 854, 875).

All of this suggests, as we would expect, that there are considerable variations in aspirations and opportunities between rich and poor. Well-paid older professionals and managers in occupational pension schemes have the greatest discretion in planning and designing a preferred future, which may or may not include elements of paid work, flexible or otherwise. The less well-paid, those with broken work histories and those with few skills may be forced to consider carrying on working through economic necessity if paid work is available. That said, the evidence presented here suggests that older workers often have a relatively positive view of work and that there is support among this group for opportunities to work flexibly, especially part-time. Research indicates that those who are trying to combine paid employment with caring responsibilities would particularly welcome a greater range of flexible work options. Thus, older workers in all three of the groups identified above might welcome greater opportunities to work flexibly but for different reasons.

The prospect for increasing flexible options

So far the supply side of the older workers question has been considered, but a much-neglected aspect of this debate is the extent to which employers are willing to employ or continue employing older workers. Research on age discrimination reveals that attitudes towards older workers are often ambiguous and contradictory (see, for example, Arrowsmith and McGoldrick, 1997; Taylor and Walker, 1998; Chui et al, 2001; Duncan and Loretto, 2004; NAO, 2004, p 27). Employers may see older workers as having particular beneficial attributes. For example, employers target mature women for housekeeping and care work, which is seen as 'familiar' employment for them (Adam-Smith et al, 2003, p 37; Jenkins, 2004, pp 317-18, 321). Older people are also perceived to be more reliable than younger people and may be expected to be flexible in attitude (Adam-Smith et al, 2003, p 38; Jenkins, 2004, p 323). Qualitative research on the New Deal for Long Term Unemployed People, however, reported that older workers felt that employers were resistant to recruiting older workers (Legard et al, 2000).

In order to retain or recruit older workers, employers have been urged to adopt flexible work practices in the face of demographic pressures.

However, McGregor's research in New Zealand (2001) showed that few employers were responding. Among just over 1,000 employers who were surveyed, some 11% offered gradual or phased retirement, and about 25% had job-sharing schemes. While over 700 employers employed part-time or casual workers, McGregor (2001, p 46) concluded that employers were being 'driven by work functionality relating to cost effectiveness of an organization's labour force rather than by human resource policies aimed at attracting or retaining older workers'. A more recent survey of 122 employers (Goodwin, 2004), covering over half a million employees, found an increased spread of flexible work options for older workers.

As yet, relatively few employers formally extend their work–life balance policies to cover the full range of caring responsibilities beyond parenting (Phillips et al, 2002; Evandrou and Glaser, 2003, p 597). A survey sponsored by the Department of Trade and Industry found that younger employees (under the age of 35) were more likely than older workers to request a change in working pattern, although 10% of 45- to 54-year-olds and 13% of 55- to 64-year-olds had made such a request (Holt and Grainger, 2005, p 12). The reported results do not indicate whether older groups were more or less successful in achieving changes to their work routine, although employees without dependent children were less successful overall than those with children.

Access to flexible work options clearly has a role to play in facilitating the management of health issues in the work context both for those still in work and those currently economically inactive. The DWP has recently acknowledged that employers must play an enhanced role in the rehabilitation of employees with health issues (DWP, 2005, pp 8, 43-4). An organisation's response, or failure to respond, to an individual's changing health status, by modifying the work, changing shift patterns or reducing hours, can mean that the same health issue might lead to continued employment in one case and withdrawal from employment in another (Vickerstaff et al, 2004, p 28). A study of older nurses found that relatively minor changes to work patterns could affect whether someone felt able to carry on working or not (Watson et al, 2003, pp 14-22).

Loretto and White (2004a) found little evidence that employers would make adjustments to accommodate the situation of individuals, whether in terms of the hours worked or the tasks performed, and there was scant evidence of the interventions for IB claimants that have been urged by the DWP (2002a). The 37 employers in the study were asked whether they had devised special arrangements for older workers, but only a minority had done so. For example, 17 allowed for a switch to part-time work; 10 provided for phased retirement; but only one employer offered an 'age-sensitive' retraining programme. Nevertheless, there were some examples of positive approaches by employers, including a preparedness to 'work their way round' an applicant's disability.

Those on benefits may face other constraints on returning to work. Despite the government's focus on activation, that is, encouraging those on benefits back into work, there are still perverse incentives in the way benefits operate, especially for couples. If one partner enters poorly paid work, the household may be worse off than if it had stayed on benefits (for examples, see Arrowsmith, 2004, p 36). This may make part-time work or temporary work particularly unattractive.

For more privileged groups in the labour market, disincentives may come from their pension arrangements. Final salary or defined benefit pension schemes, which put a premium on retiring at the point of highest earnings, are seen to discourage downshifting, while career average schemes would not have this impact. However, it is clear from research evidence that many people do not understand their pensions (Loretto et al, 2000b; DWP, 2002a, p 36; Bunt et al, 2003; Mayhew, 2003, pp 73-93; Vickerstaff and Cox, 2005; Chapter Six of this volume). Qualitative research by Vickerstaff et al (2004, p 38) found that this lack of understanding acted as a block to thinking about gradual retirement or downshifting prior to retirement. Tax treatment of pensions has also acted as a disincentive to gradual retirement in the past; new rules introduced in April 2006 allow people to continue working and draw an occupational pension from the same employer.

Although the main question in increasing flexible work options for older people is whether there is employer demand for such workers, it is clear also that some individuals will face perverse incentives in the benefit and pension systems. The 'success' stories in terms of employers' attitudes towards older workers seem to be largely confined to those sectors such as retail where there is a strong business case for employing older staff and in which there are strong operational pressures to use flexible working patterns (Loretto et al, 2005, p 65).

More flexible options: opportunity or threat?

The broad conclusions of this chapter are as follows: unsurprisingly, patterns of employment for older workers are gendered; older women are more likely to work flexibly than men. The majority of older workers currently work standard full-time patterns of work; with the exception of part-time work, there is relatively little evidence of other forms of flexible working such as temporary work or term-time working. Over the past decade, there has been a substantial increase in the proportion of older men who work part-time. The majority of older workers who work part-time say that they choose to do so, although it is important to be aware of the constraints on 'choice', especially for women who are reconciling paid employment with domestic responsibilities. Nevertheless, attitudes towards part-time work are relatively positive in the UK. Yet, the focus so far has tended to be on women in certain occupations in which part-time working is dominant, and on flexible arrangements for working parents. Reducing hours, and moving to part-time work, seems the most viable and the most popular option for older workers looking to downshift their work commitments. This might also fill the vacuum left by younger women who now prefer to work full-time.

It is a supportable assumption that if more flexible work options were available older workers would return to or remain longer in employment. However, there are question marks over the quality of flexible work available, especially for older women. Phillipson (2002, p 2) observed that flexibility can have perverse consequences. Such devices as changes in working hours, early retirement, or working beyond expected retirement date, are often 'externally directed rather than something that individuals are able to determine for themselves'. By deploying part-time workers into a non-central role, managers may be accused of marginalising the workers, lowering their status, and restricting their career opportunities.

Other studies of part-time working among professionals have shown that managers complain of employee inflexibility, while the employees complain of being underused and at risk of skill erosion (Edwards and Robinson, 2004, p 169). Jenkins (2004, p 315), in a case study of part-time employment in a local authority, found that access to training was compromised for part-time employees, who were mainly women. As Jenkins (2004) argues, it is very important to focus on the motivations of employers and investigate the uses to which part-time workers are put. She makes a distinction between three types of part-time worker – core, peak and ancillary – and argues for the importance of considering whether part-time practices serve to integrate or marginalise part-time workers. Older women workers are concentrated in certain sectors, such as hotels and restaurants and retail, where part-time work is commonly used strategically to cover for peak periods of activity (Jenkins, 2004, p 314). Older non-managerial men are concentrated in skilled trades and manufacturing, where the gendered division of labour has traditionally meant that men work full-time and part-time jobs, if available, are seen as women's work.

There are significant age, sector and regional differences in the patterns of economic activity of older workers, which are reflected in access to flexible working opportunities. In terms of sustaining the labour force participation rates of older workers, the research is clear that it is imperative that, wherever practicable, older people are kept in employment; once older workers are out of work for any period of time, they find it much more difficult to re-enter employment. For those with health issues or caring responsibilities that have interrupted their working life, or threaten to do so, flexible employment can be a highly effective option.

At present, the right to request flexible working is open only to parents of young children. As such, it infers an age bias, and could potentially be considered as indirect age discrimination after October 2006. The UK government has been under some pressure (from bodies such as the Employers Forum on Age and the Chartered Institute of Personnel and Development) to extend the right to cover the entire workforce. To date, it has resisted such large-scale change, but has extended the right to request flexible working to carers of adults (Amendments to Maternity, Paternity, Parental and Adoption Leave and Flexible Working Regulations October 2006).

Government's aim to reduce the numbers of IB claimants and increase the participation rates of older workers will be highly dependent on employers' willingness to offer employment that meets the work–life balance needs and aspirations of older workers. As a recent White Paper put it:

We need to:

help employers to examine their recruitment and retention practices and encourage them to support flexibility in employees' working patterns up to and beyond the State Pension Age. (DWP, 2006a, p 69)

The main potential disadvantages for older workers taking up flexible work options are the lower availability of part-time options where men predominate; lower levels of earnings; limited prospects of training or promotion; limited access to fringe benefits; and lower pensions later in life (Dex and McCulloch, 1995, p 28). As yet, we know relatively little about the experiences of older workers who work flexibly or have sought to downshift towards the end of their working life.

We need more research on the extent to which the commercial and organisational pressures that encourage employers to offer flexible working arrangements produce the kinds of work that older workers want.

Notes

[1] Dex and McCulloch (1995, pp 5-6) differentiate between the following 12 descriptive forms: self-employment; part-time work; temporary work; fixed-term contract work; zero-hours contract employment; seasonal work; annual hours, shift work, flexitime, overtime, or compressed working weeks; working at home; teleworking; term-time only working; Sunday working; and job sharing.

[2] These questions were not asked in January to March 2006.

[3] Although the LFS does not differentiate between parenting and grandparenting, analysis of other variables indicates that only a very small minority of older men and women have dependent children under the age of 19.

[4] This question is asked of employees only and therefore excludes the self-employed.

[5] The pattern of self-employment among women and men aged 25-49 shows a steady increase across the five-year age bands, rising to 9% of women aged 45-49 and 20% of men aged 45-49.

References

Adam-Smith, D., Norris, G. and Williams, S. (2003) 'Continuity or change? The implications of the national minimum wage for work and employment in the hospitality industry', *Work, Employment and Society*, vol 17, no 1, pp 29-47.

Arrowsmith, J. (2004) *A review of 'what we know' about partners of benefit recipients*, Department for Work and Pensions Report WAE200, London: DWP.

Arrowsmith, J. and McGoldrick, A. (1997) 'A flexible future for older workers?', *Personnel Review*, vol 4, pp 258-73.

Barham, C. (2002a) 'Economic inactivity and the labour market', *Labour Market Trends*, vol 110, no 2, pp 69-77.

Barham, C. (2002b) 'Patterns of economic inactivity among older men', *Labour Market Trends*, vol 110, no 6, pp 301-10.

Barham, C. (2003) 'Life stages of economic inactivity', *Labour Market Trends*, vol 111, no 10, pp 495-502.

Barnes, H., Parry, J. and Lakey, J. (2002) *Forging a New Future: The Experiences and Expectations of People Leaving Paid Work Over 50*, Bristol: The Policy Press for Joseph Rowntree Foundation.

Barnes, H., Parry, J. and Taylor, R. (2004) *Working after State Pension Age: Qualitative Research*, Department for Work and Pensions Research Report 208, Leeds: HMSO.

Bunt, K., Adams, L. and Kuechel, A. (2003) *Pension Scheme Changes and Retirement Policies: An Employer and Employee Perspective*, Department for Work and Pensions Research Report 199, Leeds: HMSO.

Chui, W.C.K., Chan, A.W., Snape, E. and Redman, T. (2001) 'Age stereotypes and discriminatory attitudes towards older workers: an East-West comparison', *Human Relations*, vol 54, no 5, pp 629-61.

CROW (Centre for Research into the Older Workforce) (2004) *Are Older Workers Different?*, Briefing Paper 1, Guildford: CROW, University of Surrey.

Dex, S. and McCulloch, A. (1995) *Flexible Employment in Britain: A Statistical Analysis*, Equal Opportunities Commission Research Discussion Series, Manchester: Equal Opportunities Commission.

Duncan, C. and Loretto, W. (2004) 'Never the right age? Gender and age-based discrimination in employment', *Gender, Work and Organisation*, vol 11, no 1, pp 95-115.

DWP (Department for Work and Pensions) (2002) *Simplicity, security and choice: Working and saving for retirement*, Cm 5677, London: HMSO.

DWP (2005) *Department for Work and Pensions Five Year Strategy*, Cm 6447, London: HMSO.

DWP (2006a) *A New Deal for Welfare: Empowering People to Work*, Cm 6730, London: The Stationery Office.

DWP (2006b) *Security in Retirement: Towards a New Pension System*, Cm 6841, London: The Stationery Office.

Edwards, C. and Robinson, O. (2004) 'Evaluating the business case for part-time working amongst qualified nurses', *British Journal of Industrial Relations*, vol 42, no 1, pp 167-83.

Emmerson, C. and Tetlow, G. (2006) 'Labour market transitions' in J. Banks, E. Breeze, C. Lessof and J. Nazroo (eds) *Retirement, Health and Relationships of the Older Population in England: The 2004 English Longitudinal Study of Ageing (Wave 2)*, London: Institute for Fiscal Studies, pp 41-82.

Evandrou, M. and Glaser, K. (2003) 'Combining work and family life: the pension penalty of caring', *Ageing and Society*, vol 23, no 5, pp 583-601.

Evandrou, M. and Glaser, K. (2004) 'Family, work and quality of life: changing economic and social roles through the lifecourse', *Ageing and Society*, vol 24, no 5, pp 771-91.

Francesconi, M. and Gosling, A. (2005) *Career Paths of Part-time Workers*, Equal Opportunities Commission Working Paper Series 19, Manchester: Equal Opportunities Commission.

Fredman, S. (2004) 'Women at work: the broken promise of flexicurity', *Industrial Law Journal*, vol 33, no 4, pp 299-319.

Godwin, K. (2004) 'Age diversity: the story so far', *Equal Opportunities Review*, no 131, pp 7-16.

Hart, M, Anyadike-Danes, M. and Blackburn, R. (2004) 'Spatial differences in entrepreneurship: a comparison of prime age and third age cohorts', Paper presented at IGU Congress, Glasgow.

Henz, U. (2004) 'The effects of informal care on paid-work participation in Great Britain: a lifecourse perspective', *Ageing and Society*, vol 24, no 6, pp 851-80.

Holt, H. and Grainger, H. (2005) *Results of the Second Flexible Working Employee Survey*, Employment Relations Research Series 39, London: Department of Trade and Industry.

Hotopp, U. (2005) 'The employment rate of older workers', *Labour Market Trends*, February, pp 73-88.

Howard, M. (2004) *Support for working carers*, Carers UK paper presented to Joseph Rowntree Foundation Seminar, Transitions after 50: Workshop Older People in the Workforce – Mechanisms for Change, October, London.

Humphrey, A., Costigan, P., Pickering, K., Stratford, N. and Barnes, M. (2003) *Factors Affecting the Labour Market Participation of Older Workers,* Department of Work and Pensions Research Report 200, Leeds: HMSO.

Jenkins, S. (2004) 'Restructuring flexibility: case studies of part-time female workers in six workplaces', *Gender, Work and Organization*, vol 11, no 3, pp 306-33.

Legard, R., Molloy, D., Ritchie, J. and Saunders, T. (2000) *New Deal for Long Term Unemployed People: Qualitative Work with Individuals, Stage One*, ESR38, London: Employment Service.

Lissenburgh, S. and Smeaton, D. (2003) *The Role of Flexible Employment in Maintaining Labour Market Participation and Promoting Job Quality*, York: Joseph Rowntree Foundation.

Loretto, W. and White, P. (2004) *An Investigation of Older Workers and the Scottish Labour Market*, Report to Scottish Enterprise, Edinburgh: University of Edinburgh.

Loretto, W., Duncan, C. and White, P.J. (2000a) 'Ageism and employment: controversies, ambiguities and younger people's perceptions', *Ageing and Society*, vol 20, no 3, pp 279-302.

Loretto, W., Vickerstaff, S. and White, P. (2005) *Older Workers and Options for Flexible Work*, Manchester: Equal Opportunities Commission.

Loretto, W., White, P. and Duncan, C. (2000b) 'Something for nothing? Employees' views of occupational pension schemes', *Employee Relations*, vol 22, no 3, pp 260-71.

Mayhew, V. (2003) *Pensions 2002: Public Attitudes to Pensions and Saving for Retirement*, Department of Work and Pensions Research Report 193, Leeds: HMSO.

McGregor, J. (2001) *Employment of the Older Worker: Helping to Build a Better Workplace*, Palmerston North: Massey University.

McNair, S., Flynn, M., Owen, L., Humphreys, C. and Woodfield, S. (2004) *Changing Work in Later Life: A Study of Job Transitions*, Report commissioned by South East England Development Agency, Guildford: Centre for Research into the Older Workforce, University of Surrey.

Meadows, P. (2003) *Retirement Ages in the UK: A Review of the Literature*, London: Department of Trade and Industry.

Mooney, A., Statham, J. and Simon, A. (2002) *The Pivot Generation: Informal Care and Work after 50*, Bristol: The Policy Press for Joseph Rowntree Foundation.

NAO (National Audit Office) (2004) *Welfare to Work: Tackling the Barriers to the Employment of Older People*, House of Commons HC 1026, London: The Stationery Office.

Phillips, J., Bernard, M. and Chittenden, M. (2002) *Juggling Work and Care: The Experience of Working Carers of Older Adults*, Bristol: The Policy Press for Joseph Rowntree Foundation.

Phillipson, C. (2002) *Transitions from Work to Retirement*, Bristol: The Policy Press for Joseph Rowntree Foundation.

Phillipson, C. and Smith, A. (2005) *Extending Working Life: A Review of the Research Literature*, Department for Work and Pensions Research Report 299, Leeds: DWP.

PIU (Performance and Innovation Unit) (2000) *Winning the Generation Game*, London: The Stationery Office.

Scales, J. and Scase, R. (2000) *Fit and Fifty?*, Swindon: Economic and Social Research Council.

Smeaton, D. and McKay, S. (2003) *Working after State Pension Age: Quantitative Analysis*, Bristol: The Policy Press for Joseph Rowntree Foundation.

Taylor, P. and Walker, A. (1998) 'Policies and practices towards older workers: a framework for comparative research', *Human Resource Management Journal,* vol 8, no 3, pp 61-76.

Vickerstaff, S. and Cox, J. (2005) 'Retirement and risk: the individualisation of retirement experiences?', *The Sociological Review,* vol 53, no 1, pp 77-95.

Vickerstaff, S., Baldock, J., Cox, J. and Keen, L. (2004) *Happy Retirement? The Impact of Employers' Policies and Practice on the Process of Retirement,* Bristol: The Policy Press for Joseph Rowntree Foundation.

Wareing, A. (1992) 'Working arrangements and patterns of working hours in Britain', *Employment Gazette,* March, pp 88-100.

Watson, R., Manthorpe, J. and Andrews J. (2003) *Nurses over 50: Options, Decisions and Outcomes,* Bristol: The Policy Press for Joseph Rowntree Foundation.

Whiting, E. (2005) 'The labour market participation of older people', *Labour Market Trends* 113, no 7, pp 285-296.

Office for National Statistics. Social and Vital Statistics Division and Northern Ireland Statistics and Research Agency. Central Survey Unit, *Quarterly Labour Force Survey, January–March 2006* [computer file]. Colchester, Essex: UK Data Archive [distributor], June 2006. SN: 5396.

The source of this dataset is duly acknowledged. The analyses presented in this chapter were carried out by the authors. The original data creators, depositors and the UK Data Archive bear no responsibility for these analyses or interpretation.

TEN

The employability of older workers: what works?

Tony Maltby

Introduction

The everyday, localised experiences and perceptions of older people in accessing paid work, and their retention and progression in employment, are under-researched and under-documented. More often studies consider the implementation of policy at the national level and at the level of the firm, that is, at a macro level of analysis. This chapter[1] provides something unique, since it reports on a participatory and empowering qualitative 'action research' project conducted and funded as part of the Equal Community Initiative's Forward Development Partnership, which was based in and focused on two communities in central England (Birmingham and Solihull). The Development Partnership was established to consider issues of access, retention and progression in employment and offer both practical localised policy implementation and research evidence to enhance the employability of people with disabilities, those requiring 'basic skills' and 'older workers'. The main policy-focused output of the 'older workers' research was the derivation of a 'What works?' list of policy initiatives based on the key research findings (see Appendix), and the primary objective of the research was to enhance the employability of this age cohort. The research demonstrated that continuing institutional age discrimination by employers, unsatisfactory training provision and limited accommodation of health problems as they affect the ability to engage in paid work were the key limiting factors affecting access, retention and progression of 'older workers' (that is, those aged over 50 years). The chapter builds on this evidence to suggest that better progress might be achieved at the national level through the application of the more holistic 'work ability' approach. This has the overall aim of enhancing productivity and promoting the sustainability of the workforce. Conceptually, work ability considers the interplay between all the factors that enable a person to function well in a job. It aims to balance the personal factors, such as physical and mental health, skills and motivation, with the job itself; how it is managed, what the working environment is like and what the role actually entails. The work ability concept of age management aims to encourage employers to tailor work to individuals as they age – and also to improve those individuals' health and skills or knowledge needed for the job (see Ilmarinen and Tuomi, 2004, for a comprehensive discussion).

This chapter therefore offers a review of the salient policy-focused issues followed by a detailed report on the Equal-funded research, including methodology and findings (separated into key themes). It concludes by suggesting that a much more proactive and holistic approach to policy implementation is urgently required in this area.

The current state

As has been well documented in recent years and reinforced within this volume, the United Kingdom, like many OECD countries, is facing a number of major socioeconomic challenges arising from population ageing (Clasen and Clegg, 2003; OECD, 2004; Taylor, 2004). Here the predominant concerns include the ageing and shrinking labour force and the sustainability of the public pension systems. Allied to these worldwide concerns, there is continued evidence of age discrimination in the labour market; acting in contradiction to this is the potential influence of the 'grey' vote (Platman and Taylor, 2004). Moreover, the continued unemployment of older people[2] results in their social exclusion and contributes to their poverty in retirement. Indeed, Bradshaw and Finch (2003) have suggested that this problem leads not only to poverty, but also to isolation, mental as well as physical ill health, distress and disillusionment.

Recent upturns in labour market activity among older people are attributable in part to New Labour's commitment to promoting active ageing as a central feature of its policy and practice (DWP, 2004; Phillipson, 2004; HM Government, 2005a). Yet it is clear that they are also directly attributable to a combination of factors, including a period of economic growth and changes in the attitude of the over-50s and those of their employers towards their employment (Hotopp, 2005). Others suggest that choice is being offered to older people in place of the abrupt, non-negotiable 'guillotine' of retirement (Platman, 2004), even if this is sometimes a forced choice borne out of financial expediency. Even so, 1.3 million people over 50 are claiming incapacity benefits while vacancies remain unfilled, mainly in areas requiring technical and craft skills, people skills (including communication and customer care), and management and supervisory skills (LSC, 2004; House of Commons, 2005). The reform of Incapacity Benefit (IB) and the extension of the Pathways to Work pilots (HM Government, 2005a) may be two ways of reducing this figure, yet the suggested success of the less recent New Deal 50+ scheme as the mechanism for the sustainability of employment is not convincingly supported (Karagiannaki, 2005).

These less practical concerns aside, encouraging and facilitating the skills, experience and potential of older people will result in the filling of unfilled job positions, as is clear both from the Equal-funded research and from other studies (see, for example, OECD, 2004). The policy lacunae between social assistance and the labour market may result in a policy failure and restrict people from working (Gebauer and Vobruba, 2003). Thus, in many cases older people's 'failed' transition into employment is shifted from the state towards the individual (Fergusson, 2004). In policy terms, such generalisations are not aligned with the stated policy of 'support (to) those who cannot work' and speak instead to a 'blaming the victim' culture.

The main aim of this chapter, however, is to examine the employability of unemployed people over the age of 50 in the UK labour market based on the recently completed Equal-funded research. Among other things, this investigated the access, retention and progression of older people in the labour market in Birmingham and Solihull. This geographical area typifies the effects of the decline of manufacturing and is one of great ethnic and cultural diversity.[3] The work was funded through the European Social Fund (ESF), under Round One of the Equal Community Initiative working within the Forward Development Partnership between May 2003 and 2005.[4]

Among the many initiatives ESF embraces, Equal tests and promotes new means of combating all forms of discrimination and inequality in the labour market. Its work includes actions for the integration of asylum seekers. The principal themes of Equal are employability, entrepreneurship, adaptability and equal opportunities, with the work of the development partnership focusing on employability. The overall rationale of the partnership is to develop, test, deliver and 'mainstream' models of intervention that focus on access, retention and progression in relation to the labour market. The partnership has affiliations with key agencies in Birmingham and Solihull that provide a range of complementary skills, and specifically with those involved in the areas of basic skills, 'older workers' and disability. It has also developed 'transnational' links with similar projects in Finland, Italy and Germany, which has led to the joint development of new products and methodologies and the sharing of research and, to a lesser extent, policy outputs.

Methodology

A basic tenet of the action research project was to encourage the democratic participation and empowerment of older people (Barnes, 1999, 2005; Lewis, 2005). It can be argued that outcomes of political decision making reflect the concerns of older people if and when activities and views from 'ordinary' people's lives are incorporated in the process of a political democracy (Barnes, 2005). As Lewis (2005) indicates, the tension between dirigisme and pluralism can be remedied when bottom-up approaches are promoted.

A qualitative approach was selected as the project needed to be developed organically in keeping with the participative framework adopted. Thus, emerging themes could be pursued, inconsistencies checked, and ad hoc and face-to-face discussions given credit (Gebauer and Vobruba, 2003). This method was strongly favoured, since most quantitative empirical studies divorce participation from the delicate link it has with politics and ideology. In addition, technical knowledge alone is inadequate for the resolution of policy problems (Beresford, 2002; Barnes, 2005). Thus, an action research outlook was introduced. The regressive potential of participation, such as the tokenisation of people, the delaying of decisions and the legitimisation of predetermined agendas, was overcome by focusing on empowerment as a central tenet, allowing the data collected to reflect informants' own agendas and 'real' concerns (Beresford, 2002). Indeed, older people's expertise can be recognised through their active engagement in carrying out research (for example, see Warren and Maltby, 2000; Cook et al, 2004).

One aspect of the action research element was realised through the provision of accredited[5] social science research skills training for older volunteers who took part in discussion groups. After attending the course, they were encouraged to conduct one-to-one interviews as part of their accreditation as well as contributing to the project. Additional training in CV writing, job-interview skills, teamwork and other issues relevant to access, retention and progression in the labour market were also made available to all the informants via an innovative personal development programme called *Skills for a Change*, which was based on the successful Pertemps personal development programme, *Cricket without Boundaries.*[6]

The methodology employed within this action research can usefully be divided into two parts: the general discussion group and the more intensive face-to-face interview. A general outline of these is useful, since they exemplify the participative design employed and reflect the grounding of the study in the very local, micro level of policy.

Discussion groups

Between 2002 and 2004, the research team conducted 13 discussion groups with individuals over 50. The average number of individuals in each group was five and more than a quarter of the informants were women. Most members of the group were jobseekers resulting from redundancy, long-term unemployment, retirement, 'incapacity' and illness. The sample was drawn from a variety of sources, including partner client lists (for example, Dinosaurs Unlimited recruitment agency, Jobcentre Plus and the Pertemps employment agency), community-based activities supported by agencies such as Age Concern and a mosque in east Birmingham. Some were recruited through 'snowballing'. The discussion groups were distinctly different from the more structured 'focus groups' that are often used. In the case of the discussion groups, an attempt was made to encourage the active participation of participants and some flexibility in which topics were explored. Each session of the discussion groups started with an effort to create a relaxed atmosphere for the discussions to take place smoothly. For example, questions framed around personal introductions, hobbies and interests and employment histories were posed while having tea and biscuits. Informants were then encouraged to discuss and share their personal experiences of accessing employment locally and any issues arising; the usefulness of New Deal 50+ and Jobcentre Plus in this process; accessing training and its usefulness; and matters arising from the process of job applications. Participants were encouraged to discuss only the issues that were relevant to them. Furthermore, the facilitator (one of the research team) refrained from imposing his personal views and focused on finding the 'authentic voice' (Peace, 1999). The overall process gave participants insight into others' experiences, which in some cases led to self-help, and in others the furthering of contacts among group members. The whole process could be seen as 'redressing the power imbalance' of voices that are under-represented in both research and government consultation (Peace, 1999; Barnes, 2005).

Training provision

Building on the successful discussion groups, letters were sent out to all participants inviting them to be peer research interviewers. Those who volunteered undertook accredited training to equip them with social research interviewing skills paid for by the development partnership. A total of eight people expressed their interest, four of whom undertook the training and assisted the research team in conducting the next phase, the one-to-one interviews.

One-to-one interviews

Following the completion of the discussion groups, each participant was invited to take part in a one-to-one interview. Indeed, the ethos of the interviews followed the same principles and aims of the discussion groups. The themes discussed were more or less the same except for their semi-structured nature. To place the interview in a personal context, each participant was asked about his/her work history. Interviewers were careful not to use the leverage bestowed on them by their position when conducting the interviews. This was mainly achieved by letting informants lead the interviews, which might better be described as structured conversations.

Between December 2004 and February 2005, 13 interviews were conducted, of which the '50+ team' of volunteers undertook six. Heuristically, these interviews confirmed the findings from the discussion groups' analysis. The gender mix of the participants was nine males and four females with an age range of between 52 and 60. The interviews, like the discussion groups, were all conducted in private,[7] digitally recorded, and then transcribed for analysis using NVIVO software. Copies of the transcriptions were made available to each of the interviewees and members of discussion groups.

Research findings
Training

The research focused on documenting the views and opinions of 'older workers' and what follows reflects their perceptions and experiences alone. The research found that the barriers faced in accessing training have had an adverse impact on both the retention of staff and their progression within employment. The availability of finance, time and publicity regarding what is available were identified as the main hurdles. Moreover, informants who had accessed training provision emphasised the need for better quality training and indeed 'follow through' on that training, such as interviews by training providers on the effect of the training on individual trainees' job search.

The findings from the one-to-one interviews on training and

qualifications reinforced those from the discussion groups. They indicated that the training offered by Jobcentre Plus and other agencies is mostly generic in nature and often universally allocated to 'older workers' on the basis that they all require particular skills, such as computer skills, no matter how competent they might already be in that area. Indeed, such forms of training stem mainly from the assumption that 'one size fits all' and the ageist assumption that all older people lack computer skills (see Brooke and Taylor, 2005). In fact, our informants had considerable diversity of experience among them and one respondent, a former CAD/CAM[8] designer, was offered a generic computing course. Thus, consequent to their 'poor' or basic IT training, informants thought that their specific skills gaps were not addressed. For instance, one informant explained the computer training he received as follows:

> To be quite honest the training was so basic. ... I've used a computer for 30-odd years and I learnt how to programme a computer way back when computers were bigger than this table.

One of the oft-cited remarks of the New Deal 50+ informants was that all training provision they embark on should enable them to progress to real and purposeful employment. This is in direct contrast to current practice, where the main driver is meeting a predetermined internal target for jobseeking 'customers' to receive a particular training course, irrespective of its appropriateness. This research suggests that informants' pleas can only be realised when jobseeking individuals are treated as individual entities who manage a range of lifelong experiences as well as interests resulting from often long-term participation in a specific field of work.

Furthermore, career-building procedures are not in place to 'follow up' individuals once they complete such training. This results in dissatisfaction and frustration of trainees and is not cost-effective for training providers. One immediate and practical solution identified by our informants was to revive apprenticeship schemes that allow access at any age. These are disappearing in the UK, yet were the favoured approach among our informants, largely, it is assumed, because many of them originally received their trade-based skills through such schemes. Many of the informants indicated that apprenticeship schemes had worked for them in the past and were effective in securing long-term employment. This viewpoint reinforces the urgent need to exploit the real opportunities that are associated with modern apprenticeship schemes, which ameliorates mid-life career development/change.

Further findings highlighted the lack of financial support to fund training. This is detrimental and creates a barrier to accessing employment. For instance, one participant indicated that he was disheartened by the lack of financial commitment from his employer in supporting his tertiary-level education. Indeed, fair access to education and courses seems to be an issue among older individuals (DfES, 2003). In fact, they usually are pushed into participating in 'soft skill' courses.

Based on these responses, this chapter argues that training provision and advice should be tailored towards meeting the specific skills gaps and career interests of each individual jobseeker. Many of the participants in the discussion groups indicated that their own qualifications were labelled 'outdated' by both employment agencies and some employers. Some of the qualifications reported as being deemed obsolete included GCE 'O' levels as well as City and Guilds qualifications. 'Stripping off' skills and qualifications, especially for those coming from an industrial and manufacturing background, jeopardises their status and self-esteem. In most cases, the types of qualifications held do not *per se* affect jobseekers' employability, although their 'hire-ability' might be affected.[9] The updating and upgrading of some qualifications can enhance employability, along with 'hire-ability' skills such as confidence building and CV writing, hence the endorsement here of the Skills for a Change course. Such programmes are a cost-effective and an optimal option for both statutory and non-statutory training providers, as well as for older jobseekers.

However, there are several older jobseekers who possess industry-based skills and qualifications derived through lengthy employment on a particular task within a particular industry. Driven by the perceived high cost of 'training for purpose' (for example, training someone to be a plumber), government should devise a policy or a mechanism that acknowledges older 'qualifications' among employers. They should not make older people less valuable for employment (Brooke and Taylor, 2005). Rebuilding new work-based identities through tailored training specific to the needs of the localised labour market is deemed necessary. This is perhaps a huge task, as it demands the provision of targeted training and advice, real financial support and the persuading of older jobseekers to make career shifts.

In fact, there were a few informants who had gone to great lengths to invest, or who wanted to invest, in training they felt valuable to the development of a new career. The high cost of such training can create barriers, as demonstrated by the experience of one long-term unemployed informant who described his difficulty in securing £1,000 for a gas engineer training course that could have helped him achieve a qualification that would have secured his future. Devising other forms of 'follow up' is another way whereby government engages in responsive bottom-up policy consultation and restoration. Working in 'partnership' with other sectors and civil society encourages and endorses a 'follow-up' policy agenda (Lewis, 2005).

Government and other agencies

Some informants indicated that the advice provided by Jobcentre Plus and New Deal 50+ staff was not entirely satisfactory for their needs and had created barriers in accessing employment for 'older workers'. The duality of such discontent seems to boil down to the 'target-driven' approach; the lack of knowledge, time and enthusiasm of personal advisers as well as the provision of jobs that are unskilled, deskilling, untenured, low-paid or without health and safety arrangements. The main solution is to ensure individually tailored help and better or more enthusiastic advisers within a similar age range as the client group (Moss and Arrowsmith, 2003). Moreover, a 'non-target-driven' approach in service delivery (perhaps an anathema in the modern managerialist climate that prevails) contributes for better one-to-one contact with jobseekers and helps identify their individual needs (Aston et al, 2001; Atkinson, 2001).

Individuals with diverse and rich qualifications and work experiences are not attracted by so-called 'menial jobs'. The 'one size fits all' approach, where such individuals are seen simply as 'jobseekers' who must be uniformly treated, does not see them as a diverse set of human beings, nor does it encourage or motivate them to seek paid work (Bardasi and Jenkins, 2002; Moss and Arrowsmith, 2003). It precludes informed, critical, inclusive and responsive choices and decisions (Coote and Lenaghan, 1997). The advice provided often disregards the talents and work experiences of individuals and the wrong advice can provide a disincentive to locating paid work. Another interesting finding is that some respondents expressed a strong desire for earlier intervention from government schemes, for example the voluntary New Deal 50+, calling for the removal of the existing qualifying period of six months that is currently a condition of volunteering for the scheme. They could not comprehend why such a condition was placed on them, since, from their perspective, the aim of the New Deal programme is to encourage and support (principally) the unemployed to find employment as quickly as possible.

Moreover, many of the informants indicated that they have experienced little or no feedback from employers regarding their performance at job interviews. This is not a negligible problem because such feedback can be an effective mechanism by which a jobseeker's performance can be improved in future job-searching activities. The non-acknowledgement of job applications and the lack of feedback on job interviews is a widespread practice among employers. Yet our respondents indicated that even when requesting such information through direct contact, often by formal letter, their requests were at best declined or at worst ignored. Paying attention not only to the bottom line but also to the 'triple bottom line' should become an employer's responsibility to the community (Pearce et al, 1996; Davenport and Low, 2001; Henriques and Richardson, 2004).

This research has been able to elaborate at the local level that personal advisers regard older clients as an 'add-on' to their other tasks set within the pressured climate of the achievement of 'targets'. This results in their lack of know-how, a limited time devoted to each client, and a lack of empathy and understanding and a client (customer), who becomes demoralised and degraded. Some of the respondents described their journeys to Jobcentre Plus and other employment agencies as trips to fill various forms and to 'tick the right boxes'. Thus, personal advisers need to develop a more humane approach to dealing with 'older workers'; they need to spend more time with them and develop the capacity to address the low self-esteem, motivation and mental health challenges often experienced by unemployed individuals. Special advisory groups for older people, with training to equip them with the right understanding, commitment, motivation and knowledge, are crucial (Karagiannaki, 2005). Moreover, it is essential that this process includes bringing the specialities of other sectors (for example, the voluntary sector) to the fore through 'partnership' working (Lewis, 2005).

Health and work–life balance

The research informants consistently indicated that the non-existence of a systematic approach to policies enhancing their work–life balance was an impediment to their inclusion in the labour market. Fundamentally, decisions about paid work are often affected by the caring responsibilities many older people have for younger and older kin and friends. The findings thus support the work of Mooney et al (2002), which indicated the lack of policy in this area for what they describe as the 'pivot generation' (those aged 45 and over) (Hirsch, 2004; SEU, 2005). Some of the respondents indicated that they had continuing long-term health problems preventing them from working full-time, and argued for greater flexibility in their working lives (Rix, 2004; Brooke and Taylor, 2005; House of Commons, 2005). Working practices that consider the specific needs of 'older workers', for example part-time work, job sharing, temporary contracts and freelancing, are important ingredients in addressing their particular situations (Platman, 2004). The findings also indicate that individuals experiencing frailty, disability and ill health found the break into the labour market a difficult experience, especially those with a history of mental illness, who experienced an extreme level of exclusion. The acclaimed high level of Incapacity Benefit dependency can be reduced when the transition into work for such individuals is made possible through policies addressing their work–life balance and the sustainable provision of moral and physical support during the job search and even post-employment (as with the Pathways to Work approach). A more radical solution, perhaps, would be the adoption of a holistic approach to the work/life/home balance – the 'work ability' concept pioneered by Ilmarinen and his colleagues in Finland (see Ilmarinen and Tuomi, 2004, and Chapter Seven of this volume).

Age discrimination

Asked about barriers in accessing employment, informants reported that ageism was one of the major negative factors and was experienced from (potential) employers and society as a whole. In general, it was suggested that potential employers were not considering the wealth of skills and experiences older people can offer. In order to eliminate age discrimination, one of the main strategies for the UK government is the implementation of the 2006 anti-age discrimination directive. The hope is that this legislation, together with government campaigns such as Age Positive, will change attitudes that create difficulties for older people in accessing employment (Brooke and Taylor, 2005; Hirsch, 2005).

Interestingly enough, many of our informants possessed little or no direct knowledge of the Directive and its implementation. This could be the result of the government focusing publicity on employers rather than employees. The government's policy document *Opportunity Age* presents research that indicates that lack of awareness can be a real barrier to the labour market participation of older people (HM Government, 2005b). Even so, those who had some knowledge of the directive,[10] with the exception of one, were sceptical and showed lack of faith in the protective power of the proposed legislation, perhaps borne out of personal experience of past anti-discriminatory legislation.

Ageist attitudes, stereotypes and perceptions pervade all the findings discussed above. Age discrimination is society's stereo-drama, which expresses itself through training providers, personal advisers and employers. Many of our informants identified age discrimination as a deterrent to employment. The stereotypes about older people's performance at work, their 'outdated' qualifications, the 'low-level skills' they possess and their 'inability to adapt' to modern technologies are the major forms by which age discrimination is manifested. More often than not, the perception that older people do question things, stand up for their rights, claim higher wages and work for a limited length of time leaves them unpopular among potential employers (Legard et al, 2000; Gebauer and Vobruba, 2003). One respondent speaking about ageism indicated that:

> I found over the last four, five years you get a youngster applying for a job, when I say youngster, 20- to 35-year-olds, you know they stand a better chance.

Other respondents indicated that some employers are reluctant to pay pension contributions for older jobseekers. This resistance stems from the fact that 'older workers' may leave their work after few years of pension contributions. This is perhaps a rational argument for employers, as their motive is often profit maximisation, but strikingly enough, working beyond the state pension age has appealed to some of our informants. One informant, quoted below, describes how employers' concerns over pension funding contributes to the difficulty in accessing jobs:

> I have a feeling that having somebody older to go into the pension scheme seems to be some kind of a sticking point, whether they [employers] thought that I would retire in two or three years and they would be landed with paying a full pension or not.

Most of the informants indicated that age discrimination had played a role in creating barriers in their job retention and progression. For instance, a woman in her 50s with considerable experience of working for women with mental health difficulties and other related social work indicated that her three failed attempts to move to other senior positions were due to her chronological age. She sums up her struggle in job progression as:

> I am finding it difficult obviously now that it is not happening any more [getting a new job] so I can put it down just to age I suppose.

Indeed, evidence suggests that individuals working beyond state pension age have a better quality of life when compared with those who are unemployed and looking for work (Walker, 2004). Under pressure from the European Union, anti-age discrimination legislation is the centre of gravity for New Labour in eliminating ageism but does not necessarily expose age perceptions that are the foundations of discriminatory practices (Brooke and Taylor, 2005). The requirement to accept old qualifications without prejudging their value and the use of the age-neutral job application form adopted and promoted by the Employers Forum on Age can promote awareness and reverse covert assumptions among employers, especially in small and medium-sized enterprises. Indeed, we are already seeing a number of larger employers adopting age-neutral selection and recruitment strategies (for example, Tesco, B&Q, HBOS, HSBC).

Hostile and alienating working environments

Evidence from our informants suggests that job-related illnesses such as stress and nervous breakdown are commonly experienced due to what were described as unsuitable working environments, and here call centres came in for severe criticism. For instance, one participant explained her experience of working in a call centre as follows:

> The calls were coming in and I put myself on what they used to call in 'idle'. That's the term they used, 'idle' because I wanted a drink talking all day and I wanted to go to the loo. Didn't have a break. … I didn't go for the fag breaks and my boss literally said to me, 'Where are you going? I'll do it for you.' I says, 'What? You'll go to the toilet for me?'

Another respondent who had worked as a delivery van driver speaks about the increased stress he faced as a result of management-oriented pressures:

> I was expected, even on the motorways, to break the speed
> limit. ... On the Friday evening, I sat at home and I thought
> well this is ridiculous. I am going to lose my licence or kill
> somebody or kill myself. ... On the Saturday I spoke to
> the boss and I said, 'I'm not putting my licence on the line.'
> That's my experience of taking work out there.

Evidently, the working lives of the cohort in question reiterate the need
for improvement of working practices (Hirsch, 2005). Employment
policies that make work humane and rewarding that encourage
work–life balance through the provision of caring facilities and work-
related and/or non–work-related health facilities, and promote flexible
working hours and even flexi-year arrangements are required. Such
policies promote the welfare of 'older workers' and enable them to
remain in work for longer (Nordheim, 2004; Hirsh, 2005; Chapter Nine
of this volume). Indeed, Platman (2004) indicates that improving the
employment conditions of older people results in a 'win–win' solution
to the problems of skills shortages, increased longevity, growing welfare
burdens and entrenched patterns of early exit from the labour market.
Yet she warns that implementing flexibility without employment
protection leaves 'older workers' vulnerable to the vagaries of the
labour market.

As is the case in many OECD countries, the UK economy has
experienced a decline in manufacturing industry followed by an
expansion of the service sector (Taylor and Walker, 1994; Disney and
Hawkes, 2003; Glucksmann, 2004; OECD, 2004). The findings of
this research indicate that for many 'older workers' some new service
sector working environments, particularly call centres, are hostile
and alienating.[11] Such industries have intensive work targets and
arrangements for frequent monitoring of employees using computerised
technological devices (Moss and Arrowsmith, 2003). This results in the
isolation of 'older workers', as most of their time is spent keeping up
with the pace of work: the modern equivalent of 'working on the line'
(Benyon, 1973). One informant described the detrimental nature of
isolation at such a place of work as follows:

> Now to go into a call centre and to sit down and say just
> get on with the work there, 30 seconds per call, you are
> being monitored all the time and you know you are being
> assessed all the time.

The perception of our respondents therefore is the alienation of 'older workers'. This is exacerbated further, they argue, by the fact that call centres are run by the 'young', both at management and colleague level. Indeed, Brooke and Taylor (2005) indicated that young people are believed to be endowed with better knowledge and adaptability with regard to modern technology. They further argue that the myth of older people as unproductive prevails, especially when they undertake work using modern technology. In such cases, they suggest that 'age-aware' rather than 'age-free' working environments should be introduced for managing working relations and optimising employment, otherwise tension can build up between 'older workers' and their co-workers. This is consistent with the experience of some of our informants who in extreme cases walked out on their jobs.

It should be realised that some 'older workers' have fewer financial responsibilities due to the fact that they have paid off their mortgages, have children who have left home, own private pensions and certainly get better social security assistance compared with what was available in their youth (the epitome of a 'third-age' generation (Laslett, 1987)). Thus, New Labour's employment policy should further incorporate not only 'welfare to work' and an 80% employment target, but also 'welfare within work', enshrined with the work ability concept.

Based on this foregoing analysis, the most influential and important recommendations of this research have been summarised in a 'What works?' list (see Appendix) to help 'mainstream' the activity and disseminate the broad findings. These phrases, taken from the wording used by the Equal programme, have been chosen as they chime with the New Labour evidence-based approach to policy development in line with the Third Way, even though some have argued that there are difficulties with such an approach (for example, see David, 2002; Oliver and McDaid, 2002; Packwood, 2002; Young et al, 2002). It is hoped that this research will have the potential to influence and indeed change current policy and business practice and that it will be important in terms of influencing government departments and their training and work–life balance policies (particularly for those in the 'pivot' or 'sandwich' generation).

Conclusion

On the basis of the Equal-funded research outlined here and other recent work, much of it reported in this volume, the UK government's stated target of an 80% employment rate (HM Government, 2005a) can only be successfully achieved when 'older workers' are valued as individuals, better ways of working are widely supported (possibly via the Finnish concept of 'work ability' mentioned earlier) and stability to work groups is provided (Brooke and Taylor, 2005). Based on evidence from this research, the employment experience needs to be radically altered by the adoption of a 'work ability' approach encompassing the 'active ageing' agenda in full. Whereas the 20th century was the century for the creation of 'retirement', it is suggested that the 21st century will be one of changing working patterns, incorporating lifelong learning, increased leisure and an *absence* of retirement as we currently understand it. This in effect means the full expression of the 'active ageing' principle (Walker, 2002), applying it to working time as well as non-working time. People may still work but 'downscale' their employment activity consistent with the current conceptualisation of a 'partial' retirement.

The findings here clearly demonstrate that there is still much work to do, although it is recognised that there are many positive examples of good practice, mainly, though not exclusively, from large multinational companies. The focus of future research clearly needs to be on small and medium-sized businesses and in particular those companies comprising less than 10 employees; this line of research is currently being pursued by the author and colleagues.

Furthermore, it is clear from the research that although the supply side of the employment equation is widely and formally supported through a number of measures (although they require fine tuning), little localised or targeted support or advice exists for employers of the positive benefits of recruiting workers over 50 years of age and of the demographic imperatives for such transitions.

More recently, we have seen that the policy agenda is moving in this direction with recognition from the Turner Report (Pension Commission, 2005) and Hirsch (2005) among others. The strategy document for the health and well-being of working-age people jointly published by the Department for Work and Pensions and the Department of Health (DWP/DH, 2005) and the appointment of a Director of Occupational Health are positive steps forward – but only small ones. The Turner Report (Pension Commission, 2005) in particular points to the limited focus on and provision of training opportunities for those over 50. This is set against the widespread support for training for 16- to 19-year-olds, a fact highlighted in this research. Frankly, such an emphasis on the young does not reflect the widely reported demographic shifts currently taking place. Additionally, what is currently suggested is limited and piecemeal. A more radical approach and a possible solution would be for further research on the applicability of a work ability approach within the UK context, prior to its full implementation.

Notes

[1] The author wishes to acknowledge the contributions of former colleagues, Lul Admasachew and Martin Ogilvie, to the research on which this chapter is based. Thanks are also extended to lay research interviewers Anthony Gough, Graham Bagnall and Mohammed Afzal and to the informants, who have to remain anonymous.

[2] Here, the terms 'older people', 'people over age 50' and '50+ cohort' are used interchangeably (see OECD, 2004).

[3] Birmingham, the UK's second largest city and its smaller neighbour, Solihull, lie in the heart of England and more specifically the Midlands. They have been dominated by manufacturing industry, particularly automobiles and, historically, jewellery, and have felt the effects of the declines of such industries since the mid-1980s. Please note that the research was carried out and completed prior to the closure of the Rover Longbridge site.

[4] A more detailed report of this project can be obtained gratis from the author.

[5] Through the Open Colleges Network (OCN).

[6] This is a very successful personal development programme sponsored by Pertemps and supported by Warwickshire County Cricket Club. It involves skills training to support the whole recruitment and selection process and addresses issues such as presentation of self at interview; CV and application-form writing; targeting an employment search; and improvement of self-confidence and team-working skills through cricket-based exercises.

[7] Most of the one-to-one interviews were conducted in the interviewees' home.

[8] Computer Aided Design/Manufacture, which requires high competency in computer usage.

[9] Lack of employability refers mainly to lack of skills and qualifications, while lack of 'hire-ability' is more related to self-esteem and CV-writing and job-interview skills.

[10] This includes those who came to learn about the directive throughout the course of the interviews.

[11] Call centres range from those that are highly knowledge-oriented (for example, those providing medical advice) to those where employees require only basic training (for example, customer handling for a utility company) (Glucksmann, 2004).

References

Aston, J. Willison, R. and Konz, J. (2001) *Evaluation of New Deal 50 Plus: Qualitative Evidence from Clients, Third Phase*, Employment Service Report 99, London: Employment Service.

Atkinson, J. (2001) *Evaluation of the New Deal 50 Plus, Summary Report. ESR103*, London: Employment Service.

Bardasi, E. and Jenkins, S.P. (2002) *Income in Later Life. Transitions after 50 Series*, Bristol: The Policy Press for Joseph Rowntree Foundation.

Barnes, M. (1999) 'Users as citizens: collective action and the local governance of welfare', *Social Policy and Administration*, vol 33, no 1, pp 73-90.

Barnes, M. (2005) 'The same old process? Older people, participation and deliberation', *Ageing and Society*, vol 25, no 2, pp 245-59.

Benyon, H. (1973) *Working for Ford*, Harmondsworth, London: Penguin.

Beresford, P. (2002) 'Participation and social policy: transformation, liberation or regulation?', in R. Sykes, C. Bochel and N. Ellison (eds) *Social Policy Review 14, Developments and Debates: 2001–2002*, Bristol: The Policy Press, pp 265-90.

Bradshaw, J. and Finch, N. (2003) 'Overlaps in dimensions of poverty', *Journal of Social Policy*, vol 32 no 4, pp 513-25.

Brooke, L. and Taylor, P. (2005) 'Older workers and employment: managing age relations', *Ageing and Society*, vol 25, no 3, pp 415-29.

Clasen, J. and Clegg, D. (2003) 'Unemployment protection and labour market reform in France and Great Britain in the 1990s: solidarity versus activation', *Journal of Social Policy*, vol 32, no 3, pp 361-81.

Cook, J., Maltby, T. and Warren, L. (2004) 'A participatory approach to older women's quality of life', in A. Walker and C. Hagan Hennessy (eds) *Growing Older: Quality of Life in Old Age*, Maidenhead: Open University Press.

Coote, A. and Lenaghan, J. (1997) *Citizens Juries: Theory into Practice*, London: Institute for Public Policy Research.

Davenport, E. and Low, W. (2001) 'Filling in the gaps – options for developing social ethical reporting in a triple bottom line framework', Paper prepared for the Ministry for the Environment, Social Audit, July, New Zealand.

David, M. (2002) 'Introduction: themed section on evidence-based policy as a concept for modernising governance and social science research', *Social Policy and Society*, vol 1, no 3, pp 213-14.

DfES (Department for Education and Skills) (2003) 'Widening participation in higher education' (www.dfes.gov.uk/hegateway/uploads/ewparticipation.pdf).

Disney, R. and Hawkes, D. (2003) 'Why has employment recently risen among older workers in Britain?', in R. Dickens, P. Gregg and J. Wadsworth (eds) *The Labour Market under New Labour*, London: Palgrave-Macmillan.

DWP (Department for Work and Pensions) (2004) *Older Workers. Statistical Information Booklet*, Sheffield: DWP.

DWP/DH (Department for Work and Pensions/Department of Health) (2005) *Health, Work and Well Being – Caring for our Future: A Strategy for the Health and Well Being of Working Age People*, London: DWP, DH and Health and Safety Executive.

Fergusson, R. (2004) 'Discourses of exclusion: reconceptualising participation amongst young people', *Journal of Social Policy*, vol 33, no 2, pp 289-320.

Gebauer, R. and Vobruba, G. (2003) 'The open unemployment trap: life at the intersection of labour market and welfare state: the case of Germany', *Journal of Social Policy*, vol 32, no 4, pp 571-87.

Glucksmann, M.A. (2004) 'Call configurations: varieties of call centre and divisions of labour', *Work, Employment and Society*, vol 18, no 4, pp 795-812.

Henriques, A., and Richardson, J (eds) (2004) *The Triple Bottom Line: does it all add up?*, London: Earthscan.

Hirsch, D. (2004) 'Improving experiences and options in later working life – towards a framework for UK policy and practice', Unpublished issues paper for Joseph Rowntree Foundation workshop.

Hirsch, D. (2005) *Sustaining Working Lives: A Framework for Policy and Practice*, York: Joseph Rowntree Foundation.

HM Government (2005a) *Opportunity Age. Meeting the Challenges of Ageing in the 21st Century, Volume One*, Cm 6466i, London: The Stationery Office.

HM Government (2005b) *Opportunity Age: A Social Portrait of Ageing in the UK. A Snapshot of Key Trends and Evidence, Volume Two*, Cm 6466ii, London: The Stationery Office.

Hotopp, U. (2005) *The Employment Rate of Older Workers*, Office for National Statistics, London: Department of Trade and Industry.

House of Commons (2005) *Welfare to Work: Tackling the Barriers to the Employment of People, Tenth Report of Session 2004–2005*, Report together with formal minutes, oral and written evidence, London: House of Commons.

Ilmarinen, J. and Tuomi, K. (2004) 'Past, present and future of work ability', *People and Work Research Reports*, vol 65, pp 1-25.

Karagiannaki, E. (2005) *Jobcentre Plus or Minus? Exploring the Performance of Jobcentre Plus for Non-jobseekers*, CASEpaper 97, London: Centre for Analysis of Social Exclusion.

Laslett, P. (1987) 'The emergence of the Third Age', *Ageing and Society*, vol 7, no 2, pp 133-60.

Legard, R., Molloy, D. and Saunders, T. (2000) *New Deal for Long Term Unemployed People: Qualitative Work with Individuals, Stage One*, Employment Service Report 38, London: Employment Service.

Lewis, A. (2005) 'New Labour's approach to the voluntary sector: independence and the meaning of partnership', *Social Policy and Society*, vol 4, no 2, pp 121-31.

LSC (Learning and Skills Council) (2004) *National Employers Skills Survey: Key Findings*, Coventry: LSC.

Mooney, A., Statham, J. and Simon, A. (2002) *The Pivot Generation: Informal Care and Work after Fifty*, Transitions after 50 series, Bristol: The Policy Press for Joseph Rowntree Foundation.

Moss, N. and Arrowsmith, J. (2003) *A Review of 'What Works' for Clients Aged Over 50*, Sheffield: Department for Work and Pensions.

Nordheim, F.V. (2004) 'Responding well to the challenge of an ageing and shrinking workforce. European Union policies in support of member state efforts to retain, reinforce and re-integrate older workers in employment', *Social Policy and Society*, vol 3, no 2, pp 145-53.

OECD (Organisation for Economic Cooperation and Development) (2004) *Ageing and Employment Policies, United Kingdom*, Paris: OECD.

Oliver, O. and McDaid, D. (2002) 'Evidence-based health care: benefits and barriers', *Social Policy and Society*, vol 1, no 3, pp 183-90.

Packwood, A. (2002) 'Review article: Evidence-based policy: rhetoric and reality', *Social Policy and Society*, vol 1, no 3, pp 267-72.

Peace, S. (1999) 'Commentary', in S. Peace (ed) *Involving Older People in Research: 'An Amateur doing the Work of a Professional?'*, London: Centre for Policy on Ageing.

Pearce, J., Raynard, P. and Zadek, S. (1996) *Social Auditing for Small Organisations. A Workbook for Trainers and Practitioners*, London: New Economics Foundation.

Pension Commission (2005) *A New Pension Settlement for the Twenty-first Century. The Second Report of the Pension Commission*, London: The Stationery Office.

Phillipson, C. (2004) 'Older workers and retirement: critical perspectives on the research literature and policy implication', *Social Policy and Society*, vol 3, no 2, pp 189-95.

Platman, K. (2004) 'Flexible employment in later life: public policy panaceas in the search for mechanisms to extend working lives', *Social Policy and Society*, vol 3, no 2, pp 181-8.

Platman, K. and Taylor, P. (2004) 'Introduction: Themed section on age, employment and policy', *Social Policy and Society*, vol 3, no 2, pp 143-4.

Rix, S. (2004) 'Public policy and the ageing workforce in the United States', *Social Policy and Society*, vol 3, no 2, pp 171-9.

SEU (Social Exclusion Unit) (2005) *Excluded Older People. Interim Report*, Office of the Deputy Prime Minister, London: HMSO.

Taylor, P. (2004) 'Age and work: international perspectives', *Social Policy and Society*, vol 3, no 2, pp 163-70.

Taylor, P and Walker, A. (1994) 'The ageing workforce; employers' attitudes towards older workers', *Work, Employment and Society*, vol 8, no 4, pp 569-91.

Walker, A. (2002) 'A strategy for active ageing', *International Social Security Review*, vol 55, no 1, pp 121-39.

Walker, A. (2004) 'The ESRC Growing Older Research Programme, 1999-2004', *Ageing and Society*, vol 25, no 5, pp 657-74.

Warren, L. and Maltby, T. (2000) 'Averil Osborn and participatory research', in A.H. Warnes, L. Warren and M. Nolan (eds) *Care Services for Later Life*, London: Jessica Kingsley, pp 291-310.

Young, K., Ashby, D., Boaz, A., and Grayson, L. (2002) 'Social science and the evidence-based policy movement', *Social Policy and Society*, vol 1, no 3, pp 215-24.

Appendix

What works?

- *Early intervention*

  Early intervention is needed, not after a qualifying period, such as the six months of unemployment needed to qualify for New Deal 50+.

- *Job matching*

  Jobs need to match the relevant skills and experience of the client. Many Jobcentre Plus jobs have a low skill base and are often unsuitable when the experience and skills of the client are matched to the jobs available. There is also little recognition of 'older workers'' lifetime experience of work.

- *Person-specific skills*

  Training offered to unemployed 'older workers' is often too generic. What is needed is to find the specific skills gap an individual might have and address this. This needs to be informed training with real financial and trainer support.

- *Training pathways*

  Correct training pathways need to be identified to enable clients to progress to real and purposeful employment, in other words, 'training for purpose'.

- *New Deal 50+ advisers*

  New Deal 50+ advisers need to be committed, motivated and knowledgeable. This should be a specialised role rather than an 'add-on' role.

- *Career development*

  There needs to be real opportunities for mid-life career development/change. Apprenticeship-style training was favoured among the cohort.

- *Working practices*

  Better working practices should be encouraged, taking into account the needs of 'older workers' within an age-diverse workforce. Work–life balance is a real issue for 'older workers', and some of the new industries (for example, call centres) can be too youth-orientated and alienating to 'older workers' because of the working practices employed.

- *Person-specific intervention*
  The 'one size fits all' model of intervention should be avoided.

- *Support*
  Employment advisers need to provide better training and support.

- *'Older workers' as a resource*
  Employers need to recognise 'older workers' as a valuable resource. This is vital for real change to occur within the labour market.

ELEVEN

Is extending working life possible? Research and policy issues

Chris Phillipson

Introduction

In the opening decade of the 21st century, much uncertainty still surrounds the transition from work to retirement. The causal factors here come from various directions associated with economic, social and cultural change. The economic foundation of retirement has been undermined with the unravelling of state and personal pensions, and the movement of companies from defined benefit to money purchase schemes. The social desirability of retirement has also been questioned, with moves to increasing state pension age in virtually all industrialised economies (DWP, 2006a; OECD, 2006).[1] The meanings attached to retirement have, at the same time, become more complex, reflecting the varied health, financial and personal circumstances of retirees (Phillipson and Smith, 2005).

But reversing retirement trends may prove difficult – at least over the medium term. Governments, for a variety of reasons, are encouraging later retirement along with 'age diversity' in the workplace. In contrast, attitudes and aspirations on the part of working people (especially those comprising the 'baby boom' generation) may run in the opposite direction. This chapter explores tensions in current debates about retirement by:

- summarising current trends in the transition from work to retirement;
- examining the range of factors encouraging people to leave employment;
- assessing policy options for stimulating age diversity in the workplace.

Retirement trends

A well-documented trend in the UK and most industrialised countries has been the declining age of exit from the labour force (Kohli et al, 1991; OECD, 2006). Among men in the UK aged 60-64, labour force participation declined from 82.9% in 1971 to 54.1% in 1991; by 2000, the rate had declined to less than 50%. The proportion of men aged 50-64 neither in work nor looking for employment increased from 11% in 1976 to 27% by the end of the 1990s. In general, male employment rates now begin to decline from an earlier age: as early as age 50 in the UK, according to one estimate (Campbell, 1999).

The move away from paid work was accelerated by periods of high unemployment in the 1970s and 1980s. From the late 1990s, with the move out of economic recession, the shift towards earlier retirement went into reverse, with modest increases in economic activity for men and women in their late 50s. In the UK, 68.6% of men aged 50 to state pension age (SPA) were in employment in 1999, a figure that had increased to 72.8% by 2006 (equivalent figures for women were 63% and 68.4%). Increases in employment were also recorded for people of SPA and over; taking the same years, the figures increased from 7.6% to 9.6% for men and 8.1% to 11.1% for women. The overall employment rate for adults aged 50-69 increased from 50.1% in 1999 to 55.2% in 2006 (DWP, 2006b).

These changes illustrate modest upturns in economic activity among older workers. Together with cyclical recovery, some determining factors include:

- closure or restriction of pathways encouraging early retirement (for example, reduced opportunities for early retirement on grounds of ill health as a result of tax penalties on early retirement 'packages' in the private sector and a range of restrictions on retirement ahead of SPA in the public sector);
- development of programmes encouraging training and returning to work (for example, in the UK, New Deal 50+);
- encouragement of gradual pathways to retirement (for example, expansion of part-time working among men aged 60-64);
- introducing work incentives in pension schemes (for example, the switch from defined benefit to defined contribution plans – retirement behaviour in the latter tending towards later retirement, given the context of a fall in equity markets and a reduction in annuities).

While these measures have produced a modest reversal in trends towards earlier retirement, the evidence suggests that many women and men will be reluctant, or at the very least find it difficult, to return to paid employment. The next section of this chapter reviews the reasons for this, highlighting issues of poor health and disability, and problems within the workplace, as major factors limiting the desirability of paid employment.

Older workers and employment

The research literature identifies a mixture of factors 'pushing' and 'pulling' people out of the labour force. Poor health and disability have been identified in a range of studies as the most important factors 'pushing' people out of employment, although this may not be described as 'retirement', and may not be recognised at the time as a permanent move. Cappellari and colleagues' (2005) analysis of British Labour Force Survey (LFS) data found 45% of men aged 50-65 and 41% of women aged 50-60 experiencing a health problem for a year or longer. The association between poor health and early retirement has been further examined in a range of quantitative (for example, Humphrey et al, 2003; McNair et al, 2004; Haardt, 2006) and qualitative (Barnes et al, 2002; Irving et al, 2005) studies. Humphrey and colleagues (2003) examined factors behind labour market participation and withdrawal among those aged 50-69. Among those respondents who had taken early retirement, 49% (53% of men and 44% of women) gave ill health as one of the reasons. The lower a person's retirement age, the more likely it was that they would have left because of an illness or disability of some kind; they were also less likely to have an income from a personal pension.

A range of 'pull' factors (mostly positive) has been identified, encouraging people to leave work ahead of SPA. Financial security is one highly significant element here, identified in research by, for example, Humphrey et al (2003), Smeaton and McKay (2003) and Lissenburgh and Smeaton (2003). Humphrey and colleagues (2003, p 48) found that those retiring early reported higher incomes than those expecting to retire at SPA. They comment that: 'This suggests that those expecting to retire early were more likely to have had the financial resources to enable them to do this.' Of those expecting to take early retirement, 45% said that this was because they could afford to do so.

The above finding is supported by Smeaton and McKay's (2003) analysis of Family Resources Survey (FRS) data. Their research confirmed the extent to which access to an occupational pension was associated – especially in the case of men – with more rapid exit out of the labour market. Lissenburgh and Smeaton (2003) and Arthur (2003) link access to financial resources to the idea, following Richard Titmuss (1958), of 'two nations' of early retirees. On the one hand, older workers from a disadvantaged background are more likely to leave employment *involuntarily* due to unemployment or ill health, while on the other hand their more advantaged counterparts are more likely to leave *voluntarily* due to their acquired wealth or entitlement to a private pension (see also Whiting, 2005; McNair, 2006).

An important 'pull' factor for some individuals may be a desire to find a new direction to their lives. In the survey by Humphrey and colleagues (2003), of those who had taken early retirement, close to one in four (23%) had done so to 'enjoy life while they were still fit and young'. Among those intending to retire early, 83% gave this response. The desire to spend more time with partners is also important in this context. In the Humphrey et al (2003) survey, this factor was mentioned by 16% of the early retired, and by 50% of those expecting to retire early (see also Barnes et al, 2004).

The idea of professional and managerial groups viewing their 50s as an appropriate point to 'take stock' and possibly leave full-time employment was identified by Scales and Scase (2001, p 5) in their report *Fit at Fifty*, published by the Economic and Social Research Council (ESRC). They make the point that among some groups an 'expectation of early retirement' had become entrenched by the end of the 1990s, with a desire for building a new life beyond main career employment – notwithstanding potential financial pressures. This study points to changes in priorities over the life course, with an increasing number of people wanting a different direction to their lives – released from major financial commitments such as those associated with a mortgage and childcare (see, further, Phillipson, 2002).

Whether the above change will be mainly short term (characteristic of the first baby boom generation) or become more deeply rooted has important implications for policies associated with attempts to extend working life (Phillipson and Smith, 2005; Biggs et al, 2006). On the one hand, changing attitudes to early retirement may encourage flexible working of different kinds; on the other hand, there may be resistance to closer involvement with types of work that fail to add to the quality of daily living in middle and older age (Ginn and Arber, 2005).

Smeaton and McKay (2003, p 54) demonstrate through analysis of a variety of data sets that working beyond pension age is only a strong possibility for those working in the run-up to this stage (see, further,

Haardt, 2006). They go on to make the important observation that:

> It is difficult to re-enter the labour market having left it. Moreover, many of those leaving work may be doing so on health grounds, or because they have sufficient resources to live on in retirement. Rates of leaving work for those who do continue to work drop relatively quickly after SPA for men and women. Even if more people can be encouraged to work after this age, on current trends they could not work for many more years.

McNair and colleagues (2004) grouped their sample of respondents aged 50-69 into 'choosers', 'jugglers' and 'survivors', with the first of these most amenable either to returning to or staying in work. Mostly male, this was the most highly qualified group in the sample; less than one in 10 were unqualified. 'Jugglers' were mainly female and had been out of work the longest; they were much more likely to consider voluntary rather than paid work. 'Survivors' were the most resistant to returning to work: a high proportion had left employment for health reasons; most were men and three quarters were on low incomes. From their analysis of these groups, McNair and colleagues (2004, p 61) drew the conclusion that economic inactivity is 'self-reinforcing', with those leaving the labour market in their 50s standing a poor chance of making a successful return (see, further, Haardt, 2006).

Findings such as the above are highly significant in the context of proposals to raise pension ages (Pensions Commission, 2004; DWP, 2006a). They also create issues for governments attempting to encourage new approaches to productive ageing, these including:

- promoting a switch from an 'early exit' to a 'late exit work culture' (de Vroom and Guillemard, 2002);
- developing strategies encouraging 'active ageing' (PIU, 2000);
- promoting 'age diversity' (DWP, 2002);
- encouraging flexible retirement (Loretto et al, 2005);
- removing incentives to leave the labour force (OECD, 2006);
- combating age discrimination in the labour market through legislation.[2]

Given the research evidence suggesting the range of factors 'pushing' and 'pulling' people out of employment, what are the policy responses that might either help delay retirement or bring people back into the labour market? The next section of this chapter identifies a range of possible responses that might be considered by government, employers and trade unions.

Policy issues in extending retirement

This section examines a number of policy measures that might be considered in order to consolidate the gains in employment made by older workers. Four areas will be examined:

- improving training and lifelong learning;
- developing health interventions and improving the quality of work;
- extending the scope of flexible employment;
- providing integrated public policies to support older workers.

Before examining these areas, it is worth underlining the general point made by Hirsch (2005, p 3; see also Chapter Seven in this volume) that '... a strategy to improve the position of older workers and to give them more options about how they make the transition to retirement needs to rest on creating more *sustainable working lives*' (emphasis in original). Hirsch goes on to argue that:

> Helping older workers in this way is not fundamentally different from helping other subgroups of workers. Older workers are not a separate group within society; later working life is a stage that most of us will pass through. So it is not just a matter of ensuring that a disadvantaged minority gets extra assistance or does not face discrimination, important as these things may sometimes be for older workers confronting labour market disadvantage. Solutions need also to think about ageing in work as a *process* that needs to be better managed. (2005, p 3; emphasis in original)

Extending work life must then be supported through measures that promote attachment to employment *throughout* the life course. Achieving this will require interventions in the four areas identified above, which will now be discussed in turn.

Training and lifelong learning

Access to training and continuing education is a highly significant issue for older workers. Ford (2005a) makes the point that, although many adults aged 50–SPA have highly developed skills and experience currently lost to the economy, learning requirements are higher for them than for younger age groups. He notes that *one in three* in this age group has literacy or numeracy problems, compared with *one in five* of those 26–35. Current research evidence suggests that the 50+ age group often misses out on courses provided by their employer. At the same time, systematic evidence about what works in training older workers is lacking and there is a clear need to know what can best meet the diverse needs of this age group, as well as the range of benefits (for employer and employee) that training is likely to bring.

The Age and Employment Network (TAEN) argues that adult learning and training is still relatively low in national priorities, receiving whatever resources from the Department for Education and Skills as are left over after schools and higher education needs have been satisfied. TAEN concludes that this is leading to a reduction of public resources for adult learning. In consequence, it puts forward the following suggestions in respect of the £9 billion currently allotted to adult learning: first, publicise performance data for advice and adult learning services by age group; second, extend apprenticeships beyond the current age ceiling of 25; third, raise the profile of adult advice services; fourth, remove the ceiling of age 30 on the proposed free entitlement to Level 3 technical qualifications; and finally, ensure that the take-up of entitlement to free Level 2 qualifications reflects the fact that the majority of those who do not have these basic qualifications are aged 40+ (Grattan, 2005, p 7).

McNair (2005), however, cautions that while prioritising Level 2 qualifications and basic skills is important, the strong emphasis on the needs of people aged 14–19 runs the risk of intensifying the neglect of the older workforce. Encouraging Learning and Skills Councils (LSCs) to give greater priority to this group may be important in this respect. The National Audit Office, in its report *Welfare to Work: Tackling the Barriers to the Employment of Older Workers*, notes the limited range of actions currently undertaken by the LSC:

> All 47 local Learning and Skills Councils have now produced Equality and Diversity Impact Measures. However, only seven Councils specifically address issues relating to older learners. These include targets to increase participation, retention and achievement in learning of people aged 50 plus, targets to improve further education data quality in terms of age, and identifying discriminatory practices within the local labour market. All seven have relatively high

levels of inactivity among older people, but there are other
Councils with higher inactivity rates that currently have no
measures for older learners. (NAO, 2004, p 39)

Mayhew and Rijkers (2004) stress the importance of 'continuous
learning during the whole of working life as a means of reducing
the dangers of labour market disadvantage in the older years'. Ford
(2005b, p 10) makes the case for an 'overall national third age guidance
and learning strategy', one that would be linked to the national skills
strategy and would enable adults from mid-life onwards to maximise
their skills and potential. An important element of this might be closer
involvement from higher education and further education institutions
in responding to the needs of older learners, with the development
of new programmes or the adaptation of existing ones to the needs
of 'third-age employees'. Higher education summer schools might be
run for the 'third age' in parallel to those being organised for those in
the 'first age', with a specific focus on issues surrounding maintaining
'sustainable working lives'. Lifelong Learning Networks, to take a
further example, funded by the Higher Education Funding Council
for England (HEFCE),[3] now cover much of England and should be
encouraged to include specific initiatives for supporting older workers
into higher education.

Developing health interventions and improving the quality of work

As discussed earlier, research has confirmed the importance of ill health
and disability as factors that can lead to premature withdrawal from the
workplace. This is especially the case for men and women in routine
or manual jobs, with one third of men in their 50s reporting a long-
standing limiting illness. By comparison, similar rates for men from
professional and managerial backgrounds are not reached until they
are aged over 75: what Yeandle (2005, p 2) refers to as a '20 year "illness
gap"'. The significance of this needs greater recognition in respect
of a preventative approach to health issues at work. Awareness of the
importance of this area is long-standing, both in the British context (for
example, HEA, 1994) and elsewhere in Europe – notably the Finnish
Older Workers' Programme (1998-2002) (see Chapter Eight in this
volume for a discussion). McNair (2005, p 36) argues that the Finnish
experience indicates that explicit health interventions, including job
redesign, for people in their 40s and early 50s can significantly increase
the employability of older workers. He concludes:

Helping people to understand the ways in which work damages their health, and helping employers to design work to impose fewer physical stresses would help with this. So would strategies to encourage employers to review the balance of work across the life course, employing older people on less physically demanding jobs to conserve their skills and knowledge.

Taylor (2002) confirms the importance of this point, arguing: 'A focus on the needs of older workers is almost certainly too late in some cases, although safety nets are essential' (p viii). He argues for preventive support coming through the provision of grants for ergonomic improvements in order to reduce the risk of disability among workers of all ages, and to make work more attractive to older workers. Hirsch (2003, p 17) summarises the issues in terms of developing policies that would '... change the character of work to take account of older people's characteristics as workers'. He argues, however, that '... we are still a long way from the philosophy in Finland that work needs to adapt to help older workers remain engaged and healthy'.

At the same time, it remains the case that extending working life will prove difficult unless more general steps are taken to improve the quality of work. Research such as the Whitehall II study confirms the role of stress in the workplace as a factor precipitating early retirement (Higgs et al, 2003). A range of studies over the 1990s highlighted the general decline in employee job satisfaction (Green, 2005; Ginn and Arber, 2005). Many of the studies in the Joseph Rowntree Foundation Transitions after 50 programme confirmed how pressures at work motivated people to take early retirement (Barnes et al, 2002; Arthur, 2003). Further research is needed to identify specific policies aimed at improving quality of life in the workplace and their possible benefits for extending working life. More information is also required about the problems facing specific groups – notably those from routine and manual work occupations but some white-collar groups as well.

Extending the scope of flexible employment

Despite interest in and attention to promoting flexible pathways from work to retirement, the evidence at present suggests that these remain limited to particular groups of workers and specific occupations. The lack of progress must be a concern, given the extensive debate around encouraging gradual forms of retirement. Platman (2004, p 3) makes the following point:

Policy-makers and campaigning groups have been advocating a more flexible approach to later careers for many years. In 1980, the International Labour Organisation recommended that its member states introduce measures which ensured a gradual transition from work to retirement, by adopting voluntary, flexible ages for retirement and pension eligibility ... Since then, flexible employment as a solution to 'the problem' of older workers has surfaced with increasing regularity in a broad range of international policy briefings, research reports, academic texts and good practice guides.

Loretto and colleagues (2005) have highlighted some of the difficulties in this area, notably around problems of providing high-quality flexible employment and resolving difficulties presented by tax and occupational rules.

Currently, the research evidence to date suggests that very few workers gain access to high-quality flexible employment, and that flexible work options remain limited in scope. What can also be said is that flexible retirement is failing to fulfil its potential in helping people to delay their retirement. Further research examining some of the reasons for the current weaknesses and limitations in this policy would seem strongly justified if progress with extending working life is to be achieved. Much of this will need to focus on *organisational* (firm-specific) as well as *policy* (tax and pensions) issues limiting the development of flexible retirement (Vickerstaff, 2006). In relation to the former, examination of the role of human resource policies and line managers will be a significant dimension. In respect of the latter, the simplification of tax and pension rules will be an essential component.

Hirsch (2003, pp 45-6) makes the point that a key problem is that high-quality bridging employment from work to retirement tends to go to those who were in the best occupational positions before retirement. He identifies a number of possible responses, for example: creating greater flexibility in the benefit system to allow payment for activities such as volunteering within the community; encouraging employers to make greater use of the skills of older employees; and implementing public subsidies to widen the range of employment open to individuals after they have left their main careers.

Providing integrated public policies to support older workers

Finally, an important issue to address will be embedding policies for older workers within the broad policy levers available to encourage labour market attachment. Taylor (2002) argues that 'the current fragmentation of policy responses has often resulted in a range of similar initiatives targeting different so-called "disadvantaged" groups. This has been inefficient and may have weakened their effectiveness' (2002, p 40). Taylor identifies a number of areas for development if this fragmentation is to be overcome:

- Linking policies on age and employment with other areas of public policy such as lifelong learning and equality more generally (see, also, Ford, 2005b).
- Recognition of the associated costs as well as benefits of extending working life policies, for example training costs to help retain workers in the labour market.
- The importance of targeting particular groups in recognition of the diversity of the older workforce (see also Loretto et al, 2005).
- The importance of localised initiatives from regional, local government and trade union bodies.
- The value of providing long-term support to older workers, given a context of increasing risk in respect of career and retirement planning (see also Vickerstaff and Cox, 2005).

More broadly, the task of government policy will be managing the greater complexity of work and retirement transitions in the 21st century. A retirement where *everyone* finishes at 60, 65 or 67 (to take three possible ages) is no longer feasible (nor indeed desirable). This was characteristic (albeit only for men) of what might be termed the *traditional life course* built around three clear stages of education, work and retirement (Marshall et al, 2001). The reality now (itself partly a *consequence* of public policy) is for greater fluidity and flexibility in movement across the boundaries separating each stage (Phillipson, 2002). Policies aimed at extending working life reflect this development. Schuller and Walker (1990) summarised this in terms of seeing the period of the 60s as part of a 'decade of retirement', that is, 'the idea that when people reach 60 they should benefit from a number of years of transition between full-time work and complete retirement' (Reday-Mulvey, 2005, p 37).

Central tasks for public policy arising from implementing this approach include, first, ensuring that significant numbers of people are not excluded from the benefits of greater flexibility in moving from work to retirement; and second, helping people to secure greater control over transitions after 50. The basis for this might be supporting extending working life measures with three types of policy:

- Those designed to create greater choice and flexibility about moves in and out of work (such as career breaks and time credit systems), with the possibility of spreading work more evenly across the life course (Simeons and Denys, 2001).
- Those that enhance the capacity of older workers as a group – through training, improvements to the work environment, lifelong learning and the development of anti-discrimination policies (Ford, 2005b; Hirsch, 2005).
- Those that encourage support towards the end of the working life, with the promotion of gradual retirement and preparation for retirement (McNair, 2005a).

Action on these points will be essential for tackling what has been termed the 'cycle of deskilling' (Platman, 1999) affecting older workers, this arising from limited educational opportunities and restricted job-related training. The challenge for public policy is to create the conditions for greater choice within the various transitions experienced by those aged 50-69. Promoting extending working life as an inclusive policy, one that can meet the diversity of groups among older workers, will be a crucial test for the implementation of policy provision in this area.

Conclusion

This chapter has reviewed factors taking people out of, or limiting the likelihood of their returning to, paid employment ahead of pension age. The areas identified, notably problems relating to poor health, responsibilities for informal care, stress within the workplace and changing attitudes to work, indicate potential obstacles to implementing policies for extending working life. Meeting this objective will require further progress on the policies discussed, with major attention to areas such as health promotion in the workplace, improving the quality of employment, and raising the profile of training for those aged 50-SPA.

Central tasks for public policy in supporting older workers include, first, ensuring that significant numbers of people are not excluded from the benefits of greater flexibility in moving from work to retirement; and second, helping people to secure greater control over transitions after 50, for example through measures aimed at improving financial security and alleviating poverty and social exclusion. Critical thinking will also be required on the major questions raised by the policy debates running through work and retirement issues. In particular:

- What are the social and economic implications of rising aspirations and expectations about retirement? How are these likely to vary within and across cohorts? To what extent do these aspirations reflect and reinforce existing patters of inequality?
- What are the likely obstacles (and potential solutions) to achieving 'age diversity' within the workplace? What forms of job redesign might be appropriate to assist those willing to continue in work into their 60s and beyond?
- What are the problems that might be encountered (by organisations and individuals) in implementing flexible employment policies such as gradual retirement, time credit systems and career breaks? If considered desirable and appropriate, what sort of incentives would be needed to introduce such policies?
- If work-to-retirement transitions are becoming more complex, what implications does this have for supporting people combining different transitions associated with family, working and retirement lives? What is the balance of individual and government responsibility in this area?

In conclusion, the underlying theme of this chapter would support the view of Ghilarducci (2006), who in a recent study makes the point: 'Just because some of us will expect to live longer than our parents does not mean that [we] should work longer.'[4] In other words, we should be careful about accepting the assumption that living longer means retiring later – a policy that is now being pursued with vigour in public and social policy (OECD, 2006). Many people may still want to embrace a 'culture of retirement', even if it means a 'trade-off' with a lower standard of living (Costa, 1998). Many people, as the research suggests, are unable to continue working because of poor health or a disability of some kind. And work environments do not make continued employment a satisfactory experience for a significant number of workers – especially those who move into part-time or casual forms of employment. So we need to be careful about abandoning retirement as a social as well as an economic institution (one that might be regarded as a major triumph of the previous century), and we will certainly need to be mindful of the new insecurities that older workers will experience in the turbulent labour markets of the 21st century.

Acknowledgements

I am grateful to Sarah Vickerstaff, Phil White and Wendy Loretto for the opportunity to present these findings at the ESRC seminar. The research on which the chapter is based was supported by the

Department for Work and Pensions (DWP) and I am grateful to David Johnson at DWP for his help during the project. Allison Smith provided considerable help in the collection of data for the study and I am much in her debt for her assistance.

Notes

[1] The OECD (2006) monograph *Live Longer, Work Longer* provides an assessment of current work and retirement policies across the major industrialised economies.

[2] The 2006 Employment Equality (Age) Regulations were introduced on 1 October 2006 in the UK to protect workers from age discrimination.

[3] See the website of the Higher Education Funding Council for England for further information about the characteristics of Lifelong Learning Networks.

[4] www.monthlyreview.org/0506ghilarducci.htm (accessed 4 November 2006.

References

Arthur, S. (2003) *Money, Choice and Control*, Bristol/York: The Policy Press for Joseph Rowntree Foundation.

Barnes, H., Parry, J. and Lakey, J. (2002) *Forging a New Future: The Experiences and Expectations of People Leaving Paid Work over 50*, Bristol: The Policy Press.

Barnes, H., Parry, J. and Taylor, R. (2004) *Working After State Pension Age: Qualitative Research*, Department for Work and Pensions Research Report 208, London: Department for Work and Pensions.

Biggs, S., Phillipson, C., Leach., R and Money, A.-M. (2006) *Baby Boomers and Adult Ageing in Public Policy: The Changing Relationship between Production and Consumption*. Cultures of Consumption Working Paper No 27, ESRC/AHRC Research Programme (www.consume.bbk.ac.uk).

Campbell, N. (1999) *The Decline of Employment Among Older People in Britain*, London: Council for Advancement and Support of Education.

Cappellari, L., Dorsett, R. and Haile, G. (2005) *Labour Market Transitions among the Over-50s*, London: Department for Work and Pensions.

Costa, D. (1998) *The Evolution of Retirement*, Chicago, IL: University of Chicago Press.

de Vroom, B. and Guillemard, A.M. (2002) 'From externalisation to integration of older workers: institutional changes at the end of the worklife', in J.G. Anderson and P.H. Jensen (eds) *Changing Labour Markets, Welfare Policies and Citizenship*, Bristol: The Policy Press, pp 183-208.

DWP (Department for Work and Pensions) (2002) *Being Positive about Age Diversity at Work*, London: DWP.

DWP (2006a) *Security in Retirement: Towards a New Pension System*, London: DWP.

DWP (2006b) *Older Workers: Statistical Information Booklet*, London: DWP.

Ford, G. (2005a) *Am I Still Needed? Guidance and Learning for Older Adults*, Derby: Centre for Guidance Studies, University of Derby.

Ford, G. (2005b) 'Am I still needed?: Guidance and learning for older adults', in D. Hirsch (ed) *Sustaining Working Lives: A Framework for Policy and Practice*, York: Joseph Rowntree Foundation.

Ghilarducci, T. (2006) 'The end of retirement', *Monthly Review*, vol 58, no 1 (www.monthlyreview.org).

Ginn, A. and Arber, S. (2005) 'Longer working: imposition or opportunity? Midlife attitudes to work across the 1990s', *Quality in Ageing*, vol 6, no 2, pp 26-35.

Grattan, P. (2005) *Third Age Employment Network (TAEN): Submission to the Pensions Commission*, London: TAEN.

Green, F. (2005) *Understanding Trends in Job Satisfaction: Final Report*, Report to the Economic and Social Research Council, Swindon: ESRC.

Haardt, D. (2006) *Transitions out of and back to Employment among Older Men and Women in the UK*, Working Paper 2006-20, Essex: Institute of Economic and Social Research.

HEA (Health Education Authority) (1994) *Investing in Older People at Work*, London: HEA.

Higgs, P., Mein, G., Ferrie, J., Hyde, M. and Nazroo, J. (2003) 'Pathways to early retirement: structure and agency in decision-making among British civil servants' *Ageing and Society*, vol 23, no 6, pp 761-78.

Hirsch, D. (2003) *Crossroads after 50: Improving Choices in Work and Retirement*, York: Joseph Rowntree Foundation.

Hirsch, D. (2005) *Sustaining Working Lives: A Framework for Policy and Practice*, York: Joseph Rowntree Foundation.

Humphrey, A., Costigan, P., Pickering, K., Stratford, N. and Barnes, M. (2003) *Factors Affecting the Labour Market: Participation of Older Workers*, London: Department for Work and Pensions.

Irving, P., Steels, J. and Hall, N. (2005) *Factors Affecting the Labour Market: Participation of Older Workers: Qualitative Research*, Department for Work and Pensions Research Report 281, London: Department for Work and Pensions.

Kohli, M., Rein, M., Guillemard, A.-M. and van Gunsteren, H. (1991) *Time for Retirement: Comparative Studies of Early Exits from the Labour Force*, Cambridge: Cambridge University Press.

Lissenburgh, S. and Smeaton, D. (2003) *Employment Transitions of Older Workers: The Role of Flexible Employment in Maintaining Labour Market Participation and Promoting Job Quality*, Bristol/York: The Policy Press for Joseph Rowntree Foundation.

Loretto, W., Vickerstaff, S. and White, P. (2005) *Older Workers and Options for Flexible Work*, Working Paper Series No 31, Manchester: Equal Opportunities Commission.

Marshall, V.W., Heinz, W.R., Krüger, H. and Vermer, A. (eds) (2001) *Restructuring Work and the Life Course*, Toronto: University of Toronto Press.

Mayhew, K. and Rijkers, B. (2004) 'How to improve the human capital of older workers, or the sad tale of the magic bullet', Paper prepared for the joint EC/OECD seminar on Human Capital and Labour Market Performance, 8 December, Brussels.

McNair, S. (2005) 'The age of choice: a new agenda for learning and work', in A. Tuckett and A. McAulay (eds) *Demography and Older Learners*, Leicester: National Institute of Adult Continuing Education, pp 27-38.

McNair, S. (2006) 'How different is the older labour market? Attitudes to work and retirement among older people in Britain', *Social Policy and Society*, vol 5, no 4, pp 485-94.

McNair, S., Flynn, M., Owen, L., Humphreys, C. and Woodfield, S. (2004) *Changing Work in Later Life: A Study of Job Transitions*, Guildford: Centre for Research into the Older Workforce, University of Surrey.

NAO (National Audit Office) (2004) *Welfare to Work: Tackling the Barriers to the Employment of Older People*, Report by the Comptroller and Auditor General, HC1026 Session 2003-04, London: The Stationery Office.

OECD (Organisation for Economic Co-operation and Development) (2006) *Live Longer, Work Longer*, Paris: OECD.

Pensions Commission (2004) *Pensions: Challenges and Choices*, First Report of the Pensions Commission, Norwich: The Stationery Office.

Phillipson, C. (2002) *Transitions from Work to Retirement: New Patterns of Work and Retirement*, Bristol: The Policy Press.

Phillipson, C. and Smith, C. (2005) *Extending Working Life: A Review of the Research Literature*, London: Department for Work and Pensions.

PIU (Performance and Innovation Unit) (2000) *Winning the Generation Game*, London: The Stationery Office.

Platman, K. (1999) *The Glass Precipice: Employability for a Mixed Age Workforce*, London: Employers Forum on Aging.

Platman, K. (2004) 'Flexible employment in later life: public policy panaceas in the search for mechanisms to extend working lives', *Social Policy and Society*, vol 3, no 2, pp 181-8.

Reday-Mulvey, G. (2005) *Working Beyond 60: Key Policies and Practices in Europe*, London: Palgrave Macmillan.

Scales, J. and Scase, R. (2001) *Fit and Fifty*, Swindon: Economic and Social Research Council.

Schuller, T. and Walker, A. (1990) *The Time of our Life: Education, Employment and Retirement in the Third Age*, London: Institute for Public Policy Research.

Simeons, P. and Denys, J. (2001) 'The career break as an alternative to early-exit schemes', in V.W. Marshall, W.R. Heinz, H. Krüger and A. Vermer (eds) (2001) *Restructuring Work and the Life Course*, Toronto: University of Toronto Press, pp 360-74.

Smeaton, D. and McKay, S. (2003) *Working after State Pension Age: Quantitative Analysis*, Department for Work and Pensions Research Report 182, London: Department for Work and Pensions.

Taylor, P. (2002) *New Policies for Older Workers*, Bristol/York: The Policy Press for Joseph Rowntree Foundation.

Titmuss, R.M. (1958) *Essays on 'The Welfare State'*, London: Allen and Unwin.

Vickerstaff, S. (2006) 'Entering the retirement zone: how much choice do individuals have?', *Social Policy and Society*, vol 5, no 4, pp 507-17.

Vickerstaff, S. and Cox, J. (2005) 'Retirement and risk: the individualisation of retirement and experiences?', *The Sociological Review*, vol 53, no 1, pp 77-95.

Whiting, E. (2005) 'The labour market participation of older people', *Labour Market Trends*, vol 113, no 7, pp 285-96.

Yeandle, S. (2005) *Older workers and work–life balance* (www.jrf.org.uk/bookshop/ebooks/olderworkersandworklifebalance.pdf)

TWELVE

The future for older workers: opportunities and constraints

Sarah Vickerstaff, Wendy Loretto and Phil White

This concluding chapter reviews the common and emerging themes from the contributions to this collection and points to what are likely to be the key issues for older workers, their employers and their governments in the coming decades. Following an initial assessment of the concerns, problems and opportunities expressed by the contributors, the chapter is divided into four sections: first, a discussion of government policy and legislative developments that are changing the employment landscape for older workers; second, a consideration of the perspectives of employers as to the threats and opportunities they associate with an ageing workforce; third, an assessment of what older individuals themselves aspire to; and, finally, a conclusion about the main opportunities and constraints that an ageing workforce implies.

Certain key themes emerge from the chapters in this volume, which should guide future research and policy development in the field. The first of these to note, which is easy to attest to and sometimes more difficult to genuinely build into research and policy, is the heterogeneity of older workers. The shorthand of an age cohort (50 years old and over) can all too easily lead us down the road of forgetting that, among those in this age bracket, we are talking about a number of different generations, individuals differentiated by gender, ethnic origin, levels of income, health status and domestic circumstances, never mind differences in outlook and aspirations. In the ESRC seminar series from which this volume springs, there were participants who wanted to reject the very notion of 'older workers' for this reason. However, other available terms, such as seniors (Aliaga and Romans, 2006), common in the United States, have yet to take hold in the UK context. The diversity of the older population must be acknowledged and explored in research and policy but another aspect is also worthy of attention; namely, that each generation faces different challenges with regard to continuing to work and to retirement timing. The economic, social and political context is not stable, and hence each generation has a different pattern of saving and pension entitlement and different expectations about extending or restricting working life, and faces varying retirement ages and pension values according to economic and political developments. This is no more aptly demonstrated than by the current generation of older women (in their 80s) for whom female employment outside the home was more exceptional compared with younger generations of women who will be engaged in paid employment for more of their lives and will face different state pension rules and entitlements. Another factor associated with current low labour market participation rates for older groups, that of low or no qualifications (see, for example, Zaidi et al, 2006), is similarly something that is changing as younger generations are more likely to have stayed in education longer and are less likely to have left without any qualifications. Thus, in some sense each generation faces a unique bundle of incentives and disincentives to continue working into older age.

This leads us on to two other very important themes that emerge from the chapters in this volume: the importance of a life-course perspective and the increasing role of uncertainty within it. With respect to the life course, it is clear that choices and opportunities around retirement are heavily conditioned by individuals' work histories in terms of wealth and pensions, but also in how these affect health and attitude and motivation to work. As if to underline the intractability of certain issues here, a recent report produced jointly by a pension provider (Scottish Widows) and the Equal Opportunities Commission (EOC) found that almost one third of women had no pension provision at all, and half of all women who were saving for retirement stopped doing so when they had children (Inman, 2006). So we need to map further how work history opens up or shuts off possibilities in later life.

Another feature of taking a life-course perspective is the need to consider the extent to which transitions, such as that from work to retirement, are, in the contemporary world, less patterned and predictable than they may have been in the past (see Vickerstaff and Cox, 2005; Vickerstaff, 2006). In the work of sociologists such as Ulrich Beck (2000), changes in the labour market, and especially the increased insecurity associated with changing employment patterns, have overturned the old certainties. The experience of retirement, the degree of volition the individual has over its manner and timing, and the degree of financial security that can be expected, has become individualised, unpredictable and risky. As one example of such risk, those who have been adversely affected by endowment mortgage mis-selling may now have to prolong their working lives to pay off their mortgages, let alone providing for their old age. However, such shocks may, paradoxically, induce people to eschew planning, on the grounds that such efforts are futile. It may be that the past 30 years or so comes to be seen as a golden age, an era that will not be repeated, in which many were able to retire early with good occupational pensions (Walker et al, 2006, p 13).

The life-course perspective is also very instructive in reminding us that older workers share much with workers of all ages in wanting a better balance between work and the rest of life and the ability to make choices about how and when they work. Increasingly, opportunities to work flexibly, in terms of hours and roles, are thought to be crucial in extending working lives (see Chapter Nine of this volume). This train of thought is taken further by a number of contributors who have argued that we need to rethink the concept of working lives and move away from the assumption that a working life starts after school or college and continues uninterrupted until retirement; we need to build flexibility into our concept of a working life (see Chapter Seven of this volume) as well as our concept of retirement (Schultz, 2002).

It seems clear from the contributions throughout the book that we are in some senses at the threshold of a new era when many people will either want or have to work for longer and paths into full retirement will become more varied and diverse. Crucial to how this new period will develop are the roles of the various stakeholders: governments who want people to work for longer; employers who will employ older workers; and individuals who will seek to make decisions about when and how to retire. This chapter turns now to consider the view from the bridge for these different stakeholders. Although a discrete section has been devoted to each, it should be borne in mind that the issues discussed, for example legislation, are often pertinent to all the parties.

The government role in extending working life

Governments across Europe, the US, Canada and Australia are keen to encourage people to delay retiring and to extend their working lives. There are a number of different ways in which a government can try to have an impact in this area: through legislation designed to reduce or eliminate discrimination; by raising state pension ages; by reducing incentives in the benefit and pensions regimes to retire early or take ill-health or disability pathways out of the labour market; by active supply-side labour market policies, such as measures to encourage and subsidise people into or back into work, measures to make work pay or a range of training policy measures; or by its own actions as a major employer.

In October 2006, Britain, under obligation to implement the European Community Directive on Equal Treatment in Employment and Occupation, joined a band of countries with explicit anti-age discrimination legislation. It is as yet too soon to comment on the impact of the new Employment Equality (Age) Regulations. The regulations make it unlawful to directly or indirectly discriminate against someone on the basis of their age, but, as with other discrimination legislation, the individual may be subject to complex and multiple forms of discrimination (such as 'gendered ageism', Duncan and Loretto, 2004) and be poorly briefed as to what protection the law conveys. The new law also maintains a default normal retirement age of 65 (which in itself might appear discriminatory). It will not be legal to retire someone before they are 65 unless it is by agreement or for a reason with 'objective justification'.

International experience of the impact of age discrimination legislation on the labour market participation of older workers is mixed (see Chapters Three and Four of this volume; Hornstein et al, 2001). As Macnicol demonstrates in Chapter Three, legislation is not a panacea and may simply benefit some groups (for example, white males) more than others. The American legal position may have served to create a difference between the opportunities for insiders and outsiders, as Lahey comments: 'Although the laws as they currently exist provide a boon for older men who remain in their jobs and are more difficult to fire, they harm those seeking employment' (2006, p 5). On balance, the evidence suggests that legislation does have some impact on employer behaviour with respect to hiring, promotion and redundancy practices; however, it is less clear whether social attitudes to older workers have been dramatically altered through such legislation (Hornstein et al, 2001, pp viii–ix). As Casey argues in Chapter Four of this volume, structural features of the economy and the prevailing economic climate are central factors in the attractiveness of older workers to employers. Hornstein and colleagues, in their review of the impact of legislation in the US, Canada and Australia, conclude:

> A clear observation on the effectiveness of age discrimination legislation, based on the experience of several countries, is that it is greatly helped by operating in conjunction with other policies to promote equal rights and educate employers and workers about their obligations and rights. There is no real choice between legislation and other methods of promoting non-discriminatory behaviour. The various approaches interact and enhance the overall impact.

> Certainly legislation on its own is unlikely to change the employment culture. (2001, p viii)

In the British case, there are grounds for expecting that litigation over the age regulations in the employment tribunals will be inhibited in the early stages of the new law, because there is currently no commission to bring test cases to tribunals, in the manner of such bodies as the EOC. The Commission on Equality and Human Rights, covering issues of gender, disability and age discrimination, will operate from October 2007, eventually also covering race discrimination from 2009. Until then, individuals are left very much to their own devices, and may feel daunted by the prospect of litigation.

There are, however, other grounds for envisaging considerable tribunal scrutiny. First, in contrast to other anti-discrimination measures, focusing on segments of employees, the age regulations apply to all persons, whether at the younger or older end of the spectrum. Second, the very basis of the regulations was already being challenged before they came into force. The charge is that the government, by allowing employers compulsorily to retire employees at or beyond the age of 65, was in breach of the 2000 directive. The case was brought by Heyday, a body giving advice on retirement issues (www.heyday.org.uk). The High Court, exceptionally, allowed for an initial oral hearing in early December 2006, in order to expedite matters. At the time of writing, the case has been referred to the European Court of Justice for its ruling.

The third justification for expecting litigation lies in the framing of the regulations: some are drawn so loosely that tribunal cases may be the only way to make the law somewhat clearer. For example, while it is generally unlawful for employers to specify the age requirements sought from applicants, the Department of Trade and Industry gave minimal guidance as to what words or phrases in job adverts would fall foul of the law. The fourth, and perhaps the most fundamental, justification stems from the extraordinary complexity of age discrimination itself (Macnicol, 2006, pp 17-18). The vagaries of policy making aside, that perspective helps to explain why those parts of the regulations concerned with pension schemes and discrimination were deferred until December 2006.

Another way in which governments can try to have an impact on retirement ages is by raising state pension ages and/or 'loosening' retirement ages in the sense of providing incentives to retire later by beneficial deferral rates for those who take up their state pension later than the norm. A recent OECD review of age and employment policies in 21 countries concluded that 'the overall trend is for the official pension age to rise' (2006, p 90) and that women have seen the most significant changes as their state pension ages are equalised with those of men. Government policy is now firmly in place for a raising of the state pension age in Britain: after the equalisation of men's and women's ages at 65 by 2020, a progressive raising for both sexes, from age 65 to 68, will get under way from 2024 to 2044 (DWP, 2006a). Such moves are not well liked with populations at large. There is evidence to suggest that people generally look forward to retirement and see it as a just reward for a long working life. In the past 30 years, 'early retirement' for professionals and managers has to some extent become entrenched as an expectation in Britain (Meadows, 2003, p vii; Phillipson, 2002; Scales and Scase, 2000, p 5), or at least as a possible choice. The social acceptability of working longer is therefore another important factor in older individuals' orientation to paid employment. Increasing opportunities for flexible retirement is seen as one way of making working for longer more attractive to individuals (DWP, 2006b).

The structure of available state benefits for older workers who lose their jobs and the rules of pension provision (both public and private) can have an impact on the decisions made by individuals about whether to continue in employment or not. The government in Britain is keen that the benefit system does not encourage people to stay out of the labour market if they are able to participate (DWP, 2002, p 24). The move to an active welfare state regime for those out of work through the New Deal programmes, which provide one-to-one support and guidance for those out of work, has also had the effect of pushing more older workers on to benefits other than jobseeker's allowance, as Beatty and Fothergill demonstrate in Chapter Five of this volume. In the past, incapacity benefit (IB) appears to have provided a route to early withdrawal from the labour market in the face of redundancy or unemployment, especially for unskilled or skilled manual working men. Alcock et al (2003) have characterised this as 'hidden unemployment'. Government efforts are now firmly focused on reducing the numbers of people on IB and getting as many as possible of them back into work through the Pathways to Work programme (Chapter Five of this volume; see also Pendleton, 2006). It is expected that opportunities to work part-time or other forms of flexible employment will be very significant for those with long-standing health conditions who are trying to get back into work. However, there are still perverse incentives in the way benefits operate, especially for couples. If one partner enters poorly paid work, the household may be worse off than if they had stayed on benefits (for examples, see Arrowsmith, 2004, p 36).

Government can also seek to have an impact on the employability of older workers by encouraging continuing training and education throughout the working life. Training has been an option for unemployed older workers going through the New Deal 50+ programme but take-up has been low (Platman and Taylor, 2006, p 279). It is well documented that older workers are less likely to receive training at work than prime-age workers (see Platman and Taylor, 2006 for a review of the evidence). Despite government rhetoric around the need for a 'learning society', the Pensions Commission final report concluded:

> At present training expenditure is skewed towards younger workers. Government should ensure that all public programmes which support or encourage training are not age specific, and should work collaboratively with business to encourage best practice in the training of older workers. (2005, p 24)

Tax and the inflexibility of occupational pension rules have been another barrier in the past to individuals' downsizing and opting for flexible or gradual retirement policies. Hitherto tax rules inhibited taking paid work while also drawing a pension from the same employer. Occupational pensions based on final salary have also had the negative incentive of the potential pension penalty of reducing hours or downscaling work activity prior to retirement. Changes to tax rules, which came into force in April 2006, allow the individual to draw on an occupational pension while continuing to work for the same employer (see HM Revenue and Customs, undated). This may be expected to encourage more people to consider gradual retirement, although for many the need to keep building a pension or simply maintaining current income will continue as a disincentive to downscale their employment activity.

Finally, government can act as a role model by the policies it adopts for its own employees. Thus, the British government has decided that the pension age for new entrants to the civil service, from 2006 onwards, should be 65. The pension age of existing civil servants will rise to 65 in April 2013. By means such as these, government could be said to be sending a 'signal' about the duration of working life to employers more generally, although there is rumbling discontent in the private sector about the cost of final salary pension schemes in the public sector, which serves to undercut government's credibility as a role model (Clark, 2006, p 162).

From this discussion, it is clear that governments have a number of tactics and inducements that can be employed to encourage individuals to work for longer and delay retiring. However, government does not have that many levers over the actions of employers when it comes to the demand for older workers. Discrimination legislation can affect employer behaviour, but the extent to which private sector organisations can be forced to recruit and retain older workers is due largely to factors beyond government's direct control. Management practice within the public sector can also present a contradictory face when, along with government championing the business case for retaining older workers, we witness major workforce reductions in the ministry responsible for spearheading the Opportunity Age strategy and Age Positive policy, namely the Department for Work and Pensions (see Pendleton, 2006, pp 535-6), and when local government continues to use early retirement as a means for saving money. It is very important, therefore, that we adequately understand the factors driving employers' orientations towards older workers, and it is to this we now turn.

The role of employers

The attitudes and practices of employers towards older workers will remain key. However, reflecting on changes across Europe over the past decade, Walker (2006) comments that 'good practice in the employment of older workers remains a minority pursuit'. In the UK, this viewpoint is supported by two key studies conducted in the run-up to the implementation of the Employment Equality (Age) Regulations in October 2006. First, a large-scale study of 2,087 work establishments, each with five or more employees, found that although 56% of organisations had an equal opportunities policy covering age, age still played a direct role in a wide range of policies and practices, especially in relation to recruitment and selection and to redundancy and retirement (Metcalf and Meadows, 2006). It was often the case that age was not directly mentioned; rather criteria related to age, such as length of service, or experience (measured by time) would be used. While such criteria, where used as a proxy for age, may constitute indirect discrimination under the new regulations, we will have to wait for the emergence of case law to provide guidance. Age factors in relation to training (for example, maximum age for training) affected a smaller proportion of organisations; however, these were often larger employers and thus accounted for a sizeable number of employees. In general, the authors concluded that larger organisations, the public sector, the financial intermediation industry and establishments with a recognised union seemed best placed (Metcalf and Meadows, 2006, p 9). At the same time, they noted that age awareness needs to be raised, especially in (smaller) organisations that may not have human resource specialists.

The second key study, based on in-depth case study research in 14 organisations, also expressed concern over levels of awareness. McNair and Flynn (2005) found that while employers demonstrated basic awareness in the sense of knowing that legislation was forthcoming, they did not demonstrate comprehension of the possible implications of the law in that it was not considered a high priority and was not viewed as a major driver for change.

The centrality of employers to the future for older workers is explicitly recognised by the government in the UK and endorsed widely in its promotion of the age regulations through the Age Positive campaign and the Age Partnership group. The unequivocal message is that of the benefits to the business of adopting an age-diverse approach, with particular emphasis on older workers. However, based on contributions to this book and other previous research, we would contend that the business benefits of positive approaches to older workers are not always obvious, and may in some cases not be real.

Most importantly, issues surrounding costs have been and will remain crucial to employers' treatment of older workers. As older workers are generally deemed more expensive, early retirement has been a key cost-control mechanism adopted by employers in recent years. (As an aside, we would point to the Japanese experience, outlined in Chapter Four of this volume, as an illustration of the perils of making older workers cheaper.) Moreover, the cost situation is bound up with the notion that older workers' marginal productivity diminishes and many employers would not expect to receive a return on training investment given to those aged 55 or above. Employers may legitimately claim to be receiving mixed messages from the legislation in that, as Walker (2006) has acknowledged, as long as there is a retirement age, there will be an upper barrier to recruitment and training.

A concern with cost issues almost invariably leads to a short-term perspective. As Mike Danson points out in Chapter Two of this volume, the current supply of migrant labour in Scotland may mean that employers there cannot see any benefits of employing older workers. This short-term, cost-based perspective has also been noted across Europe more generally (Walker 2006, p 86). A combination of short-term, ad hoc approaches to resourcing, together with a sense of complacency (employers not currently facing labour problems) and fatalism (often linked to globalisation), work together to reinforce passivity and inaction (Loretto and White, 2006a).

The business case is also predicated on dismissing outmoded, mainly negative, stereotypes of older workers. However, we maintain that the situation is more complex. As several authors (for example, Oswick and Rosenthal, 2001 and Loretto and White, 2006a) have argued, very often the *positive* stereotypes attached to older workers – for example, that older workers are more dependable than their younger counterparts – are used to assign them to certain jobs, often those at the bottom of the hierarchy. This leads to a situation of conditional acceptance of older workers; they are welcome, provided they are flexible and healthy, and for certain jobs only (Loretto and White, 2006b). Thus a challenge to employers would be to remove this 'age typing' of jobs in order to widen the employment opportunities available to older workers.

While acknowledging the desirability of reducing age discrimination in recruitment, McNair and Flynn (2005) maintain that encouraging employers to retain their older workers for longer is the focus most likely to produce 'significant change'. To this end, Chapters Seven, Nine and Eleven in the volume have explored the extent to which more flexible working options at the end of working life will be key to extending working lives, while also, importantly, giving individuals more choice over the manner and timing of their retirement. As yet, flexible or gradual retirement, much heralded as a positive response to older worker issues, remains largely untested in the British case (Vickerstaff, forthcoming). In its recent review of ageing and employment policies in 21 countries, the OECD argued for 'a new agenda of age-friendly employment policies and practices' (2006, p 14). In addition to the need for pension and benefits reform, improved training and career advice for older workers, and an assault on ageist ideas and assumptions, the report argued for flexible pathways to retirement as a means of increasing the length of the working life (2006, pp 98-101).

Although desirable, this focus on flexible retirement perhaps serves to obscure a more important theme to emerge from the contributions to this volume, namely that we need to think more radically not only about the end of working life, but also about the prevailing concept of 'working lives' that is built in large measure on the old male breadwinner model of an unbroken work history stretching from entry into the labour market after schooling and education until retirement. We need to consider policies and practices on flexible working across the life course to encompass ideas like career breaks (Chapter Seven of this volume) and lifelong learning and to think more clearly about the impact of work on health (Chapter Eight). Designing and managing healthy work not just for older workers but for all workers is crucial. Such an approach is critical to the concept of active ageing, which combines the notion of productive ageing with a strong emphasis on quality of life and physical and mental well-being (see Walker, 2006 for a discussion). Although active ageing is not restricted to employment, in that it considers people holistically, the principle of active age management by employers across the life course is central.

It may well be that the regulations spur employers to look more systematically at the life course. One such focus might be on the link between benefit entitlement and length of service. If the length of service required is more than five years, employers would have to show, with evidence, that such a requirement meets a business need. The provision of 'lifestyle', or 'cafeteria', benefits might be one solution to difficulties with compliance; the benefit needs of employees might be expected to vary by age, and be tailored accordingly. Another area that might receive greater employer attention is that of performance management. A systematic approach to monitoring an individual's performance over the course of employment would throw into sharper relief the requirement that employers must now give a minimum of six months' notice to employees of their retirement dates. Such notice could come to be seen as a phase in, rather than the culmination of, the employment relationship.

A further priority within active age management is that of adopting a life-course approach to training and development. Previous research has confirmed that older workers are less likely to receive training in general, but especially in relation to production (Brooke and Taylor, 2005) and information (Duncan and Loretto, 2004) technologies. This inequity of treatment often arises from the perception that older people lack the capability to learn new technologies (Brooke and Taylor, 2005) or are generally resistant to change (Chiu et al, 2001). Such assumptions and stereotypes are often internalised by the older workers themselves (Ford, 2005, p 9) and lead to institutionalised ageism (Loretto and White, 2006c). The consequences are obsolescence of skills, plateaus in careers and early exit from employment (Brooke and Taylor, 2005, p 426), which in turn reinforce employers' assumptions that training older workers will not net them a return on their investment. In Chapter Seven of this volume, Donald Hirsch has maintained that a key aspect of making working lives more sustainable is an ongoing commitment to skills training and development, with both employers and older workers learning to manage the development of their own 'human capital'. Brooke and Taylor (2005) emphasise the importance of developing training and development strategies that integrate workers of different ages.

Currently, we have significant gaps in our knowledge and

understanding of employers' approaches to older workers. While a body of research maintains that larger employers are more responsive to older workers (see, for example, Metcalf and Meadows, 2006, and Chapter Ten of this volume), it has also been suggested that, in many respects, smaller organisations are more likely to exhibit good practice (Loretto and White, 2006a, 2006b). One possible reason for such contradictory evidence is the difference between espoused policy and day-to-day lived practice. While larger employers may be more likely to have age-friendly policies in place, this does not always translate into positive practice (Loretto and White, 2006a, p 326). In their case studies, McNair and Flynn (2005) also acknowledged concern about potential enactment gaps. Once again, employer passivity would seem to be an issue. For example, they found that even among those (two) organisations with formal schemes for flexible retirement, the onus was on employees to ask about such opportunities. Such an approach assumes that individual employees have the knowledge and confidence to approach their employers; however, we question the notion of the 'empowered' older worker in the final section of this chapter. The voice of the individual (older worker) has been distinctly lacking in research into employment practice; more detailed and comprehensive case study research would be beneficial here. The next section examines the perspective of the individual in some detail.

Individuals

The heterogeneity of those over 50 years of age means that there is no simple answer to what older workers want towards the end of their working lives. If there is any constant, it appears to be that people value choice and would like to be able to make their own decisions about when and how to retire (Vickerstaff, 2006, pp 509-10). Such choices are, of course, heavily constrained by the individual's financial position (of which pension status is a key part), their health, domestic circumstances and employer.

Financial security is a major factor encouraging people to leave work before state pension age. Men who are working and contributing to a defined benefit pension are much more likely to leave employment before state pension age than those contributing to a defined contribution pension (Emmerson and Tetlow, 2006, p 41; see also Phillipson and Smith, 2005, pp 27-8). It might be expected, therefore, that the move away from defined benefit pensions will encourage people to work for longer in the hope of securing a better pension.

Income remains a significant barrier to many people achieving their retirement aspirations and it is likely that many people will extend their working lives if they can because they cannot afford to do otherwise. Another important financial dimension is the help and support people get in planning for their retirement. Research indicates that many people do not understand their occupational pension or know the amount of state pension they will receive (Vickerstaff et al, 2004; Sykes et al, 2005; Barnes and Taylor, 2006). In Chapter Six of this volume, Sue Ward has shown that people are reluctant to engage with financial planning, and other research indicates that married women in particular may be lacking in knowledge about their pension prospects (Sykes et al, 2005).

In addition to financial situation, attachment to work and job satisfaction may provide other motives encouraging or discouraging people to continue at work (Vickerstaff et al, 2004, pp 18-19; Loretto et al, 2005, p 45; for those working over state pension age, see Smeaton and McKay, 2003, p 36). Reporting on two national surveys, McNair (2006) found that older people generally viewed work positively. He concluded that 'older people are strongly attached to work (though not always to their current job)' (2006, p 492). There is also evidence to suggest that those older workers on part-time contracts express the highest ratings of life satisfaction (Dean, 2003, p 8; McNair, 2006, p 492). In a Finnish study, it was found that those in higher occupational groups who had good control over their work were more likely to stay in work until the official retirement age (Gould, 2006, p 525).

These findings suggest that opportunities to work flexibly and gradual retirement may particularly resonate with older workers' desires to manage the end of their working lives. There is evidence of considerable support for the idea of gradual or flexible retirement but in truth it is something that most people in the UK have not practically thought about or tried to activate (Vickerstaff et al, 2004; Vickerstaff, forthcoming). The American tradition of seniors taking 'bridge jobs' after retiring from their career job or organisation but before full retirement is less common in the British case (on the situation in the US, see Ruhm, 1990; Quinn and Kozy, 1996; Cahill et al, 2006). However, the evidence from Britain suggests a similar pattern to the American situation in that well-qualified professional and managerial-level employees may choose to leave a career job to take up something new or interesting or work for themselves, whereas the less qualified and less well-paid may be forced to take whatever bridge jobs are available to sustain their income until they reach state pension age (Lissenburgh and Smeaton, 2003).

Research on current opportunities for flexible working (see Chapter

Nine of this volume) demonstrates that they are relatively limited for older workers, although other research indicates that there is likely to be considerable hidden demand for options to change and improve the balance between their work and non-work lives. This is likely to involve not only being able to find flexible work, but also, as Hirsch points out in Chapter Seven, contributing value to society in other ways such as voluntary work and caring. As argued by a recent Work Foundation report:

> When designing products, companies understand that at different times in their lives, different people need and want different things. It is not such a giant leap to apply this to the labour market: to start talking not just about working hours, but about working lives, which helps encompass the way each person can and wants to work may change over the lifetime. (Williams and Jones, 2005, p 2)

From a survey of 1,000 adults aged 16 and over, the authors found that employees of every age welcomed the opportunity to work flexibly. Notably, the precise format of desired flexibility varied across the life course. For example, most men and women with older dependent children (over 16), and most empty nesters, ideally wanted flexible full-time working. They also found that men in their 40s and above were more willing to change their working arrangements to fit in with elder-care responsibilities than for childcare responsibilities. The authors suggest that this reflects the notion of career progression − that men did not want to hamper their career opportunities at a younger age by working flexibly, but by the time they were faced with caring for elderly relatives, they had progressed sufficiently up the career hierarchy to be able to vary their work patterns. Despite demonstrating enthusiasm for flexible working across the ages, the Work Foundation report found that older workers were less likely to have the opportunities to work flexibly. They found that two thirds of respondents aged 16-24 work in a job that allows flexible working, but this figure drops to under 50% for respondents aged 55 or over (Williams and Jones, 2005, p 10).

One notion underlying issues related to individual decision making over the timing and manner of retirement, including options to work flexibly, is that of the 'empowered' older worker. It is often assumed, albeit implicitly, that older workers are taking decisions with adequate financial awareness, knowledge of their employment and legal rights, and confidence to pursue these with their employers. As Ward (this volume) illustrates, individuals are very definitely not empowered in terms of financial knowledge, awareness and autonomy. Moreover, it has been noted that the 'empowered worker', who is aware of their employment rights and is confident in asserting them, is more myth than reality: instead, the norm is low awareness of legislative rights and a reluctance to approach employers for fear of negative reprisal (Dwelly and Bennion, 2003).

Other factors mitigating older workers' ability to make choices are ill health and disability, factors strongly related to withdrawal from the labour market before state pension age. As indicated in Chapters Five and Eleven of this volume, chronic or long-standing limiting illnesses disproportionately affect the working classes who have spent working lives in routine or manual jobs. In 2004, there were 2.7 million recipients of IB (the principal welfare benefit paid to those who cannot work because of long-term illness or disability). A substantial proportion of this total is aged over 50, and around three quarters of a million would like to work (NAO, 2004, p 4). As discussed earlier, the government is targeting this group but is also beginning to recognise the importance of encouraging employers to keep employees with health issues in work and to minimise the risk of ill health in the first place (HM Government, undated).

A recent review of the evidence on older women, work and health concluded that:

> Workplace health promotion programmes are becoming increasingly common. However, they have often been criticised for failing to meet the needs of older workers in general and older women in particular. (Doyal and Payne, 2006, p 6)

In Chapter Eight of this volume, Amanda Griffiths argues the need for a coordinated occupational health strategy in which the emphasis moves away from an exclusive focus on adjustments that can be made to support a particular individual to an approach that also recognises the need to understand how the design, organisation and management of work can lead to potential risks to employees' health. Stress and mental health issues are steadily rising as reasons for people becoming economically inactive; the quality of work available and the nature of the work culture can be major factors in what might be termed the psychosocial aspects of work (Doyal and Payne, 2006).

Another factor conditioning older workers' orientation to paid employment is the caring activities they may be engaged in. With an ageing population, the issue of how older workers, especially women, can combine employment with caring responsibilities is likely to become an increasingly important issue. A recent report commissioned by the Joseph Rowntree Foundation found that care giving is associated with disadvantage in terms of income, access to employment and own health: 'analysis indicates that midlife caregivers for 20+ hours a week had lower levels of employment than those who provided no care or less care .... lower employment rates and poorer health are likely to have consequences for carers' quality of life and future opportunities' (Young et al, 2006, p 33).

The English Longitudinal Study of Ageing provides a clear picture of the caring activities of those over 50 (see Hyde and Janevic, 2003, Annex 5.1, Tables 5A.1-8). A minority of those between 45 and 65 find themselves as the 'sandwich or pivot generation', combining care for their own children with informal care for elderly parents (Mooney et al, 2002, p 1; Evandrou and Glaser, 2004, p 771). The number of people who, at some time, experience the combination of all three roles of employment, looking after dependent children and caring for elderly relatives is increasing (Evandrou and Glaser, 2004, p 778). Caring responsibilities for sick or elderly relatives or partners present particular problems for employed carers because the onset and nature of caring needs tend to be more unpredictable and can occur suddenly and develop in intensity rapidly. For workless households, caring responsibilities are a key reason given for not wanting or seeking work (Arrowsmith, 2004, p xv). Nevertheless, evidence suggests that many older carers value the opportunity to continue paid employment (Loretto et al, 2005, pp 42-4).

Flexible working options are likely to be welcomed by those trying to combine employment and caring. In particular, better access to flexible working hours, the opportunity to reduce working hours if necessary, the right to time off for caring responsibilities and the ability to work from home where feasible are seen as highly desirable (Mooney et al, 2002; Howard, 2004). However, research also indicates that, as yet, relatively few employers extend their family-friendly or work–life balance policies to cover the full range of caring responsibilities beyond parenting (Phillips et al, 2002; Evandrou and Glaser, 2003, p 597). The 2004 Workplace Employment Relations Survey (WERS) asked managers for the first time whether carers of older adults had a specific entitlement to leave. Only 6% of workplaces offered such leave (Kersley et al, 2006, pp 258, 265). The role of the employer therefore may be crucial in responding or failing to respond to individual health issues or a change in an employee's domestic caring commitments. The individual may also not know whether their employer would respond favourably to requests to change work routines. The 2004 WERS showed that although 70% of organisations said that reducing hours was an available flexible working arrangement, only 32% of employees thought it was an option open to them (Kersley et al, 2006, pp 250-2).

From the discussion in this section, it is clear that individuals are often grappling with the complex interplay of a range of factors: income, health, experience of employment and current job satisfaction, caring responsibilities and other opportunities or threats in terms of their aspirations for continuing working, retiring gradually or retiring completely. Another important constraint or context in which individuals make choices about continuing working or retiring might be referred to as structural features. Do workers want the jobs that are available? As Beatty and Fothergill argue in Chapter Five of this volume, there is a problem with the geographical dispersion of jobs: large numbers of older inactive people live in areas with depressed labour markets. Availability of work is often especially poor in those areas with high numbers of people claiming IB. In other areas, there may be work but not in those sectors favoured by older workers. As Tony Maltby found in Chapter Ten of this volume, some older workers perceive particular service sector environments such as call centres as hostile and alien. In traditional manufacturing and industrial areas, older men may not view the influx of new service sector or light industry jobs as work suitable for them. The jobs may also not pay enough to make it worthwhile coming off benefits. From our discussion of individuals' aspirations, it is clear that people's orientation towards paid work differs, as does their ability to find and retain the kinds of work they might want to engage in.

Conclusion

It is now barely contested that, in the coming years, more people will be working for longer and retiring fully later compared with those who have reached their 60s in the past three decades. For some, working longer may seem an 'unavoidable obligation' (Reday-Mulvey, 2005, p 195) in an era when the workforce is ageing and life expectancy is increasing. Government's urge to extend our working lives is summed up in the title of the recent OECD (2006) review of policies, *Live Longer, Work Longer*.

It could be argued that the 'problem' of an ageing workforce can be solved by continued economic growth in the context of other current policy trends. If the economy expands and demand for labour is strong, and if the security of occupational pensions is reduced and access to state pensions comes later in life, employers will be forced to employ older workers as the available labour supply, and older workers will be forced to accept the work available to maintain their incomes. However, as a recent review of equality and diversity in the UK workplace commented: 'Whilst market forces and demographics may create a diverse workforce they do not ensure best practice' (ACAS, 2006, p 2).

This suggests that we need to move the debate on from an emphasis on numbers (of older people in employment) to focus on the key question of the quality of work available for older workers. The outlook here is not especially comforting. Walker and colleagues report research that suggests that, because of globalisation, we will see increased polarisation between good and bad jobs and that the proportion of middling occupations will decline, creating an 'hour glass' distribution of jobs (2006, p 15). Thus, the scope for exit routes out of low-paid, low-skilled employment (for older workers) will be limited, and the availability of bridge jobs will be concentrated in sectors with poor-quality work. This vision of the older workforce becoming part of the reserve army of labour in the secondary labour market is hardly appealing, although already acknowledged by Seager with reference to a recent OECD report in which 'figures show immigration and rising participation rates among older workers and women has pushed wage inflation down this year' (Seager, 2006).

In this context, the calls for an active ageing approach that incorporates a focus on quality of work and of life (Walker, 2002; Reday-Mulvey, 2005, pp 32-5; Walker et al, 2006) become increasingly urgent. The emphasis in active ageing is on individuals as active agents in conjunction with employers' policies of active age management. This contrasts with the largely reactive and seemingly passive approaches adopted by governments, employers and individuals to date. Several authors in this volume have commented favourably on the Finnish 'work ability' model in adopting a holistic approach to age management and sustaining employment up to and beyond retirement ages. In the mid-1990s, the Finnish National Programme on Ageing Workers aimed to increase the employability of older workers by focusing on personal factors (such as health, motivation and job satisfaction) alongside aspects of jobs and how they are managed (Chapter Ten of this volume; OECD, 2004). This programme incorporated research, training and information dissemination covering employers and individual workers, and is believed to have contributed to the substantial rise in employment of older workers in Finland (OECD, 2004; Gould, 2006).

While undoubtedly laudable, in particular for adopting an active and holistic approach to age awareness and age management, we would guard against viewing this model – in isolation – as a panacea for older workers. As Gould (2006) points out, other factors, notably legal intervention that restricted early retirement options and a period of sustained economic growth, all acted in conjunction with work ability to increase employment rates. Moreover, Gould's recent longitudinal analysis of retirement behaviours in Finland show that people working in higher-status jobs and who report better health are those most likely to delay retirement. This serves to remind us that despite the general acceptance of lengthening working lives and delayed retirement, there is much less certainty over the extent to which the effects and impacts of these changes will be fairly distributed among the older population.

It seems increasingly clear that a good future for older workers and, we would argue, for *all* workers, can only come about with a major culture shift among policy makers, employers and employees of all ages. Solutions to some of the longer-term problems signalled here require action on a broad range of fronts (quality and health impacts of work, lifelong learning, flexibility in work hours and roles, increased social standing for non-paid work such as caring and volunteering) and a major reconceptualisation of the relationship between paid work and the life course that poses questions for all sections of the population, not just those approaching retirement. An important part of this will be building a new basis for intergenerational solidarity. Optimistically, it may be that the advent of an ageing workforce will put health, safety and welfare at work and the need for a good balance between work life and the rest of life firmly on the political agenda with potential benefits for everyone in society.

References

ACAS (Advisory, Conciliation and Arbitration Service) (2006) 'Back to basics. ACAS' experience of equality and diversity in the workplace', ACAS Policy Discussion Papers No 5, London: ACAS.

Alcock, P., Beatty, C., Fothergill, S., Macmillan, R. and Yeandle, S. (2003) *Work to Welfare: How Men Become Detached from the Labour Market*, Cambridge: Cambridge University Press.

Aliaga, C. and Romans, F. (2006) 'The employment of seniors in the European Union', *Statistics in Focus Population and Social Conditions*, 15/2006, Brussels: Eurostat, European Communities.

Arrowsmith, J. (2004) *A Review of 'What we Know' about Partners of Benefit Recipients*, Department for Work and Pensions Report WAE200, London: Department for Work and Pensions.

Barnes, H. and Taylor, R. (2006) *Work, Saving and Retirement among Ethnic Minorities: A Qualitative Report*, Department for Work and Pensions Research Report 396, Leeds: Department for Work and Pensions.

Beck, U. (2000) *The Brave New World of Work*, Cambridge: Polity Press.

Brooke, L. and Taylor, P. (2005) 'Older workers and employment: managing age relations', *Ageing and Society*, vol 25, no 3, pp 415-29.

Cahill, K.E., Giandrea, M.D. and Quinn, J.F. (2006) 'Employment patterns from career employment', *Gerontologist*, vol 46, no 4, pp 514-23.

Chiu, W., Chan, A., Snape, E. and Redman, T. (2001) 'Age stereotypes and discriminatory attitudes towards older workers: an East-West comparison', *Human Relations*, vol 54, no 5, pp 629-61.

Clark, G.L. (2006) 'The UK occupational pension system in crisis', in H. Pemberton, P. Thane and N. Whiteside (eds) *Britain's Pensions Crisis: History and Policy*, Oxford: Oxford University Press.

Dean, M. (2003) *Growing Older in the 21st century*, Report on the ESRC Growing Older Programme, Swindon: Economic and Social Research Council.

Doyal, L. and Payne, S. (2006) *Older Women, Work and Health: Reviewing the Evidence*, London: Help the Aged/The Age and Employment Network.

Duncan, C. and Loretto, W. (2004) 'Never the right age? Gender and age-based discrimination in employment', *Gender, Work and Organisation*, vol, 11, no 1, pp 95-115.

DWP (Department for Work and Pensions) (2002) *Opportunity for All Fourth Annual Report 2002*, Cm 5598, London: HMSO.

DWP (2006a) *Security in Retirement: Towards a New Pensions System*, Cm 6841, London: DWP.

DWP (2006b) *Flexible Retirement: A Snapshot of Employer Practices 2006* London: DWP.

Dwelly, T. and Bennion, Y. (2003) *Time to go Home – Embracing the Homeworking Revolution*, London: Work Foundation.

Emmerson, C. and Tetlow, G. (2006) 'Labour market transitions', in J. Banks, E. Breeze, C. Lessof and J. Nazroo (eds) *Retirement, Health and Relationships of the Older Population in England: The 2004 English Longitudinal Study of Ageing (Wave 2)*, London: Institute for Fiscal Studies, pp 41-82.

Evandrou, M. and Glaser, K. (2003) 'Combining work and family life: the pension penalty of caring', *Ageing and Society*, vol 23, no 5, pp 583-602.

Evandrou, M. and Glaser, K. (2004) 'Family, work and quality of life: changing economic and social roles through the lifecourse', *Ageing and Society*, vol 24, pp 771-91.

Ford, G. (2005) *Am I Still Needed?*, Derby: Centre for Guidance Studies, University of Derby.

Gould, R. (2006) 'Choice or chance – late retirement in Finland', *Social Policy and Society*, vol 5, no 4, pp 519-31.

HM Government (undated) *Health, Work and Well-being – Caring for our Future; A Strategy for the Health and Well-being of Working Age People*, Report produced by the Department for Work and Pensions, Department of Health and Health and Safety Executive (www.dwp. gov.uk/publications/dwp/2005/health_and_wellbeing.pdf, accessed 28 November 2006).

HM Revenue and Customs (undated) *Pensions Tax Simplification* (www. hmrc.gov.uk/pensionschemes/pts.htm, accessed 7 June 2006).

Hornstein, Z., Encel, S., Gunderson, M. and Neumark, D. (2001) *Outlawing Age Discrimination Foreign lessons, UK Choices*, Joseph Rowntree Foundation Transitions after 50 series, Bristol: The Policy Press for The Joseph Rowntree Foundation.

Howard, M. (2004) 'Support for working carers', Carers UK paper presented to Joseph Rowntree Foundation Seminar, Transitions after 50: Workshop Older People in the Workforce – Mechanisms for Change, October, London.

Hyde, M. and Janevic, M. (2003) 'Social activity', in M. Marmot, J. Banks, R. Blundell, C. Lessof and J. Nazroo (eds) *Health, Wealth and Lifestyles of the Older Population in England: The 2002 English Longitudinal Study of Ageing*, London: Institute for Fiscal Studies.

Inman, P. (2006) 'Reforms leave women still short of pensions', *The Guardian*, 21 November, p 25.

Kersley, B., Alpin, C., Forth, J., Bryson, A., Bewley, H., Dix, G. and Oxenbridge, S. (2006) *Inside the Workplace: Findings from the 2004 Workplace Employment Relations Survey*, Abingdon: Routledge.

Lahey, J.N. (2006) *How do Age Discrimination Laws Affect Older Workers?*, Work Opportunities for Older Americans, Series 5, Boston, MA: Center for Retirement Research.

Lissenburgh, S. and Smeaton, D. (2003) *Employment Transitions of Older Workers. The Role of Flexible Employment in Maintaining Labour Market Participation and Promoting Job Quality*, York: Joseph Rowntree Foundation.

Loretto, W. and White, P. (2006a) 'Employers' attitudes, practices and policies towards older workers', *Human Resource Management Journal*, vol 16, no 3, pp 313-30.

Loretto, W. and White, P. (2006b) 'Population ageing and older workers: employers' perceptions, attitudes and policies', *Population, Space and Place*, vol 12, no 5, pp 341-52.

Loretto, W. and White, P. (2006c) 'Work, more work and retirement: older workers' perspectives', *Social Policy and Society*, vol 5, no 4, pp 495-506.

Loretto, W., Vickerstaff, S. and White, P. (2005) *Older Workers and Options for Flexible Work*, Manchester: Equal Opportunities Commission.

Macnicol, J. (2006) *Age Discrimination: An Historical and Contemporary Analysis*, Cambridge: Cambridge University Press.

McNair, S. (2006) 'How different is the older labour market? Attitudes to work and retirement among older people in Britain', *Social Policy and Society*, vol 5, no 4, pp 485-94.

McNair, S. and Flynn, M. (2005) *The Age Dimension of Employment Practices: Employer Case Studies*, DTI Employment Relations Research Series No 42, London: DTI.

Meadows, P. (2003) *Retirement Ages in the UK: A Review of the Literature*, London: Department of Trade and Industry.

Metcalf, H. and Meadows, P. (2006) *Survey of Employers' Policies, Practices and Preferences Relating to Age*, Department for Work and Pensions Research Report 325/Department of Trade and Industry Employment Relations Research Series 49, Leeds: HMSO.

Mooney, A., Statham, J. and Simon, A. (2002) *The Pivot Generation: Informal Care and Work after 50*, Bristol: The Policy Press for the Joseph Rowntree Foundation.

NAO (National Audit Office) (2004) *Welfare to Work: Tackling the Barriers to the Employment of Older People*, House of Commons HC 1026, London: The Stationery Office.

OECD (Organisation for Economic Co-operation and Development) (2004) *Ageing and Employment Policies: Finland* (www.oecd.org/dataoecd/30/55/35050387.pdf).

OECD (2006) *Live Longer, Work Longer*, Paris: OECD.

Oswick, C. and Rosenthal, P. (2001) 'Towards a relevant theory of age discrimination in employment', in M. Noon and E. Ogbonna (eds) *Equality, Diversity and Disadvantage in Employment*, Basingstoke: Palgrave Macmillan.

Pendleton, N. (2006) 'Getting people back into work: the experience of Jobcentre Plus', *Social Policy and Society*, vol 5, no 4, pp 533-9.

Pensions Commission (2005) *A New Pensions Settlement for the Twenty-First Century*, Second Report of the Pensions Commission, London: HMSO.

Phillips, J., Bernard, M. and Chittenden, M. (2002) *Juggling Work and Care: The Experience of Working Carers of Older Adults*, Bristol: The Policy Press for the Joseph Rowntree Foundation.

Phillipson, C. (2002) *Transitions from Work to Retirement*, Bristol: The Policy Press for the Joseph Rowntree Foundation.

Phillipson, C. and Smith, A. (2005) *Extending Working Life: A Review of the Research Literature*, Department for Work and Pensions Research Report 299, Leeds: Department for Work and Pensions.

Platman, K. and Taylor, P. (2006) 'Training and learning in the workplace: can we legislate against age discriminatory practices?', in L. Bauld, K. Clarke and T. Maltby (eds) *Social Policy Review 18: Analysis and Debate in Social Policy 2006*, Bristol: The Policy Press.

Quinn, J.F. and Kozy, M. (1996) 'The role of bridge jobs in the retirement transition: gender, race and ethnicity', *Gerontologist*, vol 36, no 3, pp 363-73.

Reday-Mulvey, G. (2005) *Working Beyond 60*, Basingstoke: Palgrave Macmillan.

Ruhm, C.J. (1990) 'Bridge jobs and partial retirement', *Journal of Labor Economics*, vol 8, no 4, pp 482-501.

Scales, J. and Scase, R. (2000) *Fit and Fifty?*, Swindon: Economic and Social Research Council.

Schultz, J.H. (2002) 'The evolving concept of "retirement": looking forward to the year 2050', *International Social Security Review*, vol 55, no 1, pp 85-105.

Seager, A. (2006) 'OECD backs immigration policy as source of UK growth', *The Guardian*, 29 November, p 25.

Smeaton, D. and McKay, S. (2003) *Working after State Pension Age: Quantitative Analysis*, Bristol: The Policy Press for the Joseph Rowntree Foundation.

Sykes, W., Hedges, A., Finch, H., Ward, K. and Kelly, J. (2005) *Financial Plans for Retirement; Women's Perspectives*, Department for Work and Pensions Research Report 247, Leeds: Department for Work and Pensions.

Vickerstaff, S. (2006) 'Life course, youth and old age', in P. Taylor-Gooby and J. Zinn (eds) *Risk in Social Science*, Oxford: Oxford University Press.

Vickerstaff, S. (forthcoming) 'What do older workers want? Gradual retirement?', *Social and Public Policy Review*.

Vickerstaff, S. and Cox, J. (2005) 'Retirement and risk: the individualisation of retirement experiences?', *The Sociological Review*, vol 53, no 1, pp 77-95.

Vickerstaff, S., Baldock, J., Cox, J. and Keen, L. (2004) *Happy Retirement? The Impact of Employers' Policies and Practice on the Process of Retirement*, Bristol: The Policy Press for the Joseph Rowntree Foundation.

Walker, A. (2002) 'A strategy for active ageing', *International Social Security Review*, vol 55, no 1, pp 121-39.

Walker, A. (2006) Active ageing in employment: its meaning and potential, *Asia-Pacific Review*, vol 13, no 1, pp 78-93.

Walker, A., Barnes, M., Cox, K. and Lessof, C. (2006) *Social Exclusion of Older People: Future Trends and Policies*, New Horizons Research Programme, London: Office of the Deputy Prime Minister.

Williams, L. and Jones, A. (2005) *Changing Demographics*, London: The Work Foundation.

Young, H., Grundy, E. and Jitlal, M. (2006) *Care Providers, Care Receivers; A Longitudinal Perspective*, York: Joseph Rowntree Foundation.

Zaidi, A., Makovec, M. and Fuchs, M. (2006) 'Transition from work to retirement in EU25', CASEpaper 112, London: Council for Advancement and Support of Education.

Index